Economies in Transition

Contributions to Economics

Albrecht Ritschl
Prices and Production
- Elements of a System - Theoretic
Perspective -
1989. 159pp. Softcover DM 59,-
ISBN 3-7908-0429-0

Arnulf Grübler
The Rise and Fall of Infrastructures
- Dynamics of Evolution and
Technological Change in Transport -
1990. 305pp. Softcover DM 85,-
ISBN 3-7908-0479-7

Peter R. Haiss
Cultural Influences on Strategic Planning
1990. 188pp. Softcover DM 65,-
ISBN 3-7908-0481-9

Manfred Kremer/Marion Weber (Eds.)
Transforming Economic Systems: The Case of Poland
1992. 179pp. Softcover DM 69,-
ISBN 3-7908-91415-3

Marcel F. van Marion
Liberal Trade and Japan
1993. 298pp. Softcover DM 90,-
ISBN 3-7908-0699-4

Michael Carlberg
Open Economy Dynamics
1993. 203 pp. Softcover DM 75,-
ISBN 3-7908-0708-7

Hans Schneeweiß/
Klaus F. Zimmermann (Eds.)
Studies in Applied Econometrics
1993. 238 pp. Softcover DM 85,-
ISBN 3-7908-0716-8

Gerhard Gehrig
Wladyslaw Welfe (Eds.)

Economies in Transition

A System of Models and Forecasts for Germany and Poland

With 41 Figures

Physica-Verlag
A Springer-Verlag Company

Series Editor
Werner A. Müller
Peter Schuster

Editors
Professor Dr. Gerhard Gehrig
Institute for Development, Environment and
Quantitative Economic Research
Johann Wolfgang Goethe-University
Mertonstraße 17/21
D-60054 Frankfurt/Main, Germany

Professor Dr. Wladyslaw Welfe
Institute of Econometrics and Statistics
University of Lodz
41 Rewolucji 1905 r.
90214 Lodz, Poland

ISBN 3-7908-0721-4 Physica-Verlag Heidelberg
ISBN 0-387-91468-4 Springer-Verlag New York

CIP-Titelaufnahme der Deutschen Bibliothek
Economies in transition: a system of models and forecasts for
Germany and Poland / Gerhard Gehrig; Wladyslaw Welfe. -
Heidelberg: Physica-Verl. 1993
ISBN 3-7908-0721-4 (Physica-Verl.) brosch.
ISBN 0-387-91468-4 (Springer)
NE: Gehrig, Gerhard [Hrsg.]

88/7130-543210 – Printed on acid-free paper

PREFACE

It has been quite a challenge for econometricians to model economies in transition. There is no textbook at hand to master that task. Economic theory cannot be applied without adaptations to the characteristic change of a whole economic system. Regression analysis, taking into account past economic development only, is of limited use for the econometrician.

Having econometric models at hand would be very helpful for an active economic policy to guide the transition process. Various scenarios representing strategies could be simulated in their consequences to the economy. The best alternative in respect to the government's objectives could be chosen.

This very situation has born the idea of co-operation between Lódz and Frankfurt in 1990. There are problems of this kind in Poland and in Germany. The German situation is somewhat better than that of Poland as a relatively small centrally planned economy is being united with a substantial social market economy taking over a lot of the burden of the former mismanagement. Thus, it might be possible to share the experience in modelling the united Germany and preparing forecasts with the Polish model builders. In addition, it would be profitable for both model establishing teams to link their models in order to improve the forecasting potential. Moreover, the Polish partner has a broad national and international experience in econometric model building which makes co-operation smooth and fruitful. His experience in modelling countries with a centrally planned economy would also help to master the transition problems.

In realising the idea of co-operation in modelling economies in transition it seemed useful to set up not a single model, but a system of models. As the first step, both partners have concentrated their efforts to model their economies and to try to prepare a basis for policy simulations. The results of this research are subject of this publication.

The concept of a system of models and related system of forecasts at the macro level was developed by W. Welfe and its description opens the monograph. The first part demonstrates the results obtained by the Frankfurt team led by Professor G. Gehrig. They cover the construction of an annual econometric model for the united Germany composed of sub models for former East and West Germany. This model is being used in policy simulations aimed at showing the path of transition of the former GDR towards the standards of West Germany to be reached by the year 2000. The second part illuminates the results obtained by the Lódz team headed by Professor W. Welfe. They consist in deriving the concept of a quarterly macro model - suitable for the short-term analysis for the period of transition from centrally planned to a market economy. The empirical results of estimating the parameters of the model equations are shown and its properties as a demand driven system with distorted responses to the market signals analysed.

As the co-operation continues, another publication will follow when the total research has been finished. The work in progress concentrates on improvements of the presented models, concerning mainly the money and labour market fòr Germany and the linking of models for countries in transition most favourably that of Poland. The latter will include a new version of the annual macro econometric model W-5 of the Polish economy. Simulation strategies will help to produce short and long term forecasts. Last but not least, forecasts based on simulations will be checked by statistical data published during the period of co-operation.

The appendices contain comprehensive information on data bases, empirical results of estimation and simulation exercises. They also cover the information on the new computer software. The appendix of part 1 includes information on subsidiary and preparatory research work. It incorporates the description of ETAS which is a software to generate regression models. This generator is of great importance for establishing the German models and to exchange data and models by telecommunication. The work on portfolio models of the Federal Republic of Germany is also preparatory for the current research by improving the money and capital market description for the German model. The appendices of part 2 concentrate on detailed description of the data base and results of estimation of parameters of the quarterly model equations.

As the co-operation is promising for both partners there is a chance to share the results of our common research with other countries in transition and even to broaden international co-operation.

Lódz, May 5, 1992 — Feldafing, May 5, 1992

Wladyslaw Welfe — Gerhard Gehrig

Contents

CHAPTER 1

ON THE CONCEPT OF A SYSTEM OF ECONOMETRIC FORECASTING AND SIMULATION MODELS FOR THE PERIOD OF TRANSITION TOWARDS THE MARKET ECONOMIES

Wladyslaw Welfe

Institute of Econometrics and Statistics, University of Lódz

1.1 Introduction

In the developed market economies there has been observed, over the last decades, a tendency in the macro-modelling activities towards an increase of frequency both for the econometric models and forecasts being based on these models. The early annual models for the USA were supplemented by quarterly models, which as soon as in the '70s, played major role in forecasting and macroeconomic policy analysis (Duesenberry et al. [1963], Evans, Klein [1968], Fair [1971], McCarthy [1972], Andersen, Carlson [1973]). With some delay, this development spread over major industrial market economies: Canada, Japan, Australia and Western Europe (Waelbroeck [1975], Bodkin et al. [1990]). Let us mention: Malgrange [1983], Courbis, Salmon [1986] for France and Hansen, Westphal [1975], Macroeconometric... [1988] for Germany; see also d'Adda et al. [1976] for Italy, Fase [1984] for the Netherlands and Ball et al. [1973] for the United Kingdom.

More recently, an increasing demand for economic information, supplied with rising frequency, was observed. Not only more quarterly forecasts and evaluations than annual were presented, but also more monthly forecasts and quarterly forecasts updated each month. This demand comes not only from the central and local administration, but increasingly from large firms, associations, etc., interested in observing the quickly changing environment.

In Central-Eastern Europe, in the former command type, centrally planned economies, the demand for high frequency data was underdeveloped. The annual central planning system which, in principle, did not assume plan adjustments within the yearly period, required mainly the development of medium-term macro economic models. The quarterly models aimed at evaluation of the likely annual plan fulfilment were developed in a few countries only. For the CSRS they became operational (Sujan, Kolek [1974] and Sujan, Olexa [1984]). For Poland there were two attempts to build the quarterly models. The model KP-3 was for a short period of time used in the evaluation of annual plan implementation (Kalinin et al. [1977]). Later, an attempt to construct a new quarterly model in the mid of the 80's ended up with its first use (Kudrycka [1990]). The constructed models were not maintained.

For the period of transition towards market economies, where the market mechanisms and adjustments play an increasing role (including free negotiated prices clearing the markets), it becomes obvious that the major economic information has to be generated with much higher frequency, i.e. within quarterly and monthly periods. On the other hand, more emphasis must be put on forecasts and policy analyses related to financial flows and prices which were nearly completely neglected in the past (see, however, Lapinska-Sobczak et al. [1979]). It must be noticed that the official statistics over the last years have been developed to meet these demands by means of supplying, mainly on the monthly and quarterly base, more and more information on the financial flows (and prices) and also on expanding private business activities starting, in Poland, from 1989 or 1990.

1.2 Towards a system of economic forecasts and policy simulations for the transition period

Many academic and governmental research centres have recognised the above mentioned needs. Only few, however, developed research in this area. They are, among others, the Institute of Econometrics and Statistics, University of Lódz (team led by W. Welfe) for Poland and the Institute for Development, Environment and Quantitative Economic Research, Johann Wolfgang Goethe-University, Frankfurt (team led by G.Gehrig) for Germany. These two research groups supported by R.Courbis (Universite Paris X, Nanterre) started in 1991 under ACE Project a research project aimed at elaborating the concept of a system of economic forecasts and policy simulations based on econometric macro models for the transition period [1)]. The results are summarised below. They cover the description of the concept of a system of models, its exemplification's related to an annual model for united Germany (in fact modelling the new Lands i.e. former GDR was a specific problem) and a quarterly model for Poland, and also their first

(1) The project "The concept of a system of econometric forecasts for a market economy (with special emphasis to the period of transition towards a market economy)" was financed from the ACE Project grant no ERB 4012PL90003 - (F90100031). Prof. W. Welfe was the Project co-ordinator.

applications. The details are being reported in two separate parts, prepared by the Frankfurt and Lódz teams.

After two years since the economic reforms in Eastern and Central Europe gained a new impetus, many crucial questions still remain open. They are: - which empirical model of a market economy (social market or liberal) will these countries approach, what will be the timing of the commercialisation and privatisation process etc.[2]. Nevertheless, it seems that all these countries either already have had or will depart from a shortage economy towards a demand constrained economic system, suffering from inflation and high costs of adjustment (recession, growing unemployment). The transformation of the behaviour of producers, originally representing state owned firms - to the efficient managers sensitive to market signals seems a long-lasting process. One has to take into account also the high degree of monopolisation and the underdevelopment of institutional infrastructure in the financial sector. Hence, the market mechanisms of adjustment may differ from those observed in developed market economies.

Having these general findings in mind, we decided to develop a concept of an information system composed of regular forecasts and scenario analyses based on macro models, that might help in the decision making both by the representatives of private and public business and by the policy makers. It will be briefly discussed below.

1.3 On a system of macro models

A system of economic forecasts and policy simulations, which can guarantee a minimum level of consistency, must be based on a system of macro models of structural simulation type. If this system is aimed at yielding short- and medium-term (up to the year 2000) forecasts[3] - then it should be composed of: a/ annual, simulation macro econometric models, b/ quarterly forecasting and simulation macro econometric models supplemented by c/ monthly statistical forecasting sub models. Let us discuss these types of models in some more detail.

---

(2) Compare the opinions expressed by R. Portes et.al. in European Economy [1991].
(3) We do not include into our discussion the long term forecasts (of the horizon of 15-20 years) and analyses of long-term structural changes, typically based on structural models using the I-O framework. See Orlowski, Tomaszewicz [1991].

An annual simulation macro model of econometric type must cover both the real and financial sectors of the national economy built within the framework of national accounts (for the future within the SNA system - but for the present also within the MPS system for Poland to preserve the continuity). Thus, it should include all the macro aggregates, observing the conventional national accounting identities.

The changes in the economic regimes and mechanisms which took place during the transition period (first of all switching from shortage economy to demand determined systems) must be reflected in the annual macro models. Hence, extraneous information must be used to allow for parameter changes. It may rely on recent I-O tables, cross-section data, on estimates obtained from models of higher frequency or models for neighbouring developed market economies. The annual macro models for Poland (Welfe [1985], [1989], [1991], Juszczak et al. [1991]) constructed in the '80s and especially the demand-oriented version of the model W-5 (exceeding 1000 equations) has a sufficiently elastic structure, which made it possible to use it in forecasting and simulation exercises in the early '90s. Nevertheless, its equations need serious respecification mainly in order to include the responses of producers and investors to market signals and to extend the financial and price sector. It needs reestimation using the updated sample (up to 1990). These developments will be the subject of a separate monograph.

Modelling united Germany is a special case. The concept of an annual model for Germany and its use had to be developed, taking into account the severe data constraints for the former GDR. This model constructed by the Frankfurt team splits the German economy into West Germany (FRG up to unification) and former GDR, essentially in order to make possible the study of the transition from centrally planned economy of the former GDR to social market economy. The parameters for the new Lands were mostly calibrated looking into their estimates for West Germany. It shifted the applications towards an analysis of final results of the process of transformation by means of simulations performed up to the year 2000. The detailed description of these findings is to be found in part 1 of the monograph. The structure of the model was outlined by G.Gehrig. The details of the BRD-DDR Model (version 2) were discussed by G.Gehrig and others in Chapter 2. The first empirical results of policy simulations were reported by K. Behle, G.Gehrig and P.Tomczyk, supported by detailed description of simulation exercises in Chapter 3.

A quarterly simulation macro model of econometric type must stress, first of all, the changes in financial flows, prices and related changes in real flows. It will be aimed at forecasting and policy simulations. They should cover the major topics of fiscal and monetary policies, including the policy of stabilisation, anti inflationary measures, budget deficit, balance of payments deficit/surplus, etc. The properties of the major West-European quarterly models (especially for France, Germany and Italy) and their applications were examined first, before the concept of a new quarterly model for Poland was developed. It turned out, however, that the structure of the new quarterly model for the economies in transition cannot simply follow the specifications of the above West-European models. It is because, as it was mentioned above, the infrastructure of the financial sector is underdeveloped, the market mechanisms are not full at work and the sensitivity of many economic agents (first of all of the state-owned enterprises) to market signals is low, asymmetric and lagged. Hence, the models constructed for the transition period must allow for specific structure of particular equations and specific properties of the whole equation system.

The idea of constructing a quarterly model for Germany (covering former GDR) was abandoned because of complete lack of quarterly data for former GDR. Instead, a study of portfolio models for FRG (by T.Gehrig) was included in the hope that it will help to illuminate the ways the specification of financial models for Poland and united Germany should follow.

The discussion of the major topics related to the construction of a quarterly model for Poland is to be found in part 2, Chapter 4. The coverage of the quarterly model for Poland compared to that of Western countries will be constrained, especially with respect to financial flows to those phenomena, which really exist and are observable, (for instance, no transactions on capital markets were reported up to 1990). The concept of the quarterly model for Poland was formulated by W. Welfe and developed by the members of the Lódz research team including G.Juszczak, M.M.Kazmierska, N.Lapinska-Sobczak and W.Welfe and was the subject of systematic testing and revisions. The basic assumptions were formulated first supplemented by a discussion of the major relationships of a demand determined economic system reflected in the quarterly macro model. The specification of equations for the following blocks (except for macro aggregates) was outlined next: production sector, households, government (budget), banking system, foreign trade, prices and labour force. The major technical problems related to the data scarcity are also discussed, i.e. the calibrating procedures applied to estimate the parameters of structural equations, including the lags distributions in case the sample is composed of 8-12 observations. The construction of "composite" variables using extraneous information (mainly from I-O tables) was described and the search procedures outlined. Details of model specification (list of variables, the structure of the simulation model and the results of estimation) are given in the Appendices 1 and 2.

The model validation as a system of equations was performed in a standard fashion. It was supplemented by an additional attempt to introduce the expectations on prices, interest rates and profits into some of the model equations. Chapter 5 by M.M.Kazmierska and W.Zaton provides the summary of findings. It also shows the results of multiplier analysis comparing the impact of external shocks (in exports, imports, interest rate and wages) on major endogenous variables including and excluding expectations.

The construction of the quarterly data base poses many problems being due to discontinuity of old data, emerging of new information, changes in definitions and coverage. The constructed data base which includes more than 200 variables was described by G.Juszczak in Chapter 6. The quarterly models should apply the macroeconomic concepts, including the generation of macro variables covering the gross domestic product and its use, despite the fact that in some countries, like for example in Poland, the quarterly and monthly time series related to the above macro variables are simply not available. The techniques were developed in order to devise the estimates of macro variables being the function of observable, related variables (e.g. indicators like sales of production in industry which can be used to estimate GDP originating in industry). They are discussed by M.M.Kazmierska and S.Narel. The first computations of quarterly GDP and its components for Poland were also included.

A set of monthly statistical forecasting models must be developed - for selected variables (time series) related to 1) exogenous variables of the quarterly model, 2) endogenous variables explained by the quarterly model. The spectrum of these variables must be broad enough in order to identify short-term changes in "strategic" endogenous variables of the quarterly macro-models. Various procedures of the time series analyses had to be tried and their accuracy empirically assessed [4)].

The concepts and research results, outlined above, were the subject of numerous discussions led within and between the research teams. Most stimulating were the presentations of papers at two ACE sponsored workshops. The first, aimed at discussion on the intermediate results was held in Mittelberg in May 1991 (ACE Seminar: "Simulations and Financial Models"). The second, covering the final results was held in Paris in October 1991 (ACE Seminar: "The Concept of a System of Models and Forecasts").

---

(4) See Lapinska-Sobczak, Narel [1992]

1.4 The system of economic forecasts and policy simulations

The natural requirement for a system of forecasts based on a system of macro models is that they should be consistent. In its simplest notion it might be required that the quarterly forecasts for the flows must add up to the annual forecasts (respectively averages of quarterly ratios must be equal to the annual ratio). The same applies to the monthly series which might add up to the quarterly data. This natural, but strong criterion may be neither automatically nor exactly fulfilled because of differences in definitions and coverage, lags and non-linearity. Hence, special estimating procedures must be used. They are discussed in Chapter 6 by S.Narel and M.M.Kazmierska.

On the other hand, there is a rising demand for presenting updated forecasts with much higher frequency.

a/ The annual forecasts (of 2-5 year horizon) must be updated not only once for year, but twice a year or each quarter; then a use can be made of the most recent quarterly information (for instance in April after the results of the 1st quarter are known, etc.). To formalise the updating procedures we have a/ to establish the relationships for the exogenous variables between the annual and quarterly (by adding up quarters) values, b) to establish also the relationships for the "strategic" endogenous variables between their annual and quarterly values in order to discover likely distortions of structural relationships and allow for them by means of structural parameters (typically constant) adjustments;

b/ More complex is the problem of linking the quarterly forecasts based on the econometric (structural) models with the high frequency forecasts (monthly, weekly) being generated from statistical forecasting models. The consistency criterion only rarely applies, because of the differences in coverage and definitions. On the other hand, the same concepts can be approached using a set of variables, sometimes from different sources. The rules here are frequently heuristic and ad hoc, appealing to the discrimination analysis, principal components being the most familiar method. The strategy of using this high frequency data in updating the quarterly (or annual) forecasts will be similar to those above.

We have to clarify here the following misunderstanding. Sometimes it is claimed that using monthly models, say, to "improve" quarterly models, simply means that the latter are less accurate, less reliable, and the conclusion is: why not to use the monthly models only. The following arguments can be forwarded in order to justify quite an opposite opinion. First, only the structural relationships can be used to perform meaningful policy simulations (and also forecasts where policy instruments are exogenous variables), and the annual models only can give full account of the economic system. The quarterly structural models represent - to some extent - approximations of the major components of the economic system, whereas monthly models cover typically selected variables (this situation will change in the future, however). Secondly, the annual or quarterly forecasts are based upon assumptions with respect to exogenous variables (policy instruments) which may change during the period preceding the forecasting period, but coming after the forecast was made. The same applies to likely changes in structural parameters (especially if they reflect policy changes, for instance in taxation rules). Hence, it seems fully justified to implement the updated information with respect to the assumptions being previously made by the forecasters.

A survey of the above procedures will be provided, taking into account in the first line the experience gathered by GAMA for France, but also being the result of international co-operation to be demonstrated in the proceedings of the Paris ACE Seminar on "High frequency data" (October 1991) to be published elsewhere.

1.5 The numerical techniques

The empirical results in modelling the economies under transition were obtained in a relatively short time. It was due to the availability of new numerical techniques. The model generator ETAS developed by D.Hubrich and M.Rohner (from the Frankfurt team) was used in construction of the annual model for united Germany described in an annex to part 1. On the other hand, the Lódz team used the G and STS estimation packages as well as the most powerful SIMUL simulation system (A.Welfe, W.Zaton [1991]).

1.6 Further research plans

It is hoped that in the next stage the research will cover with respect to a) the annual models - the restructuring of the macro models for Poland and the new applications to study medium-term transformations of the German and Polish economies, and b) the quarterly models - the construction of a complete, maintained model for Poland. This will lead towards the construction of a system of interlinked models to be used in forecasting and policy simulations postulated in our concept referred to in this chapter.

REFERENCES

Anders, H., D. Schilar, M. Woelfling (eds.) [1981] - Planungs und Prognosemodelle, Erfahrungen, Probleme, Entwicklungs-tendenzen, Akademie-Verlag, Berlin.

Andersen, L. C., K. Carlson [1976] - St. Louis Model Revised, in: (eds.) L. R. Klein, E. Burmeister, Econometric Model Performance, University of Pennsylvania Press, Philadelphia.

Ball, R. J., B. Boatwright, T. Burns, P. Loban, G. Miller [1973] - The London Business School Quarterly Econometric Model of the UK. Economy, in: G. A. Renton (ed.). Modelling the Economy, Heineman Educational Press.

Bodkin, R. G., L. R. Klein, K. Marwah [199] - A History of Macroeconometric Model-Building, E. Elgar.

Courbis, R., P. Salmon [1986] - Le Modele PROTEE, un modele trimestriel de l'economie francaise, Presentation generale et utilisation, IIeme Seminaire Franco-Polonais sur la modelisation, Nanterre 29-30 mai 1986 (Papier GAMA, no 544).

D'Adda, C., E. De Antoni, G. Gambetta, P. Onofri, A. Stagni [1976] - Un Modello per l'economia italiana, il Mulino.

Duesenberry, J. M. et al. (eds.) [1963] - The Brookings Quarterly Model of the United States, North Holland, Amsterdam.

Evans, M. K., L. R. Klein [1968] - The Wharton Econometric Forecasting Model, Studies in Quantitative Economics no 2, Economics Research Unit, University of Pennsylvania, Philadelphia.

Fair, R. C. [1971] - A Short-Run Forecasting Model of the US Economy. Lexington.

Fase, M. M. G. [1984] - The Monetary Sector of the Netherlands in 50 Equations, Advanced Studies in Theoretical and Applied Econometrics vol. 2., The Hague.

Hansen, G., U.Westphal [1975] - A Quarterly Econometric Model for the Federal Republic of Germany. Special Features and Forecasting Results, paper presented at the World Congress of Econometric Society, Toronto.

Juszczak, G., M. M. Kazmierska, W. Welfe [1991] - Ekonometryczny model gospodarki narodowej Polski W-5 (wersja symulacyjna) (Econometric Model of the Polish Economy W-5), Prace IEiS UL, 93, Wydawnictwo UL, Lodz.

Kalinin, D., W. Maciejewski, J. Zajchowski, [1977] - Kwartalny model gospodarki Polski 1967-1975 KP-3K (Quarterly Model of the Polish Economy KP-3K), Gospodarka Planowa No 3, p. 128-135,

Kudrycka, I., [1990] - The Quarterly Forecasting Model of the Polish Economy, in: Problems of Building and Estimation of Large Econometric Models (part A), Proceedings of MACROMODELS'85, Wydawnictwo UL, Lodz, p. 55-95.

Łapinska-Sobczak, N., S. Narel [1992] - Metody prognozowania krótkookresowego (Methods of Short-term Forecasting of Polish Economy) Wiadomości Statystyczne no 10, p.12-14

Łapinska-Sobczak, N., L. Tomaszewicz, W. Welfe [1979] - Modelling of Financial and Monetary Flows in Poland, paper presented at the Collogue International: Models Monetaires et Financiers, A.E.A., Banca d'Italia, G.A.M.A., Rome 7-10 February 1979.

Macroeconometric Model of the Deutsche Bundesbank. Model Version 30/03/88 [1988], Deutsche Bundesbank.

Malgrange, P. [1983] - Steady Growth Paths in a Short Run Dynamic Model: The Case of the French Quarterly Model Metric", CEPREMAP, paper No 8321, Octobre.

McCarthy, M. D. [1972] - The Wharton Quarterly Econometric Forecasting Model, Mark III, Studies in Quantitative Economics No 6., University of Pennsylvania, Philadelphia.

Orłowski, W., Ł. Tomaszewicz [1991] - The Inforum Model of the Polish Economy, Economic System Research, 3, p. 85-92.

Portes, R. [1991] - Introduction, in: European Economy. The Path of Reform in Central and Eastern Europe. Special Edition no 2, Commission of the European Communities, Brussels- Luxemburg.

Sujan, I., J. Kolek [1974] - A Quarterly Forecasting Model of the Czechoslovak Economy, paper presented at the European Meeting of the Econometric Society, Grenoble 1974.

Sujan, I., M. Olexa [1984] - Kvartalnaja ekonometriczeskaja model dla kratkosrocznego analiza ekonomiki CSRS, Ekonomika i Matematiczeskije Metody, 20, No 4., p. 646-655.

Waelbroeck, J. [1975] - A Survey of Short-Run Model Research Out- side the United States, in: G. Fromm, L. R. Klein (eds.) The Brookings Model: Perspective and Recent Developments, North Holland, Amsterdam-Oxford, American Elsevier P.C., New York.

Welfe, A., W. Zatoń [1991] - Simulation System SIMUL, Prace IEiS UŁ, 82, Wydawnictwo UŁ, Łódź.

Welfe, W. [1985] - Econometric Macromodels of Unbalanced Growth, Prace IEiS UŁ, 52, Łódź.

Welfe, W. [1989] - Macroeconomic Disequilibrium Models of Poland, in C. M. Davis, W. Charemza (eds) Models of Disequlibrium and Shortage in Centrally Planned Economies, Chapman and Hall, Cambridge, p. 205 - 246.

Welfe, W. [1992] - Multisectoral Econometric Models of the Centrally Planned Economies and the Disequilibria, Economics of Planning, 24. p. 203-226.

PART 1

GERMANY

CHAPTER 2

THE SYSTEM OF MODELS[1)]

Klaus Behle, Gerhard Gehrig, Pawel Tomczyk
Institute for Development, Environment and Quantitative Economic Research,
Johann Wolfgang Goethe-University, Frankfurt/Main

2.1 Introduction

If one attempts to project the economic consequences of German unification econometrically the following problem arises: it is quite possible to construct an econometric model for West Germany using regression analysis; yet, adopting the same approach for East Germany is impossible.

There are several reasons. The macroeconomic data of the past do not correspond with the UN system of national accounts (SNA). They are instead based on the material product system (MPS). Data are very scarce and those for foreign trade are heavily distorted as an undefined money unit called 'Valuta Mark' has been used. In addition, regression analysis would not help to restructure a centrally planned economy. But this economy of the former GDR will be completely changed to a social market economy. Thus, projecting the old economy of the GDR would make no sense.

Adding up, the two economies would also prevent applying regression analysis. Moreover, the now regional effects of the former GDR and the former FRG could not be studied.

Thus, the solution of the problem might be found in the combination of regression analysis and simulation techniques. There will be a macroeconomic model for West Germany based on regression analysis for the time period 1960 to 1990. The equations of this model will be taken to form a simulation model for East Germany slightly changed and especially corrected for differences in the absolute level of some variables. This simulation model will be based on 1990, the year of unification.

---

(1) The first version of the model was established by cooperation with Thomas Gehrig, Dietmar Hubrich, Steffen Möckel, Meinrad Rohner, Andreas Storm and the students of the Proseminar WS 90/91.

By ex-post simulations it is possible to set up a simulation model for West Germany also based on the year 1990. Both models can be combined to a system of models by taking different symbols for the two economies and by adding some equations for intra-German trade.

This procedure makes it possible to study the isolated effects of economic growth and development in both former states. Taking technical, behavioural and institutional functions from the former FRG for East Germany seems to be reasonable as there are now the same laws and the same institutions and the same currency. In addition, as the inhabitants of the former GDR are Germans with the same skills and the same mentality as the inhabitants of the Western part, they will behave the same way as the Germans in the West do. Of course, there will be some time of transition but finally the economic structure will be the same.

The time horizon has been chosen until the year 2000. It might be quite possible that in the years 2000 to 2005 the transition period will come to an end or at least will have nearly passed.

2.2 The model for West Germany

There is a model for West Germany and one for East Germany. The models comprise essentially a commodity market, a rudimentary money and labour market. A model for East-West trade has been added in order to ease the fictitious subdivision of the FRG of today

.

The model is supposed to be essentially long run as it is based on a production function taking care of the degree of utilization of capital and labour. Thus, it might be used to derive annual results as well as to show the direction of economic development.

2.2.1 Commodity market

Supply is determined by a Cobb-Douglas production function with constant returns to scale and with the factors of production for used stock of capital and labour and selected real imports. Real output is given by GNP (Gross National Product) plus imports in 1985 prices. Moreover, there is a function for imports, one for real imports of services and one for imported real capital goods.

Demand is definitionally separated into private and public consumption and into private and public fixed capital formation further subdivided into equipment and construction and into changes of stocks and foreign trade. Each part of the definition is made functionally dependent on certain variables.

In general, demand is determined nominally. That makes it possible to endogenize the price index of GNP. As the components of demand have to be derived in real terms, too, some empirical price equations depending on the price of GNP and other factors had to be included in the model. But this does not mean that increases in final demand will only push up the overall price index without any effects on supply. As there is no connection to supply except that for capital formation the exogenously given degrees of utilization of capital and labour will influence the price of GNP.

In order to be able to study the development of the budget of the government the most important parts of its inputs and outputs had to be functionalized. There are functions for main taxes, subsidies, social security payments and others. On the output side there are functionalized transfers, interest payments, government consumption, fixed capital formation and others.

2.2.2 Money market

It was impossible to establish in a first attempt a complete model for the money market based on regression. This will be done by future work. Thus, this market has been designed in a rudimentary way. There is a function for the demand for money called M1 (cash plus short term deposits) given a certain level of production and the interest rate which is mainly determined in West Germany by the rate of discount which is set by the Federal Bank (Bundesbank).

2.2.3 Labour market

It is fairly difficult to determine the amount of labour. The demand for labour could be derived from the production function indicating the needed level of employment to sustain production. Thus, unemployment could be determined outside of the model by projecting the labour force in connection with the population growth. Employment could depend on the average real wage rate, the level of real production, working time and labour saving technical progress. Working time would be exogenous and due to the results of bargaining between trade unions and entrepreneurs. In order to be more flexible for simulations and intending to elaborate this market in more detail in the near future this function has been omitted from the model.

2.2.4 Technical details

The regression analyses were performed by a model generator called ETAS [1].[2)] The estimates were derived by OLS (ordinary least squares) as the model is non-linear. The resulting biases have been taken into account in favour of the structural quality of the equations. Simultaneous estimation methods tend to spread errors in one or some equations to all others in an economically uncontrolled way. The base period of the regressions differs a bit according to lags in the equations and to the available statistics. The goodness of fit of the model has been tested by an ex-post-simulation for the base period.

2.3 The model for East Germany

This sub-model could not be derived by regression analysis, therefore structural and definitional equations of the model for West Germany have been taken as proxies. In general, the national accounts statistics were taken to adjust the constant term of an equation whenever necessary. If possible, special adjustments were prepared such as that for the function of private consumption taking consumption per head. Moreover, dummies have been introduced in order to vary the impact of some variables over time mainly connected with imports and taxes. Summing up, the model for East Germany is not a regression model but a deterministic one.

2.4 The model for East-West trade

Re-naming the variables for the West German model makes it possible to add all the equations from the two models. But adding does not establish mutual interdependencies between the two economies. Thus, a set of definitional equations had to be implemented concerning trade. Total imports of West Germany were subdivided into imports from East Germany and those from the rest of the world. The exports of West Germany were analogously separated into those to East

---

(2) See also Appendix 1.

Germany and those to the rest of the world. For simulation purposes the imports from East Germany were made a variable percentage of all the needed imports. The same settings were implemented for the foreign trade of East Germany.

2.5 The equations of the system of models

2.5.1 Model for West Germany

Commodity market

Total supply:

$$QSP = BSP+M \qquad [1.1]$$

Gross national product:

$$BSP = CPR+CST+IAN+IVOR+X-M \qquad [1.2]$$

Gross national product in 1985 prices:

$$BSP85 = QSP85-M85 \qquad [1.3]$$

Net national income at factor cost:

$$NSPF = BSP-D-TIND+SUB \qquad [1.4]$$

Personal disposable income, private households:

$$YVPE = NSPF\_HH+TR\_HH\_EMP-TR\_HH\_GEL-GUOER\_N \qquad [1.5]$$

Net national income at factor cost, households:

$$NSPF\_HH = BUA+BUV\_HH-ZINS\_HH\_KR \qquad [1.6]$$

Undistributed profits of companies with a legal entity:

$$GUMER\_U = -6335.814+0.170*BUV+9548.591*DUM77+13707.996*DUM83 \qquad [1.7]$$

Supply

Total supply in 1985 prices:

$$\ln(QSP85) = -0.467+0.375*\ln(BESCH*1000)+0.399*\ln(MR\%D85)+ +0.226*\ln(KAPAM85) \qquad [1.8]$$

Consumption of fixed capital:

$$D = 0.027*BSP+0.830*LD \qquad [1.9]$$

Depreciation of fixed assets, public sector, in 1985 prices:

$$DAN85\_ST = 579.219+0.0015*KAP85\_ST+0.639*LDAN85\_ST \qquad [1.10]$$

Depreciation of fixed assets, equipment, private sector, in 1985 prices:

DAU85_PR = -4039.228+0.016*LKAU85_PR+0.796*LDAU85_PR [1.11]

Depreciation of fixed assets, construction, private sector, in 1985 prices:

DBA85_PR = -1262.044+0.000536*LKBA85_PR+0.981*LDBA85_PR [1.12]

Stock of capital, public sector, in 1985 prices (end of year):

KAP85_ST = IAN85_ST-DAN85_ST+LKAP85_ST [1.13]

Stock of capital, equipment, private sector, in 1985 prices (end of year):

KAU85_PR = IAU85_PR-DAU85_PR+LKAU85_PR [1.14]

Stock of capital, construction, private sector, in 1985 prices (end of year):

KBA85_PR = IBA85_PR-DBA85_PR+LKBA85_PR [1.15]

Stock of capital, public sector, in 1985 prices (average of year):

KAPM85_ST = KAP85_ST/2+LKAP85_ST/2 [1.16]

Stock of capital, equipment, private sector, in 1985 prices (average of year):

KAUM85_PR = KAU85_PR/2+LKAU85_PR/2 [1.17]

Stock of capital, construction, private sector, in 1985 prices (average of year):

KBAM85_PR = KBA85_PR/2+LKBA85_PR/2 [1.18]

Utilized stock of capital, equipment, private sector, in 1985 prices (average of year):

KAUMA85_PR = KAUM85_PR*CAPIFO/100 [1.19]

Stock of capital, in 1985 prices (end of year):

KAP85 = KAU85_PR+KBA85_PR+KAP85_ST [1.20]

Utilized stock of capital, in 1985 prices (average of year):

KAPAM85 = KAUMA85_PR+KBAM85_PR+KAPM85_ST [1.21]

Imports (including incomes from assets and business):

ln(M) = 0.087*ln(BSP)+0.910*ln(LM) [1.22]

Imports of services in 1985 prices:

MD85 = 22447.939+0.021*BSP85-28443.691*PMD_PBSP+
+0.639*LMD85 [1.23]

Imports of equipment, in 1985 prices:

MIAU85 = -29486.503+0.041*QSP85-0.041*LQSP85-512.995*PMIAU+
+1150.537*PIAU+19841.646*DUM90 [1.24]

Imports (including incomes from assets and business), in 1985 prices:

M85 = M/PM*100 [1.25]

Imports without capital goods and services, in 1985 prices:

MR%D85 = M85-MIAU85-MD85 [1.26]

19

Demand

Private consumption:

CPR = 16191.666+0.558*YVPE-1699.709*R_WPUM- [1.27]
-3.373*LTD_KEST+0.396*LCPR+22907.848*DUM90

Government consumption in 1985 prices:

CST85 = 18837.886+0.021*QSP85+0.822*LCST85 [1.28]

Private consumption in 1985 prices:

CPR85 = CPR/PCPR*100 [1.29]

Government consumption:

CST = PCST*CST85/100 [1.30]

Consumption:

C = CPR+CST [1.31]

Consumption in 1985 prices:

C85 = CPR85+CST85 [1.32]

Share of private consumption to GNP:

CPR_BSP = CPR/BSP [1.33]

Share of government consumption to GNP:

CST_BSP = CST/BSP [1.34]

Gross fixed capital formation, public sector:

IAN_ST = 4072.274005+0.126187*C-0.126*LC+0.018*LT+ [1.35]
+0.595*LIAN_ST

First difference of gross fixed capital formation, equipment, private sector:

DIAU_PR = 17581.831+0.222*C-0.222*LC-3011.577*R_WPUM+ [1.36]
+12921.790*DUM90

Gross fixed capital formation, construction, private sector:

IBA_PR = 0.141*QSP-0.141*LQSP+0.0042*KBAM85_PR+ [1.37]
+10147.894*DUM78+0.736*LIBA_PR

Gross fixed capital formation, equipment, private sector:

IAU_PR = LIAU_PR+DIAU_PR [1.38]

Gross fixed capital formation, public sector, in 1985 prices:

IAN85_ST = IAN_ST/PIAN_ST*100 [1.39]

Gross fixed capital formation, equipment, private sector, in 1985 prices:

IAU85_PR = IAU_PR/PIAU_PR*100 [1.40]

Gross fixed capital formation, construction, private sector, in 1985 prices:

IBA85_PR = IBA_PR/PIBA_PR*100 [1.41]

Gross fixed capital formation, in 1985 prices:

IAN85 = IAU85_PR+IBA85_PR+IAN85_ST [1.42]

Gross fixed capital formation:

IAN = IBA_PR+IAU_PR+IAN_ST [1.43]

Share of gross fixed capital formation (public sector) to GNP:

IANST_BSP = IAN_ST/BSP [1.44]

Share of gross fixed capital formation (equipment, private sector) to GNP:

IAUPR_BSP = IAU_PR/BSP [1.45]

Share of gross fixed capital formation (construction, private sector) to GNP:

IBAPR_BSP = IBA_PR/BSP [1.46]

Government, transfers and redistribution

Total government receipts:

IN_ST = TDIR+TIND+SB_ST+YUVST+IN_SONS [1.47]

Total government expenditures:

OUT_ST = CST+IAN_ST+SUB+ZINS_ST+SL_ST+OUT_SONS+
+ZU_NL_ST [1.48]

Balance of government budget:

FS_ST = IN_ST-OUT_ST [1.49]

Indirect taxes:

TIND = TI_UST+TI_MIN+TI_GEW+TI_SONS [1.50]

Direct taxes:

TDIR = TD_LOST%P+TD_KOST+TD_KEST+TD_SONS [1.51]

Direct taxes, private households:

TD_HH = -2110.955+0.853*TDIR [1.52]

Capital yields tax:

TD_KEST = -862.931+0.012*BUV+0.416*LTD_KEST+3489.291*DUM_89Q [1.53]

Corporate income tax:

TD_KOST = 2217.219+0.327*BST_KST+0.461*LTD_KOST-
-4804.207*DUM90 [1.54]

Payroll tax (without that on pensions):

TD_LOST%P = -12168.998+0.1152*BLG+0.430*LTD_LOST%P-
-14682.160*DUM90 [1.55]

Tax paid for carrying on a trade:

TI_GEW = 1944.449+0.231*GEW_BUV+1.120*GEW_LSST+
+12949.878*DUM80 [1.56]

Petroleum tax:

TI_MIN = -5876.156+18.516*VOL_MIN+1772.057*DUM82+
+4266.970*DUM90 [1.57]

Turnover tax:

TI_UST = -71076.539+0.056*BMG_UST+7145.258*MWST_SATZ+
+71772.981*DUM_MWST+10839.174*DUM90 [1.58]

Subsidies:

SUB = 0.028*T+0.701852*LSUB [1.59]

Total taxes:

T = TDIR+TIND [1.60]

Taxes and social contributions:

TSB = T+SB_PR [1.61]

Tax base of corporate income tax:

BST_KST = GUMER_U*KST_SATZ/100 [1.62]

Imputed contributions to social security:

GSV_BLG = BEI_GSV/100*BLG [1.63]

Tax base, tax paid for carrying on a trade:

GEW_BUV = GEW_SATZ*BUV/2000 [1.64]

Tax base, payroll tax:

GEW_LSST = BLG*LSST_SATZ/50000 [1.65]

Tax base of turnover tax:

BMG_UST = C+IAN-BLG_ST [1.66]

Interest on debts of the public sector:

ZINS_ST = ZINS_GK+ZINS_GSV [1.67]

Interest on government debt:

ln(ZINS_GK) = -2.426+0.447914*ln(TVS_GK)+0.288*ln(R_WPUM)+
+0.618*ln(LZINS_GK)-0.157*DUM90 [1.68]

Social contributions to the public sector:

SB_ST = -3246.425+1.073*GSV_BLG+5955.048*DUM73-
-16199.378*DUM90 [1.69]

Social contributions to the private sector:

SB_UH = 0.121*GSV_BLG [1.70]

Social contributions of private households:

SB_PR = SB_ST+SB_UH+SB_EA [1.71]

Contributions, paid by employers to public social insurance:

SB_AG = -6694.015+0.107*BLG+0.592*LSB_AG [1.72]

Balance of the government social contributions:

SL_ZU_ST = SL_ST-SB_ST [1.73]

Social contributions from the public sector to the private households:

SL_HH_ST = SL_HA_ST+SL_HN_ST [1.74]

Government social contributions (government and social insurance):

SL_ST = SL_HH_ST+SL_W_ST [1.75]

Transfer incomes of private households from other sectors:

TR_HH_EMP = SL_HA_ST+SL_U+SL_HH_H+SL_W+TR_SONS [1.76]

Transfer payments of private households to other sectors:

TR_HH_GEL = TD_HH+SB_PR+TR_HH_R [1.77]

Other transfer payments of private households:

TR_HH_R = 0.007656*BSP+0.800*LTR_HH_R [1.78]

Transfer incomes, without direct taxes, paid transfers and social contributions:

TR%T = TR_HH_EMP-TR_HH_R-TD_HH-SB_PR [1.79]

Prices

Price index, gross national product:

PBSP = BSP/BSP85*100 [1.80]

Relative prices, price of imported services to price of gross national product:

PMD_PBSP = PMD/PBSP [1.81]

Price index, private consumption:

PCPR = -29.523+0.490*PBSP+57.822*CPR_BSP+0.478*LPCPR [1.82]

Price index, government consumption:

PCST = -31.998+1.044*PBSP+140.584*CST_BSP [1.83]

Price index, gross fixed capital formation, public sector:

PIAN_ST = -12.696+0.470*PBSP+254.776*IANST_BSP+0.610*LPIAN_ST [1.84]

Price index, gross fixed capital formation, equipment, private sector:

PIAU_PR = 0.325*PBSP+49.243*IAUPR_BSP+0.642*LPIAU_PR [1.85]

Price index, gross fixed capital formation, construction, private sector:

PIBA_PR = -37.017+1.184*PBSP+201.567*IBAPR_BSP [1.86]

Money market

Money supply M1:

ln(M1) = -0.734+0.424*ln(BSP)-0.141*ln(R_WPUM)+0.600*ln(LM1) [1.87]

Labour market

Gross wage per hour in 1985 prices:

BLG_EH85 = BLG/BESVOL/PBSP*100 [1.88]

Total labour cost per hour in 1985 prices:

BUA_EH85 = BUA_EH/PBSP*100 [1.89]

Gross income of employees:

BUA = BUA_EH*BESVOL [1.90]

Gross income from entrepreneurial activity and property:

BUV = NSPF-BUA [1.91]

Gross wages and salaries, total:

BLG = BUA-SB_AG [1.92]

Wage and salary earners:

BESCH = ET-SELB [1.93]

Total man hours:

BESVOL = BESCH*EH/1000 [1.94]

2.5.2 Model for East Germany

Commodity market

Total supply:

QSP@ = BSP@+M@ [2.1]

Gross national product:

BSP@ = CPR@+CST@+IAN@+IVOR@+X@-M@ [2.2]

Gross national product in 1985 prices:

BSP85@ = QSP85@-M85@ [2.3]

Net national income at factor cost:

NSPF@ = BSP@-D@-TIND@+SUB@ [2.4]

Personal disposable income, private households:

YVPE@ = NSPF_HH@+TR_HH_EMP@-TR_HH_GEL@-GUOER_N@ [2.5]

Net national income at factor cost, households:

NSPF_HH@ = BUA@+BUV_HH@-ZINSHHKR@ [2.6]

Undistributed profits of companies with legal entity:

GUMER_U@ = -6335.814*&DUMGUMER@+0.170*BUV@ [2.7]

Supply

Total supply in 1985 prices:

ln(QSP85@) = -0.467*&DUMQSP@+0.375*ln(BESCH@*1000)+
+0.399*ln(MR%D85@)+0.226*ln(KAPAM85@) [2.8]

Consumption of fixed capital:

D@ = 922.226*&DUMD@+0.027*BSP@+0.830*LD@ [2.9]

Depreciation of fixed assets, public sector, in 1985 prices:

DAN85_ST@ = 579.219*&DUMDAN@+0.001521*KAP85_ST@+
+0.639*LDAN85_ST@ [2.10]

Depreciation of fixed assets, equipment, private sector, in 1985 prices:

DAU85_PR@ = -4039.228*&DUMDAU@+0.016*LKAU85_PR@+
+0.796*LDAU85_PR@ [2.11]

Depreciation of fixed assets, construction, private sector, in 1985 prices:

DBA85_PR@ = -1262.044*&DUMDBA@+0.000536*LKBA85_PR@+
+0.981*LDBA85_PR@ [2.12]

Stock of capital, public sector, in 1985 prices (end of year):

KAP85_ST@ = IAN85_ST@-DAN85_ST@+LKAP85_ST@ [2.13]

Stock of capital, equipment, private sector, in 1985 prices (end of year):

KAU85_PR@ = IAU85_PR@-DAU85_PR@+LKAU85_PR@ [2.14]

Stock of capital, construction, private sector, in 1985 prices (end of year):

KBA85_PR@ = IBA85_PR@-DBA85_PR@+LKBA85_PR@ [2.15]

Stock of capital, public sector, in 1985 prices (average of year):

KAPM85_ST@ = KAP85_ST@/2+LKAP85_ST@/2 [2.16]

Stock of capital, equipment, private sector, in 1985 prices (average of year):

KAUM85_PR@ = KAU85_PR@/2+LKAU85_PR@/2 [2.17]

Stock of capital, construction, private sector, in 1985 prices (average of year):

KBAM85_PR@ = KBA85_PR@/2+LKBA85_PR@/2 [2.18]

Utilized stock of capital, equipment, private sector, in 1985 prices (average of year):

KAUMA85PR@ = KAUM85_PR@*CAPIFO@/100 [2.19]

Stock of capital, in 1985 prices (end of year):

KAP85@ = KAU85_PR@+KBA85_PR@+KAP85_ST@ [2.20]

Utilized stock of capital, in 1985 prices (average of year):

KAPAM85@ = KAUMA85PR@+KBAM85_PR@+KAPM85_ST@ [2.21]

Imports (including incomes from assets and business):

ln(M@) = 0.677*&DUMM@+0.087*ln(BSP@)+0.910*ln(LM@) [2.22]

Imports of services, in 1985 prices:

MD85@ = 22447.939*&DUMMD@+0.021*BSP85@- [2.23]

-28443.691*PMD_PBSP@+ 0.639*LMD85@

Imports of equipment, in 1985 prices:

MIAU85@ = -29486.503*&DUMMIAU@+0.041*QSP85@- [2.24]

-0.041*LQSP85@-512.995*PMIAU@+1150.537*PIAU@

Imports (including incomes from assets and business), in 1985 prices:

M85@ = M@/PM@*100 [2.25]

Imports without capital goods and services, in 1985 prices:

MR%D85@ = M85@-MIAU85@-MD85@ [2.26]

Demand

Private consumption:

CPR@ = 4287.479+0.558*&DUMCPR@*YVPE@- [2.27]

-1699.709*R_WPUM@-3.373*LTD_KEST@+0.396*LCPR@

Government consumption in 1985 prices:

CST85@ = 18837.886*&DUMCST@+0.021*QSP85@+0.822*LCST85@ [2.28]

Private consumption in 1985 prices:

CPR85@ = CPR@/PCPR@*100 [2.29]

Government consumption:

CST@ = PCST@*CST85@/100 [2.30]

Consumption:

C@ = CPR@+CST@ [2.31]

Consumption in 1985 prices:

C85@ = CPR85@+CST85@ [2.32]

Share of private consumption to GNP:

CPR_BSP@ = CPR@/BSP@ [2.33]

Share of government consumption to GNP:

CST_BSP@ = CST@/BSP@ [2.34]

Gross fixed capital formation, public sector:

IAN_ST@ = 4072.274*&DUMIAN@+0.126*C@-0.126*LC@+0.018*LT@+ +0.595*LIAN_ST@ [2.35]

First difference of gross fixed capital formation, equipment, private sector:

DIAU_PR@ = 17581.831*&DUMIAU@+0.222*C@-0.222*LC@- -3011.577*R_WPUM@ [2.36]

Gross fixed capital formation, construction, private sector:

IBA_PR@ = -4801.249*&DUMIBA@+0.141*QSP@-0.141*LQSP@+ +0.00421*KBAM85_PR@+0.736*LIBA_PR@ [2.37]

Gross fixed capital formation, equipment, private sector:

IAU_PR@ = LIAU_PR@+DIAU_PR@ [2.38]

Gross fixed capital formation, public sector, in 1985 prices:

IAN85_ST@ = IAN_ST@/PIAN_ST@*100 [2.39]

Gross fixed capital formation, equipment, private sector, in 1985 prices:

IAU85_PR@ = IAU_PR@/PIAU_PR@*100 [2.40]

Gross fixed capital formation, construction, private sector, in 1985 prices:

IBA85_PR@ = IBA_PR@/PIBA_PR@*100 [2.41]

Gross fixed capital formation, in 1985 prices:

IAN85@ = IAU85_PR@+IBA85_PR@+IAN85_ST@ [2.42]

Gross fixed capital formation:

IAN@ = IBA_PR@+IAU_PR@+IAN_ST@ [2.43]

Share of gross fixed capital formation (public sector) to GNP:

IANST_BSP@ = IAN_ST@/BSP@ [2.44]

Share of gross fixed capital formation (equipment, private sector) to GNP:

IAUPR_BSP@ = IAU_PR@/BSP@ [2.45]

Share of gross fixed capital formation (construction, private sector) to GNP:

IBAPR_BSP@ = IBA_PR@/BSP@ [2.46]

Government, transfers and redistribution

Total government receipts:

IN_ST@ = TDIR@+TIND@+SB_ST@+YUVST@+IN_SONS@+ +ZU_NL_ST [2.47]

Total government expenditures:

OUT_ST@ = CST@+IAN_ST@+SUB@+ZINS_ST@+SL_ST@+ +OUT_SONS@ [2.48]

Balance of government budget:

FS_ST@ = IN_ST@-OUT_ST@ [2.49]

Indirect taxes:

TIND@ = TI_UST@+TI_MIN@+TI_GEW@+TI_SONS@ [2.50]

Direct taxes:

TDIR@ = TDLOST%P@+TD_KOST@+TD_KEST@+TD_SONS@ [2.51]

Direct taxes, private households:

TD_HH@ = -2110.955*&DUMTDHH@+0.853*TDIR@ [2.52]

Capital yields tax:

TD_KEST@ = -862.931*&DUMTDKES@+0.012*BUV@+0.416*LTD_KEST@ [2.53]

Corporate income tax:

TD_KOST@ = 2217.219*&DUMTDKOS@+0.327*BST_KST@+ +0.461*LTD_KOST@ [2.54]

Payroll tax (without that on pensions):

TDLOST%P@ = -12168.998*&DUMTDLOS@+0.115*BLG@+ +0.430*LTDLOST%P@ [2.55]

Tax paid for carrying on a trade:

TI_GEW@ = 1944.449*&DUMTIGEW@+0.231*GEW_BUV@+ +1.120*GEW_LSST@ [2.56]

Petroleum tax:

TI_MIN@ = -5876.156*&DUMTIMIN@+18.516*VOL_MIN@ [2.57]

Turnover tax:

TI_UST@ = -71076.539*&DUMTIUST@+0.056*BMG_UST@+ +7145.258*MWST_SATZ@ [2.58]

Subsidies:

SUB@ = 5788.665*&DUMSUB@+0.028*T@+0.702*LSUB@ [2.59]

Total taxes:

T@ = TDIR@+TIND@ [2.60]

Taxes and social contributions:

TSB@ = T@+SB_PR@ [2.61]

Tax base of corporate income tax:

BST_KST@ = GUMER_U@*KST_SATZ@/100 [2.62]

Imputed contributions to social security:

GSV_BLG@ = BEI_GSV@/100*BLG@ [2.63]

Tax base, tax paid for carrying on a trade:

GEW_BUV@ = GEW_SATZ@*BUV@/2000 [2.64]

Tax base, payroll tax:

GEW_LSST@ = BLG@*LSST_SATZ@/50000 [2.65]

Tax base of turnover tax:

BMG_UST@ = C@+IAN@-BLG_ST@ [2.66]

Interest on debts of the public sector:

ZINS_ST@ = ZINS_GK@+ZINS_GSV@ [2.67]

Interest on government debt:

ln(ZINS_GK@) = -2.426*&DUMZINS@+0.448*ln(TVS_GK@)+ [2.68]
+0.288*ln(R_WPUM@)+0.618*ln(LZINS_GK@)

Social contributions to the public sector:

SB_ST@ = -3246.425*&DUMSBST@+1.073*GSV_BLG@ [2.69]

Social contributions to the private sector:

SB_UH@ = 468.963*&DUMSBUH@+0.121*GSV_BLG@ [2.70]

Social contributions of private households:

SB_PR@ = SB_ST@+SB_UH@+SB_EA@ [2.71]

Contributions, paid by employers to public social insurance:

SB_AG@ = -6694.015*&DUMSBAG@+0.107*BLG@+0.592*LSB_AG@ [2.72]

Balance of the government social contributions:

SL_ZU_ST@ = SL_ST@-SB_ST@ [2.73]

Social contributions from the public sector to the East German households, total:

SL_HH_ST@ = SL_HN_ST + SL_HN_ST@ [2.74]

Government social contributions (government and social insurance):

SL_ST@ = SL_HN_ST@+SL_W_ST@ [2.75]

Transfer incomes of private households from other sectors:

TR_HH_EMP@ = SL_HH_ST@+SL_HH_H@+SL_W@+SL_U@+TR_SONS@ [2.76]

Transfer payments of private households to other sectors:

TR_HH_GEL@ = TD_HH@+SB_PR@+TR_HH_R@ [2.77]

Other transfer payments of private households:

TR_HH_R@ = 6952.018*&DUMTRHHR@+0.0076*BSP@+ [2.78]
+0.800*LTR_HH_R@

Transfer incomes, without direct taxes, paid transfers and social contributions:

TR%T@ = TR_HH_EMP@-TR_HH_R@-TD_HH@-SB_PR@ [2.79]

Prices

Prices index, gross national product:

PBSP@ = BSP@/BSP85@*100 [2.80]

Relative prices, price of imported services to price of gross national product:

PMD_PBSP@ = PMD@/PBSP@ [2.81]

Price index, private consumption:

PCPR@ = -29.523*&DUMPCPR@+0.490*PBSP@+ [2.82]
+57.822*CPR_BSP@+0.478*LPCPR@

Price index, government consumption:

PCST@ = -31.998*&DUMPCST@+1.044*PBSP@+ [2.83]
+140.584*CST_BSP@

Price index, gross fixed capital formation, public sector:

PIAN_ST@ = -12.696*&DUMPIAN@+0.470*PBSP@+ [2.84]
+254.776*IANST_BSP@+0.610*LPIAN_ST@

Price index, gross fixed capital formation, equipment, private sector:

PIAU_PR@ = -13.359*&DUMPIAU@+0.325*PBSP@+49.243*IAUPR_BSP@+ [2.85]
+0.642*LPIAU_PR@

Price index, gross fixed capital formation, construction, private sector:

PIBA_PR@ = -37.017*&DUMPIBA@+1.184*PBSP@+ [2.86]
+201.567*IBAPR_BSP@

Money market

Money supply M1:

ln(M1@) = -0.734*&DUMM1@+0.424*ln(BSP@)-0.141*ln(R_WPUM@)+ +0.600*ln(LM1@) [2.87]

Labour market

Gross wage per hour in 1985 prices:

BLG_EH85@ = BLG@/BESVOL@/PBSP@*100 [2.88]

Total labour cost per hour in 1985 prices:

BUA_EH85@ = BUA_EH@/PBSP@*100 [2.89]

Gross income of employees:

BUA@ = BUA_EH@*BESVOL@ [2.90]

Gross income from entrepreneurial activity and property:

BUV@ = NSPF@-BUA@ [2.91]

Gross wages and salaries, total:

BLG@ = BUA@-SB_AG@ [2.92]

Wage and salary earners:

BESCH@ = ET@-SELB@ [2.93]

Total man hours:

BESVOL@ = BESCH@*EH@/1000 [2.94]

2.5.3 Model for East-West trade

Imports of West Germany from East Germany:

M_O = ALPHA * M [3.1]

Imports of West Germany from the rest of the world without imports from East Germany:

M_R = M - M_O [3.2]

Exports from East Germany to West Germany:

X_W@ = M_O [3.3]

Exports (including incomes from assets and business):

X = X_R + X_O [3.4]

Imports of East Germany from West Germany:

M_W@ = BETA * M@ [3.5]

Imports of East Germany from the rest of the world without imports from West Germany:

M_R@ = M@ - M_W@ [3.6]

Exports from West Germany to East Germany:

X_O = M_W@ [3.7]

Exports (including incomes from assets and business):

X@ = X_R@ + X_W@ [3.8]

2.6 The structural equations of West Germany

2.6.1 Commodity market

Production

The production function [1.8] is a Cobb-Douglas type, restricted to returns to scale. Real output in prices of 1985 (QSP85) is defined as total supply and equals real private (CPR85) and governmental consumption (CST85) plus real capital formation (IAN85) including stocks (IVOR85) plus real exports (X85). As imports are considered as a factor of production because of their domestic capital and labour saving nature the gross concept (QSP) instead of the net concept (BSP) has to be applied for output.

Because imported capital goods are incorporated in the stock of capital the rest of imported goods without services (MR%D85) is considered to represent this additional factor of production. The philosophy for imported consumption goods is such that even if they are fairly close to private consumption they are apt to induce domestic value added and intermediate deliveries.

Labour (BESCH*1000) is defined by the number of employed persons times 1000. The product of labour and working time had no significant influence in the regression analysis.

The variable for capital (KAPAM85) has been constructed by the private stock of fixed capital in equipment (KAUMA85_PR) taking into account the degree of utilization (CAPIFO) plus the stocks of fixed capital in buildings in the private (KBAM85_PR) and public sector (KAPM85_ST). The real stocks have been calculated for the middle of the yearly period.

No variable for neutral technical progress could be found by the regressions for West Germany in the base period from 1960 to 1990 in contrast to earlier results [7]. The elasticities of production are for labour 0.37 and for capital 0.23 and for special imports 0.40. According to the Durbin-Watson-d this specification of the production function should be improved in later versions.

Imports

In order to determine GNP (BSP) a function [1.22] for all the imports (M) has been set up. The explaining variables are GNP and lagged imports (LM). This function is very sensitive to big changes in imports due to the high value of the parameter for the lagged variable and to its logarithmic nature.

Real imports of services (MD85) make it possible to compute the import factor of production (MR%D85). They are determined functionally [1.23] by real GNP. In addition, import prices for services in relation to the price index for GNP (PMD_PBSP) and the endogenous lag variable (LMD85) are involved in the explanation of these imports.

As imports of capital goods always play an important role in an economy real imported equipment (MIAU85) has been made dependent [1.24] on the change of real total supply (QSP, LQSP). Moreover, import prices of equipment (PMIAU) and those for domestic equipment (PIAU) and a dummy variable (DUM90) share the explanation of real imported equipment. The dummy tries to catch the influence of the change to the bigger economy of the united Germany in 1990.

Consumption

Private consumption (CPR) is dependent [1.27] on personal disposable income (YVPE), lagged private consumption (LCPR) and the dummy for year 1990 (DUM90).

In addition, there are two more explaining factors: interests and taxes. The average yield on circulating bearer bonds (R_WPUM) has a negative influence on the consumption behaviour of the households. The same holds for taxes on lagged capital yields (LTD_KEST). Although this tax is not included in the personal disposable income it has a significant influence on consumption. The explanation of this phenomenon might be that the households will consume more than the marginal propensity to consume suggests when this tax will be reduced and vice versa when the tax will be increased. As the money capital held by German households is quite substantial these additional explaining factors might be new. An interesting aspect is the fact that the parameter of lagged capital yield tax is significant which means that the explanation coincides with German tax laws. Non-wage income is usually taxed with a one year lag when there is an additional wage income. This new situation that wage income earners have substantial capital yields has to be considered thoroughly, especially in respect to tax laws and interest rates.

Besides these new aspects, the hypothesis of habit persistence seems to describe adequately the behaviour of the households in West Germany. The short term marginal propensity to consume is 0.56 and the long run propensity amounts to 0.92.

In contrast to nominal public consumption real public consumption (CST85) showed better regression results. Function [1.28] explains this consumption by real total supply (QSP85) and by a consumption lag (LCST85). There will be a short run marginal rate of 2.1% and a long run rate of 12% of total real supply for real consumption by the government.

Fixed capital formation

Gross fixed capital formation of the public sector (IAN_ST) is a function [1.35] of current (C) and previous total consumption (LC) and lagged total taxes (LT) and its own lag (LIAN_ST). Although gross investment will be explained, a kind of a nominal accelerator seems to be active which amounts to 13% in the short and to 31% in the long run.

In the private sector the change of fixed capital formation of equipment (DIAU_PR) is functionally [1.36] dependent not only on a change in total consumption (C,LC) but also on the average yield of circulating bearer bonds (R_WPUM) and on the dummy for 1990 (DUM90). Again the accelerator principle comes up somehow. This nominal accelerator amounts to 22%.

For the private construction (IBA_PR) the explanation of fixed capital formation [1.37] is given by changes in total supply (QSP,LQSP), the real stock of capital for construction in the middle of the year (KBAM85_PR), a dummy variable (DUM78) taking into account a change in the income tax laws in 1978 and its own lag (LIBA_PR). The capital stock variable seems to catch some influence of the difference between gross and net capital formation. The short run nominal accelerator is given by 14% and the long run one by 53%.

Depreciation

Consumption of fixed capital (D) is being made a function [1.9] of GNP and its own lag (LD). It is not dependent on all the stock of capital and its degree of utilization. As there are quite some problems in explaining statistically this variable the equation [1.9] has been selected.

The other equations for real consumption of capital [1.10 - 1.12] in the public sector (DAN85_ST) and in private equipment (DAU85_PR) and in private construction (DBA85_PR) are all depending on their own present or lagged stock of real capital and their own lag. The d-values show always significant autocorrelation. But, as these equations are technical ones with no special economic meaning, this statistical test might be irrelevant.

Taxes

Direct taxes of households (TD_HH) are functionally [1.52] dependent on all direct taxes (TDIR). In spite of unacceptable test values this institutional equation has been selected. The specification might be improved by better tax indicators.

The capital yields tax (TD_KEST) is determined [1.53] by its lag (LTD_KEST) and gross income from property of private households and entrepreneurial activity (BUV). The parameter of that variable indicates with 1.2% a fairly low tax income of government which is due to difficulties in taxation of money capital of households not violating the banking laws. The dummy (DUM_89Q) takes into account the influence of a new source taxation of money capital in 1989 which has been cancelled recently.

The corporate income tax (TD_KOST) is a function [1.54] of its tax base (BST_KOST), its own lag (LTD_KOST) and the dummy for year 1990 (DUM90).

The payroll tax without such a tax on pensions (TD_LOST%P) is determined [1.55] by the lagged variable (LTD_LOST%P), the total of gross wages and salaries (BLG) and the dummy for 1990 (DUM90). Again the parameter (12%) of the income variable (BLG) as a base for taxation gives interesting hints on the average short term rate for this tax category. The long term average income tax rate amounts to 13%.

Indirect taxes for carrying on a trade (TI_GEW) depends [1.56] on two tax bases one for trade (GEW_BUV) and one for the sum of wages and salaries (GEW_LSST). Moreover, there is a dummy variable (DUM80) indicating an additional influence on this tax income because of a change in tax laws cancelling the tax on the sum of wages and salaries in 1980.

The tax on petroleum (TI_MIN) is explained [1.57] by the volume of gasoline (VOL_MIN), the most important quantity to be taxed, and on two dummies, one for 1982 (DUM82) taking into account a change in the rate of tax and one for the 1990 phenomenon (DUM90).

The turnover tax (TI_UST) has been made dependent [1.58] on its tax base (BMG_UST), the rate of taxation (MWST_SATZ) and a dummy (DUM_MWST) considering the switch from turnover tax to value added tax in 1968. The parameter of the base of turnover indicates an average turnover tax of 5.57% which corresponded in its cumulative nature with the value added tax of 10% when the change took place.

Subsidies (SUB) could be determined [1.59] by all the taxes (T) and lagged subsidies (LSUB). The short term percentage share of all the taxes is 2.8% and the long term one amounts to 9.3%.

Transfers

Social contributions to the public sector (SB_ST) are a function [1.69] of imputed social contributions (GSV_BLG), a dummy for 1973 (DUM73) and for 1990 (DUM90). The dummy for 1973 might catch some influence of the energy crisis.

Social contributions to the private sector (SB_UH) are dependent [1.70] on imputed social contributions (GSV_BLG).

Function [1.72] explains contributions paid by the employers to public social insurance (SB_AG) by total gross wages and salaries (BLG) and by the endogenous lag variable. BLG is the main variable for computing the entrepreneurs´ social contribution which amounts to 11 % in the short run. The lag variable might catch at least partly the effect of legal tax corrections in the end of a calendar year.

The other transfer payments of private households (TR_HH_R) are explained [1.78] by GNP and its own lag (LTR_HH_R).

Bridge equations

Undistributed profits of companies with a legal entity (GUMER_U) are dependent [1.7] on gross income from property and entrepreneurial activity (BUV), two dummies taking care of the reform of the corporate tax in 1977 (DUM77) and the change of the government in 1982 (DUM83).

Interest on government debts (ZINS_GK) are explained [1.68] by the national debt (TVS_GK), the average yield on circulating bearer bonds (R_WPUM), its own lag (LZINS_GK) and the dummy for the year 1990 (DUM90).

Prices

The prices for private consumption (PCPR), for government consumption (PCST), for fixed capital in the public sector (PIAN_ST), for private fixed capital in equipment (PIAU_PR) and in construction (PIBA_PR) are all functions [1.82 - 1.86] of the overall price index for GNP (PBSP) and a variable considering the share of the relevant value in respect to GNP (..._BSP, e.g. for private consumption CPR_BSP). In some equations the endogenous lag variable has been included. Again the d-values show significant autocorrelation which is not surprising for such an auxiliary construction in order to determine prices. It might be mentioned once more that the price index for GNP is endogenous given by a definition.

2.6.2 Money market

The demand for money (M1) is explained [1.87] by GNP, the average yield on circulating bearer bonds (R_WPUM) and its own lag (LM1). Other functions for the money market for sight deposits of domestic non-banks (SE_N_K) and funds of domestic non-banks ranging from 1 month up to 4 years (TE_N_K) could have been established. But this improvement has been postponed for further and more detailed research in order to use the money and capital market for the Federal Republic of Germany in analogy by simulations for countries in transition.

2.6.3 Labour market

There is no structural equation for the labour market. The demand for labour could be derived by the production function depending on the rate of total labour costs per hour in constant prices, real total supply, annual working hours, a negative time trend and the endogenous lag. But it has been omitted in order to simulate different degrees of utilization for capital and labour. Preparing an estimate for all the labour force and confronting it with the demand for labour derived by the production function could result in an estimate for unemployment. This might be done in a later version of the model.

2.6.4 Regression results

equation [1.7]
GUMER_U = f(A0,BUV,DUM77,DUM83)
upper limit : 1990
lower limit : 1960

parameter	t-test	standard error
-6335.81378	3.21394	1971.35688
0.17020	14.38918	0.01183
9548.59067	4.53281	2106.54929
13707.99558	5.33940	2567.33062

Durbin-Watson d	:	1.42384	autocorrel. coef.	:	0.27911
variance	:	1.070E+0007	standard deviation	:	3.270E+0003
variation coef.	:	0.07492	determination coef.	:	0.99032

equation [1.8]

LN P_QSP85 = f(A0,LN A_BESCH,LN M_MR%D85)

upper limit : 1990

lower limit : 1960

parameter	t-test	standard error
-0.46730	7.90395	0.05912
0.37471	28.89952	0.01297
0.39908	16.46784	0.02423

Durbin-Watson d :	1.35877	autocorrel. coef. :	0.31047
variance :	5.536E-0005	standard deviation :	7.441E-0003
variation coef. :	-0.00617	determination coef. :	0.98517

equation [1.9]

D = f(BSP,LD)

upper limit : 1990

lower limit : 1961

parameter	t-test	standard error
0.02673	7.50455	0.00356
0.83016	26.62185	0.03118

Durbin-Watson d :	0.61921	autocorrel. coef. :	0.67621
variance :	4.985E+0006	standard deviation :	2.233E+0003
variation coef. :	0.01639	determination coef. :	0.99950

equation [1.10]

DAN85_ST = f(A0,KAP85_ST,LDAN85_ST)

upper limit : 1990

lower limit : 1961

parameter	t-test	standard error
579.21930	3.71203	156.03827
0.00152	2.24550	0.00068
0.63949	4.40613	0.14514

Durbin-Watson d :	1.87013	autocorrel .coef. :	0.05866
variance :	5.678E+0004	standard deviation :	2.383E+0002
variation coef. :	0.03949	determination coef. :	0.98415

equation [1.11]

DAU85_PR = f(A0,LKAU85_PR,LDAU85_PR)

upper limit : 1990

lower limit : 1961

parameter	t-test	standard error
-4039.22786	3.36059	1201.94141
0.01636	5.91413	0.00277
0.79637	22.17280	0.03592

Durbin-Watson d	:	1.41398	autocorrel.coef.	:	0.22799
variance	:	4.720E+0005	standarddeviation	:	6.870E+0002
variation coef.	:	0.00965	determination coef.	:	0.99959

equation [1.12]

DBA85_PR = f(A0,LKBA85_PR,LDBA85_PR)

upper limit : 1990

lower limit : 1961

parameter	t-test	standard error
-1262.04417	3.63358	347.32813
0.00054	3.17706	0.00017
0.98051	28.78295	0.03407

Durbin-Watson d	:	1.95226	autocorrel. coef.	:	0.02139
variance	:	2.365E+0005	standard deviation	:	4.863E+0002
variation coef.	:	0.03358	determination coef.	:	0.99569

equation [1 22]

LNM = f(LNBSP,LNLM)

upper limit : 1990

lower limit : 1961

parameter	t-test	standard error
0.08661	2.38142	0.03637
0.90955	22.22233	0.04093

Durbin-Watson d	:	1.68342	autocorrel. coef.	:	0.13715
variance	:	3.950E-0003	standard deviation	:	6.285E-0002
variation coef.	:	0.00510	determination coef.	:	0.99634

equation [1.23]

MD85 = f(A0,BSP85,PMD_PBSP,LMD85)

upper limit : 1990

lower limit : 1961

parameter	t-test	standard error
22447.93871	3.93278	5707.91152
0.02118	4.85057	0.00437
-28443.69146	4.91707	5784.68209
0.63930	9.75686	0.06552

Durbin-Watson d	:	1.84701	autocorrel. coef.	:	0.07175
variance	:	3.158E+0006	standard deviation	:	1.777E+0003
variation coef.	:	0.02535	determination coef.	:	0.99512

equation [1.24]

MIAU85 = f(A0,DQSP85,PMIAU,PIAU,DUM90)

upper limit : 1990

lower limit : 1961

parameter	t-test	standard error
-29486.50273	11.89554	2478.78584
0.04098	2.36744	0.01731
-512.99486	3.39348	151.17069
1150.53670	7.58282	151.72935
19841.64572	4.91969	4033.10906

Durbin-Watson d	:	1.25549	autocorrel. coef.	:	0.36130
variance	:	1.163E+0007	standard deviation	:	3.411E+0003
variation coef.	:	0.14213	determination coef.	:	0.96548

equation [1.27]
CPR = f(A0,YVPE,R_WPUM,LTD_KEST,DUM90,LCPR)
upper limit : 1990
lower limit : 1961

parameter	t-test	standard error
16191.66585	3.59301	4506.43206
0.55827	12.49549	0.04468
-1699.70908	2.47512	686.71777
-3.37262	3.17310	1.06288
22907.84807	3.09242	7407.74965
0.39626	7.52956	0.05263

Durbin-Watson d	:	1.87838	autocorrel. coef.	:	0.05824
variance	:	1.324E+0007	standard deviation	:	3.639E+0003
variation coef.	:	0.00562	determination coef.	:	0.99991

equation [1.28]
CST85 = f(A0,QSP85,LCST85)
upper limit : 1990
lower limit : 1961

parameter	t-test	standard error
18837.88577	5.06293	3720.74984
0.02098	2.30797	0.00909
0.82184	12.20471	0.06734

Durbin-Watson d	:	1.80847	autocorrel. coef.	:	0.09024
variance	:	1.884E+0007	standard deviation	:	4.340E+0003
variation coef.	:	0.01472	determination coef.	:	0.99642

equation [1.35]

IAN_ST = f(A0,DC,LT,LIAN_ST)

upper limit : 1990

lower limit : 1961

parameter	t-test	standard error
4072.27400	3.30657	1231.57002
0.12619	4.45708	0.02831
0.01848	2.79023	0.00662
0.59482	6.56400	0.09062

Durbin-Watson d :	1.85338	autocorrel. coef. :	-0.00198
variance :	4.230E+0006	standard deviation :	2.057E+0003
variation coef. :	0.05714	determination coef. :	0.97747

equation [1.36]

DIAU_PR = f(A0,DC,R_WPUM,DUM90)

upper limit : 1990

lower limit : 1961

parameter	t-test	standard error
17581.83133	3.95579	4444.58233
0.22201	4.73582	0.04688
-3011.57701	4.50529	668.45360
12921.78975	2.56623	5035.32446

Durbin-Watson d :	2.12670	autocorrel. coef. :	-0.06376
variance :	1.769E+0007	standard deviation :	4.206E+0003
variation coef. :	0.63340	determination coef. :	0.68726

equation [1.37]

IBA_PR = f(DQSP,KBAM85_PR,DUM78,LIBA_PR)

upper limit : 1990

lower limit : 1961

parameter	t-test	standard error
0.14109	5.50696	0.02562
0.00421	2.13206	0.00197
10147.89443	2.48796	4078.80734
0.73618	8.48359	0.08678

Durbin-Watson d :	1.73344	autocorrel. coef. :	0.11402
variance :	3.053E+0007	standard deviation :	5.525E+0003
variation coef. :	0.04742	determination coef. :	0.99075

equation [1.52]

TD_HH = f(A0,TDIR)

upper limit : 1990

lower limit : 1960

parameter	t-test	standard error
-2110.95526	2.37869	887.44548
0.85329	151.99266	0.00561

Durbin-Watson d	:	0.58670	autocorrel. coef.	:	0.70348
variance	:	6.315E+0006	standard deviation	:	2.513E+0003
variation coef.	:	0.02204	determination coef.	:	0.99875

equation [1.53]

TD_KEST = f(A0,BUV,DUM_89Q,LTD_KEST)

upper limit : 1990

lower limit : 1961

parameter	t-test	standard error
-862.93136	3.43298	251.36525
0.01246	5.61342	0.00222
3489.29120	7.76252	449.50520
0.41592	4.16852	0.09978

Durbin-Watson d	:	1.60594	autocorrel. coef.	:	0.16487
variance	:	1.656E+0005	standard deviation	:	4.069E+0002
variation coef.	:	0.10500	determination coef.	:	0.98418

equation [1.54]

TD_KOST = f(A0,BST_KST,DUM90,LTD_KOST)

upper limit : 1990

lower limit : 1961

parameter	t-test	standard error
2217.21942	2.87333	771.65511
0.32709	4.42450	0.07393
-4804.20763	2.40305	1999.21360
0.46075	3.49098	0.13198

Durbin-Watson d	:	1.46193	autocorrel. coef.	:	0.26901
variance	:	3.352E+0006	standard deviation	:	1.831E+0003
variation coef.	:	0.10284	determination coef.	:	0.97073

equation [1.55]

TD_LOST%P = f(A0,BLG,DUM90,LTD_LOST%P)

upper limit : 1990

lower limit : 1961

parameter	t-test	standard error
-12168.99802	3.48578	3491.04225
0.11519	4.63135	0.02487
-14682.16081	4.16633	3524.00214
0.43037	3.27602	0.13137

Durbin-Watson d	:	2.01141	autocorrel. coef.	:	-0.02004
variance	:	1.048E+0007	standard deviation	:	3.238E+0003
variation coef.	:	0.03972	determination coef.	:	0.99705

equation [1.56]

TI_GEW = f(A0,GEW_BUV,GEW_LSST,DUM80)

upper limit : 1990

lower limit : 1961

parameter	t-test	standard error
1944.44896	3.57961	543.20135
0.23063	13.45237	0.01714
1.11955	10.71097	0.10452
12949.87751	10.38696	1246.74380

Durbin-Watson d	:	1.89764	autocorrel. coef.	:	0.03882
variance	:	1.088E+0006	standard deviation	:	1.043E+0003
variation coef.	:	0.05131	determination coef.	:	0.98948

equation [1.57]

TI_MIN = f(A0,VOL_MIN,DUM82,DUM90)

upper limit : 1990

lower limit : 1961

parameter	t-test	standard error
-5876.15623	7.69685	763.44994
18.51592	26.03392	0.71122
1772.05749	2.84581	622.68982
4266.97047	3.62627	1176.68295

Durbin-Watson d	:	1.98294	autocorrel. coef.	:	0.00107
variance	:	1.204E+0006	standard deviation	:	1.097E+0003
variation coef.	:	0.06403	determination coef.	:	0.98520

equation [1.58]

TI_UST = f(A0,BMG_UST,MWST_SATZ,DUM_MWST,DUM90)

upper limit : 1990

lower limit : 1961

parameter	t-test	standard error
-71076.53936	13.13121	5412.79615
0.05569	29.96349	0.00186
7145.25789	11.80199	605.42843
71772.98095	11.81311	6075.70515
10839.17394	7.77344	1394.38518

Durbin-Watson d	:	1.50240	autocorrel. coef. :	0.24519
variance	:	1.339E+0006	standard deviation :	1.157E+0003
variation coef.	:	0.01640	determination coef. :	0.99934

equation [1.59]

SUB = f(T,LSUB)

upper limit : 1990

lower limit : 1961

parameter	t-test	standard error
0.02761	2.96091	0.00932
0.70185	5.88038	0.11935

Durbin-Watson d	:	1.81066	autocorrel. coef. :	0.08306
variance	:	3.563E+0006	standard deviation :	1.888E+0003
variation coef.	:	0.08284	determination coef. :	0.98521

equation [1.68]

LNZINS_GK = f(A0,LNTVS_GK,LNR_WPUM,DUM90,LNLZINS_GK)

upper limit : 1990

lower limit : 1961

parameter	t-test	standard error
-2.42596	4.14301	0.58555
0.44791	3.67457	0.12190
0.28757	6.50922	0.04418
-0.15707	3.33482	0.04710
0.61801	6.22990	0.09920

Durbin-Watson d	:	1.82219	autocorrel. coef. :	0.06798
variance	:	1.648E-0003	standard deviation :	4.060E-0002
variation coef.	:	0.00424	determination coef. :	0.99893

equation [1.69]

SB_ST = f(A0,GSV_BLG,DUM73,DUM90)

upper limit : 1990

lower limit : 1960

parameter	t-test	standard error
-3246.42535	4.15076	782.12867
1.07294	139.96915	0.00767
5955.04763	3.64749	1632.64159
-16199.37758	6.12713	2643.87618

Durbin-Watson d	:	1.82033	autocorrel. coef.	:	0.07883
variance	:	5.318E+0006	standard deviation	:	2.306E+0003
variation coef.	:	0.01272	determination coef.	:	0.99968

equation [1.70]

SB_UH = f(GSV_BLG)

upper limit : 1990

lower limit : 1960

parameter	t-test	standard error
0.121131	28.12115	0.00095

Durbin-Watson d	:	1.47061	autocorrel. coef.	:	0.11506
variance	:	1.139E+0006	standard deviation	:	1.067E+0003
variation coef.	:	0.05196	determination coef.	:	0.99398

equation [1.72]

SB_AG = f(A0,BLG,LSB_AG)

upper limit : 1990

lower limit : 1961

parameter	t-test	standard error
-6694.01575	5.61667	1191.81274
0.10708	9.84110	0.01088
0.59218	13.18599	0.04491

Durbin-Watson d	:	1.62939	autocorrel. coef.	:	0.14559
variance	:	2.178E+0006	standard deviation	:	1.476E+0003
variation coef.	:	0.01307	determination coef.	:	0.99962

equation [1.78]

TR_HH_R = f(BSP,LTR_HH_R)

upper limit : 1990

lower limit : 1961

parameter	t-test	standard error
0.00766	5.60906	0.00136
0.80043	17.10739	0.04679

Durbin-Watson d	:	1.28685	autocorrel. coef.	:	0.33767
variance	:	5.961E+0005	standard deviation	:	7.721E+0002
variation coef.	:	0.02217	determination coef.	:	0.99891

equation [1.82]

PCPR = f(A0,PBSP,CPR_BSP,LPCPR)

upper limit : 1990

lower limit : 1961

parameter	t-test	standard error
-29.52293	3.69646	7.98681
0.49049	7.16525	0.06845
57.82181	4.03802	14.31933
0.47816	6.35310	0.07526

Durbin-Watson d	:	0.93330	autocorrel. coef.	:	0.53180
variance	:	6.664E-0001	standard deviation	:	8.163E-0001
variation coef.	:	0.01158	determination coef.	:	0.99889

equation [1.83]

PCST = f(A0,PBSP,CST_BSP)

upper limit : 1990

lower limit : 1960

parameter	t-test	standard error
-31.99804	18.25774	1.75257
1.04378	85.96677	0.01214
140.58382	10.41066	13.50384

Durbin-Watson d	:	0.70402	autocorrel. coef.	:	0.60524
variance	:	8.182E-0001	standard deviation	:	9.045E-0001
variation coef.	:	0.01359	determination coef.	:	0.99914

equation [1.84]

PIAN_ST = f(A0,PBSP,IANST_BSP,LPIAN_ST)

upper limit : 1990

lower limit : 1961

parameter	t-test	standard error
-12.69621	2.18416	5.81285
0.47033	3.20291	0.14684
254.77623	2.47989	102.73701
0.61008	4.15433	0.14686

Durbin-Watson d	:	0.71164	autocorrel. coef.	:	0.61645
variance	:	3.908E+0000	standard deviation	:	1.977E+0000
variation coef.	:	0.02729	determination coef.	:	0.99446

equation [1.85]

PIAU_PR = f(PBSP,IAUPR_BSP,LPIAU_PR)

upper limit : 1990

lower limit : 1961

parameter	t-test	standard error
0.32535	3.16733	0.10272
49.24304	3.39345	14.51119
0.64232	5.42751	0.11835

Durbin-Watson d	:	0.64394	autocorrel. coef.	:	0.64805
variance	:	1.514E+0000	standard deviation	:	1.231E+0000
variation coef.	:	0.01690	determination coef.	:	0.99832

equation[1.86]

PIBA_PR = f(A0,PBSP,IBAPR_BSP)

upper limit : 1990

lower limit : 1960

parameter	t-test	standard error
-37.01736	7.87085	4.70309
1.18418	65.08074	0.01820
201.56735	6.04635	33.33704

Durbin-Watson d	:	0.77627	autocorrel. coef.	:	0.60981
variance	:	1.889E+0000	standard deviation	:	1.375E+0000
variation coef.	:	0.02025	determination coef.	:	0.99778

equation [1.87]

LNM1 = f(A0,LNBSP,LNR_WPUM,LNLM1)

upper limit : 1990

lower limit : 1961

parameter	t-test	standard error
-0.73438	3.67471	0.19985
0.42389	5.51611	0.07685
-0.14134	5.48512	0.02577
0.60004	8.38867	0.07153

Durbin-Watson d	:	1.62519	autocorrel. coef.	:	0.15590
variance	:	4.153E-0004	standard deviation	:	2.038E-0002
variation coef.	:	0.00170	determination coef.	:	0.99912

2.7 Future improvements

There should be some improvements by future versions of the model for the overall model and for the markets especially for those for labour and money:

It could be tested to functionalize the price index for GNP not only by definition but by several hypotheses according to economic theory.

Improvements in the commodity market could be achieved by disaggregating imports. Perhaps a better production function might result by repeated regressions with an enlarged set of data. There is a chance to improve the specification of some tax equations by introducing specific indicators.

The labour market could benefit from introducing supply and demand functions and eventually taking into account migration which will play an important role in Europe. Perhaps it will be possible to consider qualified labour, as well.

The money market needs a more subtile disaggregation for various kinds of money and capital being used to finance all the transactions of the economy. This is all the more important as the Eastern European countries which changed from a centrally planned economy to a market economy did not have any money or capital markets. Thus, planning transition without this important market would not be advisable. It might be even necessary to set up a model on high frequency data and trying to combine it with the annual model.

2.8 List of variables

The presented symbols of variables concern the model of West Germany. The notation for East Germany is identical but includes additionally "@" at the end of a symbol.

ALPHA [no dimension]
Share of West German imports from East Germany to total imports
BEI_GSV [per cent]
Rate of social insurance payment (total)
BESCH [thousands]
Wage and salary earners
BESVOL [mill. hours]
Total man hours
BETA [no dimension]
Share of imports from West Germany to total East German imports
BLG [mill. DM]
Gross wages and salaries, total
BLG_EH85 [DM/hour]
Gross wage per hour in 1985 prices
BLG_ST [mill. DM]
Gross wages and salaries, public sector
BMG_UST [mill. DM]
Tax base of turnover tax
BSP [mill. DM]
Gross national product
BSP85 [mill. DM]
Gross national product in 1985 prices
BST_KST [mill. DM]
Tax base of corporate income tax
BUA [mill. DM]
Gross income of employees

BUA_EH [DM/hour]

Total labour cost per hour

BUA_EH85 [DM/hour]

Total labour cost per hour in 1985 prices

BUV [mill. DM]

Gross income form entrepreneurial activity and property

BUV_HH [mill. DM]

Gross income form entrepreneurial activity and property, private households

C [mill. DM]

Consumption

C85 [mill. DM]

Consumption in 1985 prices

CAPIFO [per cent]

Degree of capacity utilization in the manufacturing sector

CPR [mill. DM]

Private consumption

CPR85 [mill. DM]

Private consumption in 1985 prices

CPR_BSP [no dimension]

Share of private consumption to GNP

CST [mill. DM]

Government consumption

CST85 [mill. DM]

Government consumption in 1985 prices

CST_BSP [no dimension]

Share of government consumption to gross national product

D [mill. DM]

Consumption of fixed capital

DAN85_ST [mill. DM]

Depreciation of fixed assets, public sector, in 1985 prices

DAU85_PR [mill. DM]

Depreciation of fixed assets, equipment, private sector, in 1985 prices

DBA85_PR [mill. DM]

Depreciation of fixed assets, construction, private sector, in 1985 prices

DIAU_PR [mill. DM]

First difference of gross fixed capital formation, equipment, private sector

DUM73 [no dimension]

Dummy-Variable: 1960 - 1972: 0, otherwise: 1

DUM77 [no dimension]

Dummy-Variable: 1961 - 1976: 0, from 1977 value 1

DUM78 [no dimension]

Dummy for the income tax reform (Jan 1, 1978)

DUM80 [no dimension]

Dummy-Variable: 1961 - 1979: 0, from 1980 value 1

DUM82 [no dimension]

Dummy-Variable: 1961 - 1981: 0, from 1982 value 1

DUM83 [no dimension]

Dummy, own contributions of those receiving social aid, from 1983 value 1, otherwise: 0

DUM90 [no dimension]

Dummy for 1990, 1990=1, otherwise: 0

DUM_89Q [no dimension]

Dummy: 1989=1, otherwise: 0 [taxation of the origin (Quellensteuer)]

DUM_MWST [no dimension]

Dummy variable: introduction of turnover tax: 1960 - 1967: 1, otherwise: 0

EH [hour/ET]

Annual average working hours

ET [thousands]

Workers (on the basis of resident status)

FS_ST [mill. DM]

Balance of government budget

GEW_BUV [mill. DM]

Tax base, tax paid for carrying on a trade

GEW_LSST [mill. DM]

Tax base, payroll tax

GEW_SATZ [per cent]

Rate of tax from yield of manufacturing, average

GSV_BLG [mill. DM]

Imputed contributions to social security

GUMER_U [mill. DM]

Undistributed profits of companies with a legal entity

GUOER_N [mill. DM]

Undistributed profits of enterprises without a legal entity

IAN [mill. DM]

Gross fixed capital formation

IAN85 [mill. DM]

Gross fixed capital formation in 1985 prices

IAN85_ST [mill. DM]

Gross fixed capital formation, public sector, in 1985 prices

IANST_BSP [no dimension]

Share of gross fixed capital formation (public sector) to GNP

IAN_ST [mill. DM]

Gross fixed capital formation, public sector

IAU85_PR [mill. DM]

Gross fixed capital formation, equipment, private sector, in 1985 prices

IAUPR_BSP [no dimension]

Share of gross fixed capital formation (equipment, private sector) to GNP

IAU_PR [mill. DM]

Gross fixed capital formation, equipment, private sector

IBA85_PR [mill. DM]

Gross fixed capital formation, construction, private sector, in 1985 prices

IBAPR_BSP [no dimension]

Share of gross fixed capital formation (construction, private sector) to GNP

IBA_PR [mill. DM]

Gross fixed capital formation, construction, private sector

IN_SONS [mill. DM]

Other government receipts

IN_ST [mill. DM]

Total government receipts

IVOR [mill. DM]

Changes in stocks

KAP85 [mill. DM]

Stock of capital, in 1985 prices (end of year)

KAP85_ST [mill. DM]

Stock of capital, public sector, in 1985 prices (end of year)

KAPAM85 [mill. DM]

Utilized stock of capital, in 1985 prices (average of year)

KAPM85_ST [mill. DM]

Stock of capital, public sector, in 1985 prices (average of year)

KAU85_PR [mill. DM]

Stock of capital, equipment, private sector, in 1985 prices (end of year)

KAUM85_PR [mill. DM]

Stock of capital, equipment, private sector, in 1985 prices (average of year)

KAUMA85_PR [mill. DM]

Utilized stock of capital, equipment, private sector, in 1985 prices (average of year)

KBA85_PR [mill. DM]

Stock of capital, construction, private sector, in 1985 prices (end of year)

KBAM85_PR [mill. DM]

Stock of capital, construction, private sector, in 1985 prices (average of year)

KST_SATZ [per cent]

Corporate income tax rate

LC [mill. DM]

Consumption, lagged value

LCPR [mill. DM]

Private consumption, lagged value

LCST85 [mill. DM]

Government consumption in 1985 prices, lagged value

LD [mill. DM]

Consumption of fixed capital, lagged value

LDAN85_ST [mill. DM]

Depreciation of fixed assets, public sector, in 1985 prices, lagged value

LDAU85_PR [mill. DM]

Depreciation of fixed assets, equipment, private sector, in 1985 prices, lagged value

LDBA85_PR [mill. DM]

Depreciation of fixed assets, construction, private sector, in 1985 prices, lagged value

LIAN_ST [mill. DM]

Gross fixed capital formation, public sector, lagged value

LIAU_PR [mill. DM]

Gross fixed capital formation, equipment, private sector, lagged value

LIBA_PR [mill. DM]

Gross fixed capital formation, construction, private sector,lagged value

LKAP85_ST [mill. DM]

Stock of capital, public sector, in 1985 prices (end of year), lagged value

LKAU85_PR [mill. DM]

Stock of capital, equipment, private sector, in 1985 prices (end of year), lagged value

LKBA85_PR [mill. DM]

Stock of capital , construction, private sector, in 1985 prices (end of year), lagged value

LM [mill. DM]

Imports (including incomes from assets and business), lagged value

LM1 [mill. DM]

Money supply M1, lagged value

LMD85 [mill. DM]

Imports of services in 1985 prices, lagged value

LPCPR [index, 1985 = 100]

Price index, private consumption, lagged value

LPIAN_ST [index, 1985 = 100]

Price index, gross fixed capital formation, public sector, lagged value

LPIAU_PR [index, 1985 = 100]

Price index, gross fixed capital formation, equipment, private sector, lagged value

LQSP [mill. DM]

Total supply, lagged value

LQSP85 [mill. DM]

Total supply in 1985 prices, lagged value

LSB_AG [mill.DM]

Contributions, paid by employers to public social insurance (consolidated), lagged value

LSE_N_K [mill. DM]

Domestic non banks' sight deposits, lagged value

LSST_SATZ [per cent]

Average payroll tax rate

LSUB [mill. DM]

Subsidies, lagged value

LT [mill. DM]

Total taxes, lagged value

LTD_KEST [mill. DM]

Capital yields tax, lagged value

LTD_KOST [mill. DM]

Corporate income tax, lagged value

LTD_LOST%P [mill. DM]

Payroll tax without tax on pensions and the rest of the world, lagged value

LTE_N_K [mill. DM]

Time deposits, lagged value

LTR_HH_R [mill. DM]

Other transfer payments of private households, lagged value

LZINS_GK [mill. DM]

Interest on government debt, lagged value

M [mill. DM]

Imports (including incomes from assets and business)

M1 [mill. DM]

Money supply M1

M85 [mill. DM]

Imports (including incomes from assets and business) in 1985 prices

MD85 [mill. DM]

Imports of services in 1985 prices

MIAU85 [mill. DM]

Imports of equipment in 1985 prices

MR%D85 [mill. DM]

Imports without capital goods and services in 1985 prices

MWST_SATZ [per cent]

Upper tax rate, value added tax

M_O [mill. DM]

Imports, West Germany from East Germany

M_R [mill. DM]

Imports of West Germany from the rest of the world without imports from East Germany

M_R@ [mill. DM]

Imports of East Germany from the rest of the world without imports from West Germany

M_W@ [mill. DM]

Imports of East Germany from West Germany

NSPF [mill. DM]

Net national income at factor cost

NSPF_HH [mill. DM]

Net national income at factor cost, households

OUT_SONS [mill. DM]

Other public consumption expenditures

OUT_ST [mill. DM]

Total government expenditures

PBSP [index, 1985 = 100]

Price index, gross national product

PCPR [index, 1985 = 100]

Price index, private consumption

PCST [index, 1985 = 100]

Price index, government consumption

PIAN_ST [index, 1985 = 100]

Price index, gross fixed capital formation, public sector

PIAU [index, 1985 = 100]

Price index, gross fixed capital formation, equipment

PIAU_PR [index, 1985 = 100]

Price index, gross fixed capital formation, equipment, private sector

PIBA_PR [index, 1985 = 100]

Price index, gross fixed capital formation, construction, private sector

PM [index, 1985 = 100]

Price index, imports

PMD [index, 1985 = 100]

Price index, imports of services

PMD_PBSP [no dimension]

Relative prices, price of imported services to price of GNP

PMIAU [index, 1985 = 100]

Price index, imports of equipment

QSP [mill. DM]

Total supply

QSP85 [mill. DM]

Total supply in 1985 prices

R_WPUM [per cent]

Average yield on circulating bearer bonds

SB_AG [mill. DM]

Contributions, paid by employers to public social insurance (consolidated)

SB_EA [mill. DM]

Balance of social contribution of foreign commuters

SB_PR [mill. DM]

Social contributions of private households

SB_ST [mill. DM]

Social contributions to the public sector

SB_UH [mill. DM]

Social contributions to the private sector

SELB [thousands]

Self employed persons and unpaid family members

SL_HA_ST [mill. DM]

Social contributions of the public sector to the private households in West-Germany

SL_HH_H [mill. DM]

Social contributions to private households from private households

SL_HH_ST [mill. DM]

Social contributions from the public sector to the private households

SL_HN_ST [mill. DM]

Social contributions of the West German government to the East German households

SL_ST [mill. DM]

Government social contributions (government and social insurance)

SL_U [mill. DM]

Social contributions from enterprises with own legal entity to private households

SL_W [mill. DM]

Social contributions form the rest of the world to private households

SL_W_ST [mill. DM]

Social contributions of the government to the rest of the world

SL_ZU_ST [mill. DM]

Balance of the goverment social contributions

SUB [mill. DM]

Subsidies

T [mill. DM]

Total taxes

TDIR [mill.DM]

Direct taxes

TD_HH [mill. DM]

Direct taxes, private households

TD_KEST [mill. DM]

Capital yields tax

TD_KOST [mill. DM]

Corporate income tax

TD_LOST%P [mill. DM]

Payroll tax (without that on pensions)

TD_SONS [mill. DM]

Other direct taxes

TIND [mill. DM]

Indirect taxes

TI_GEW [mill. DM]

Tax paid for carrying on a trade

TI_MIN [mill. DM]

Petroleum tax

TI_SONS [mill. DM]

Other indirect taxes

TI_UST [mill. DM]

Turnover tax

TR%T [mill. DM]

Transfer incomes without direct taxes, paid transfers and social contributions

TR_HH_EMP [mill. DM]

Transfer incomes of private households from other sectors

TR_HH_GEL [mill. DM]

Transfer payments of private households to other sectors

TR_HH_R [mill. DM]

Other transfer payments of private households

TR_SONS [mill. DM]

Other transfer incomes of the private households

TSB [mill. DM]

Taxes and social contributions

TVS_GK [mill. DM]

National debt at the end of the year

VOL_MIN [Petajoule]

Consumption of gasoline and diesel

X [mill. DM]

Exports (including incomes from assets and business)

X_O [mill. DM]

Exports from West Germany to East Germany

X_R [mill. DM]

Exports from West Germany to the rest of the world without exports to East Germany

X_R@ [mill. DM]

Exports of East Germany to the rest of the world without exports to West Germany

X_W@ [mill. DM]

Exports from East Germany to West Germany

YUVST [mill. DM]

Gross income of the government from property and entrepreneurial activity

YVPE [mill. DM]

Personal disposable income, private households

ZINS_GK [mill. DM]

Interest on government debt, government

ZINS_GSV [mill. DM]

Interest on public debt, social insurance

ZINS_HH_KR [mill. DM]

Interest on consumers' debts, private households

ZINS_ST [mill. DM]

Interest on debts of the public sector

ZU_NL_ST [mill. DM]

Payments of the West German government to the East German government

CHAPTER 3

THE BASIC SIMULATION[3)]

Klaus Behle, Gerhard Gehrig, Pawel Tomczyk
Institute for Development, Environment and Quantitative Economic Research,
Johann Wolfgang Goethe-University, Frankfurt/Main

3.1 Introduction

Forecasting will be done by simulations. There is a variety of possible scenarios to be applied. In order to ease the access to this bulk of information a baseline simulation has been set up. The basic simulation does not cope with events influenced by the European Community (EC) where in 1993 and in the following years we will have a common market with free access to labour and markets. There will be no more customs and economic borders among the EC countries. Possibly a common currency, the ECU, might be introduced later on and, last but not least a political union could be started by France and Germany and others.

The presented simulation scenario aims at analyzing the economic development of Germany from 1992 until the year 2000. Application of the available information on the present tendencies in economy has been the guiding principle in constructing the scenario analysis. This information has been based on recent press material and reports published by German research institutes or the Federal Statistical Office or others (see [3] - [6], [8]).

All the simulations have been performed by a Newton-Raphson algorithm which seems to achieve a quicker convergence than Gauss-Seidel in the case of small models like the one described above.

---

(3) We are very thankful to Dr Egon Neuthinger for helpful comments and suggestions.

3.2 Assumptions

In order to perform simulations the model has to be solved for the endogenous variables year by year given the exogenous variables. The values of these exogenous variables for the simulation period incorporate certain assumptions. The most important ones for the basic simulation are mentioned below. All the quantified assumptions (exogenous variables) are presented in detail in section 3.5 of this chapter, together with all the simulation results.

The main assumptions of the scenario analysis can be grouped into the following economic categories:

1. total labour costs per hour, gross wages and salaries, social contributions,
2. employment, average annual working hours and number of self employed persons,
3. interest rate (running yield),
4. rate of capacity utilization,
5. payments of the West German government to East Germany,
6. shares of "intra - German imports" in total imports for both parts of Germany, exports to the rest of world and import prices,
7. institutional variables, e.g. other indirect taxes, other state receipts and expenditures etc.

The average wage rate (total labour costs per hour - BUA_EH) is one of the most important exogenous variables in the model. It has been assumed a relatively stable increase of 5% - 6.5% annually from 34.45 DM per hour and worker in 1991 to 57.7 DM in the year 2000 in West Germany. The assumption of this variable for East Germany (BUA_EH@) expresses the higher growth rates, of 30% annually in the years 1991 - 1993 and about 11.7% annually in the years 1994 - 2000, starting from the level of 15.5 DM in 1991 and reaching the level of West Germany in the year 2000. In other words, the assumed values indicate the tendency to decreasing differences in the average wage rates between two parts of Germany and finally postulate the same level for the year 2000. It is worth mentioning that there are strong pressures to make these rates equal earlier, e.g. by 1995.

The next important assumptions concern the development of employment sector. Our assumption of the total employment in West Germany (ET) is based on the projection of the DIW. The assumption for the years 1991 - 1994 indicates relatively small changes in the number of employees. For the next years, an increase of 150 thousand employees (0.5%) annually in the years 1995 - 1996 and an increase of 300 thousand (1%) annually in 1997 - 2000 is assumed.

A different tendency has been assumed for the total employment in East Germany (ET@) - after a decrease of 12.5% in 1992 and a stable level for the number of employees in the years 1993 - 1995, an increase of 200 thousand (2.8% - 3.0%) annually for the period 1996 - 2000. According to this assumption, the level of employment in East Germany in the year 2000 is slightly below the number of employees in 1991. The assumed number of self employed persons and assisting family members (SELB) in West Germany is almost constant in the entire forecasted period. The assumption for this variable in East Germany (SELB@) presents an increasing tendency as a consequence of the privatization processes and structural economic changes. The number of self employed persons should increase from 317 thousand in 1990 through 490 thousand in 1991 (53% !) to 700 thousand in 2000. According to our assumptions, the annual average working hours will be diminished in both parts of Germany until the year 2000; in West Germany (EH) from the value 1590.7 hours in 1991 to 1503 in 2000 and in East Germany (EH@) from 1702.7 hours in 1991, with a stronger decreasing tendency to the level of the Western part in the year 2000.

The average values of interest rate (R_WPUM), which obviously are the same for East and West, assume a relatively high level of 8.7% - 8% in the years 1991 - 1993 and a decreasing tendency from 7.8% to 7.2% in the following years of the simulation period.

The exogenously introduced degree of capacity utilization has some impact on all the simulation results as a consequence of the important role played by the production function in the model which determines the potential of economic growth. It has been assumed that the rate of capacity utilization for West Germany (CAPIFO), constructed as an aggregated index by the IFO Institute, would have high values for the first years of simulated period, respectively 87.5% in 1991 and 84.6% in 1992 and a relatively lower level of 83% - 84% in the following years of projection. The rate of capacity utilization in East Germany (CAPIFO@) has been assumed on the level of 18% in 1991 with a considerably increasing tendency up to 80% in the year 2000.

The next assumptions concern the amounts of West German transfers to East Germany. The assumed values of the social contributions of the West German government to the East German households (SL_HN_ST) have a high level of 32.6 - 32.2 billion DM annually in the years 1992 - 1995 and a decreasing tendency from 28 billion DM in 1996 to 20 billion DM annually in the year 2000. A similar tendency has been assumed for the payments of the West German government to the East German government (ZU_NL_ST). The level of this variable is between

130.4 billion DM and 128.8 billion DM annually in the period 1992 - 1995 and decreases from 112 billion DM in 1996 to 80 billion DM annually in the year 2000.

The shares of "intra-German imports" in total imports of both parts of Germany play an important role in the model. These variables link the submodels into one coherent model and allow to investigate the mutual reactions in these two parts of the economy. The assumed shares reflect an asymmetric character of the role for particular parts of Germany in the entire German economy. The share of imports from West Germany in total East German imports (BETA) is extremely high with the value of 90.7% in 1991. It has been assumed that these shares would have similarly high levels of 93.1% - 86% in the years 1992 - 1996 and a decreasing tendency up to 63.0% in the year 2000. The high values of this share seem to be a consequence of two functioning phenomena - the effects of increasing imports from West Germany and decreasing imports from the rest of the world, especially from the East European markets, which have played a traditionally important role in the former GDR economy. The gradually increasing role of those markets has been expressed in our assumptions, especially for the last years of the simulation. Symmetrically, the share of imports from East Germany in the total West German imports (ALPHA) has been assumed to increase in the entire simulation period, from the value of 4.7% in 1991 to 11.6% in 2000. For the exports to the rest of the world (X_R) from West Germany a tendency to increase has been assumed, while these exports for East Germany (X_R@) would have a decreasing and then an increasing tendency, according to the assumed degree of capacity utilization in East Germany. The assumed import prices for West Germany (PM), have an average dynamics of 3% - 1% annually in the years 1994 - 2000, after the relatively high growth rates in the years 1991 - 1993.

The introduced assumptions for the last group of exogenous variables, covering such categories as the other indirect taxes, other state expenditures etc., generally of less meaning for the model, have been based on the tendencies of development in the last years and have been postulated similar or with the same dynamics for both parts of German economy in the simulated period.

All these basic assumptions are subject to change either by other simulations or by events just happening. Comparisons of the results of simulations might show better forthcoming economic tendencies than just one simulation will do. Most likely simulations will give hints on possible economic tendencies or bottlenecks but not exact figures for the endogenous variables.

3.3 Selected results

Production

The results of the scenario for the GNP in 1985 prices (BSP85) for West Germany indicate a decrease of 0.6% in 1993 and a moderate increasing tendency of 1.0% - 2.1% annually in the next years of projection. The GNP for East Germany (BSP85@), after the considerable decrease in 1991 has an increasing tendency with the relatively high dynamics, oscillating between 5.3% and 12.7% annually until the year 2000. The higher rate of growth in the East is subject to a relatively low starting position in 1991 and the assumed increasing rate of capacity utilization . The different dynamics for the GNP in the Eastern and Western parts of Germany leads to certain changes in the share of its economies in the total German GNP. The performed scenario indicates a gradually increasing share of the East German GNP from 7% in 1991 to 12.2% in 2000 in the total German GNP.

Consumption

The scenario analysis for real private consumption (CPR85) in West Germany predicts growth rates of 1.4% to 2.3% annually in the simulated period with a slightly higher dynamics in the years 1996 - 2000. The obtained results for the Eastern part (CPR85@) indicate different paths of development. After the moderate growth rates until 1995, an increasing tendency in dynamics of 2.7% - 4% annually in the following years is observed. The differences between the growth rates of consumption in nominal terms for both parts of Germany are much higher, especially for the years 1991 - 1994, respectively 3.0% - 5.6% annually for the West and 6% - 17% annually for the East. The differentiated dynamics in real and nominal terms for East Germany have its source in the relatively high growth rates of consumer prices (PCPR@).

Capital formation

Gross fixed capital formation in 1985 prices (IAN85) will have a cyclical development with a positive trend in West Germany until the end of the simulation period. In the Eastern part, after an increase in 1991 and 1992, the development of this category (IAN85@) has two phases - a moderate dynamics in the years 1993 - 1997 and high growth rates in 1998 - 2000. The private real gross fixed capital formation for construction (IBA85_PR) will be strongly hampered by high interest rates and laws restricting decisions of house owners in respect to rents and finishing of rental contracts. As new apartments are highly needed additional measures by the government would foster housing either by tax deductions or by quicker depreciation possibilities. There will be much housing replacement in East Germany. The same holds for the stock of capital in equipment if it should still be used in the future. Railways, public institutions, hospitals and many other stocks of capital have to be modernized. There is a big difference in the "up-to-date" status between the two former states.

Prices

The price indices (PBSP and PBSP@) for both parts of Germany have two different simulated trajectories. The scenario for the West (PBSP) projects the relatively constant dynamics of 2.4% - 4.2% annually , whereas for the East the foreseen inflation (PBSP@) has much higher growth rates of 14% annually in the period 1992 - 1993 and decreasing tendency on the level of 4% annually in the next years of simulation.

These price indices are highly sensitive in respect to the forecasted values of all the endogenous variables. As mentioned above, the values of these price indices can be taken as an overall measure of the model`s quality.

Exports

The exports (X) are exogenous in respect to that part which goes to the rest of the world (X_R). Those parts (X_O) crossing the now non-existing border between the two former states have been functionalized in order to study the impact of mutual trade. Given exogenously high rates of growth for the exports to the rest of the world the simulation shows that it is quite possible to sustain a high rate of growth for all exports without a major impact on prices in spite of the German unification. It could be even possible to increase exports to the countries of the former Eastern Block. There are no indications that development aid should be drastically reduced in favour of the East. On the contrary, there might be even more aid beyond the year 2000 than without unification.

Imports

The scenario for the real imports shows a relatively stable increase in dynamics of growth for the West (M85), between 2% and 4% annually, with the exception of decrease in 1993. The dynamics of growth for real imports in East Germany (M85@) are generally higher in the first years of the simulated period, i.e. until 1993, mainly due to the increasing imports from West Germany. The further development of East German imports is characterized by a slightly decreasing tendency of growth. A positive trade balance will result in the West and a negative one in the East, increasing until 2000. Summing both parts of the trade balance, the trade surplus is maintained for the entire Germany in the years 1996 - 2000.

3.4 Some comments

Moreover, there are some results of the baseline simulation which should be commented:

The variable FS_ST@ which is the balance of the government budget of East Germany shows positive values for the years 1991 until 1997. This might be due to the method of simulation in using the slightly adapted structural equations of West Germany for East Germany. Many variables contribute to the values of FS_ST@ according to its definition [2.49] in connection with [2.47] and [2.48]. Levying taxes is in the West more efficient than in the East due to the difficulties by transition of the whole economic system. On the one side the necessary governmental institutions have to be set up and its officials should be trained in the new tax laws. On the other side new accounting systems have to be adopted by business in order to prepare the correct accounting base for tax deductions etc. Therefore, the tax equations taken from the West overestimate the tax revenues of the East. Of course, similar arguments hold for the outputs of the budget. Thus, the difference of input and output could be less erroneous, but obviously it is not. The positive values of the variable in question do not make economic sense. As soon as there is more information on the details of this variable the simulation will be improved by changing either the relevant structural equations or the values of the relevant exogenous variables.

Another problem for the simulation is the assumed stock of capital for East Germany (KAP85@). Although the degree of utilization (CAPIFO@) has been set on a very low level (e.g. 25% in 1993) in order to compensate for parts of the stock of capítal which have not been depreciated it could be that the amount of real capital is still too high and should be stepwise reduced in the period until 2000. The relation of utilized real capital to real output measured by real GNP could perhaps give some hints for necessary corrections. Yet, again there should be more information in order to adjust the baseline simulation as the solution of the problem is very complex (interdependent) due to the investment and capital depreciation functions and the involved production function.

Very likely, there will be additional criticism of this simulation. Yet, it should be kept in mind that this is an experiment in modelling an economy without using data of the past but referring to structures and solutions mainly by analogy. Another difficulty and sometimes an advantage too, is the fictitious splitting up of the two economies. Therefore, sometimes adding up of variables for the West and the East might present more reasonable results. Thus, the simulation will show rather tendencies than exact values.

3.5 Tables (values)

3.5.1 Endogenous variables

General remarks:
- Variables for East Germany with @ at the end of the symbol

YEAR	BSP85	BSP	QSP	NSPF
1960	859800.000	303000.000	355750.000	240110.000
1961	896400.000	331400.000	387470.000	260750.000
1962	937500.000	360500.000	422460.000	282110.000
1963	963300.000	382100.000	448520.000	297800.000
1964	1026400.000	419600.000	493560.000	327250.000
1965	1080300.000	458200.000	545060.000	358450.000
1966	1111100.000	487400.000	578400.000	379780.000
1967	1108400.000	493700.000	582770.000	380740.000
1968	1172000.000	533700.000	634170.000	418090.000
1969	1259800.000	597800.000	717560.000	462940.000
1970	1322800.000	675700.000	814500.000	530400.000
1971	1363100.000	750400.000	903280.000	586240.000
1972	1422300.000	824600.000	988330.000	643470.000
1973	1491100.000	918800.000	1104370.000	720400.000
1974	1491900.000	983700.000	1216080.000	769740.000
1975	1473000.000	1027700.000	1266130.000	800570.000
1976	1554700.000	1123800.000	1401600.000	878240.000
1977	1594400.000	1195600.000	1491210.000	933700.000
1978	1649400.000	1289400.000	1592360.000	1007150.000
1979	1715900.000	1393800.000	1753730.000	1084000.000
1980	1733800.000	1477400.000	1899550.000	1139580.000
1981	1735700.000	1539600.000	2004350.000	1179810.000
1982	1716500.000	1590300.000	2067640.000	1214180.000
1983	1748400.000	1675700.000	2157270.000	1278100.000
1984	1802000.000	1763300.000	2293430.000	1347130.000
1985	1834500.000	1834500.000	2403970.000	1406770.000
1986	1874400.000	1936100.000	2462400.000	1497550.000
1987	1902300.000	2003000.000	2528040.000	1550000.000
1988	1971800.000	2108000.000	2674140.000	1635540.000
1989	2050300.000	2249100.000	2892590.000	1738100.000
1990	2149800.000	2439100.000	3157780.000	1885300.000
1991	2226800.000	2631200.000	3458410.000	2008750.000
1992	2277162.753	2794277.954	3664284.466	2152468.460
1993	2262989.186	2864798.742	3780131.076	2189394.956
1994	2285538.710	2962248.216	3923635.635	2259466.676
1995	2318360.115	3068070.839	4076418.026	2337918.322
1996	2360811.691	3235914.471	4293832.314	2475619.507
1997	2412686.614	3407782.033	4517864.691	2615937.360
1998	2464907.540	3610870.400	4776459.575	2783925.297
1999	2516104.411	3838982.283	5063946.419	2974089.304
2000	2569712.798	4044140.828	5331524.281	3139848.162

Legend :

BSP85 \ Dimension : mill.DM
Gross national product in 1985 prices
BSP \ Dimension : mill.DM
Gross national product
QSP \ Dimension : mill.DM
Total supply
NSPF \ Dimension : mill.DM
Net national income at factor cost

YEAR	QSP85	GUMER_U	NSPF_HH	YVPE
1960	987750.000	12600.000	225440.000	187960.000
1961	1035450.000	13180.000	245070.000	207090.000
1962	1090770.000	12470.000	267220.000	224100.000
1963	1123750.000	13190.000	282000.000	240580.000
1964	1201770.000	14740.000	309870.000	263170.000
1965	1280380.000	16010.000	339850.000	293440.000
1966	1316540.000	15300.000	362180.000	311130.000
1967	1312780.000	14330.000	364820.000	318130.000
1968	1402200.000	18750.000	397270.000	343870.000
1969	1528560.000	22880.000	437960.000	381540.000
1970	1635970.000	15580.000	512610.000	427970.000
1971	1702560.000	16420.000	567890.000	472900.000
1972	1779350.000	24220.000	619000.000	528060.000
1973	1864790.000	26960.000	692810.000	575430.000
1974	1871930.000	28270.000	742860.000	624640.000
1975	1853980.000	30610.000	774290.000	687490.000
1976	1974200.000	38250.000	846810.000	728800.000
1977	2032300.000	39650.000	903490.000	776820.000
1978	2105880.000	49490.000	966470.000	825740.000
1979	2216780.000	52300.000	1040680.000	894870.000
1980	2256900.000	49890.000	1101490.000	960410.000
1981	2251750.000	54900.000	1139620.000	1022420.000
1982	2232250.000	51740.000	1176270.000	1049730.000
1983	2264690.000	72140.000	1225320.000	1076670.000
1984	2344800.000	79800.000	1288040.000	1129840.000
1985	2403970.000	79630.000	1347670.000	1170110.000
1986	2463470.000	81810.000	1439040.000	1215700.000
1987	2516260.000	89430.000	1491310.000	1267580.000
1988	2621430.000	99550.000	1575910.000	1323150.000
1989	2754660.000	102190.000	1664920.000	1394270.000
1990	2937700.000	103580.000	1810610.000	1530400.000
1991	3110950.000	126950.000	1920020.000	1639970.000
1992	3183419.536	132234.435	1988289.876	1697237.844
1993	3126510.256	131027.719	2050535.965	1740883.048
1994	3166091.393	132856.680	2128564.516	1793185.613
1995	3215024.203	132188.556	2230552.582	1868586.654
1996	3292241.760	135927.634	2366840.368	1969771.461
1997	3380367.708	137641.760	2518624.519	2078579.588
1998	3470914.694	140450.526	2692668.761	2198676.098
1999	3562889.587	140097.506	2908528.327	2340321.113
2000	3658945.669	145946.121	3064650.255	2452971.652

Legend :

QSP85 \ Dimension : mill.DM
Total supply in 1985 prices
GUMER_U \ Dimension : mill.DM
Undistributed profits of companies with a legal entity
NSPF_HH \ Dimension : mill.DM
Net national income at factor cost, households
YVPE \ Dimension : mill.DM
Personal disposable income, private households

YEAR	D	DAN85_ST	DAU85_PR	DBA85_PR
1960	23630.000	2230.000	21530.000	8430.000
1961	27120.000	2610.000	22600.000	8300.000
1962	31230.000	3080.000	23960.000	8070.000
1963	34990.000	3210.000	25620.000	8220.000
1964	38960.000	3520.000	27800.000	8180.000
1965	43310.000	3880.000	30580.000	8130.000
1966	47770.000	3650.000	33900.000	8690.000
1967	50520.000	4360.000	37570.000	8320.000
1968	53650.000	4550.000	41350.000	8550.000
1969	58200.000	4840.000	45140.000	8660.000
1970	68030.000	4890.000	48980.000	9090.000
1971	78080.000	5270.000	52910.000	9200.000
1972	86730.000	5430.000	56700.000	9570.000
1973	95980.000	5810.000	59980.000	9770.000
1974	107780.000	6470.000	64400.000	9720.000
1975	117240.000	6430.000	68430.000	10430.000
1976	125770.000	6500.000	72890.000	11180.000
1977	134010.000	6360.000	77510.000	12460.000
1978	144390.000	6710.000	81760.000	13290.000
1979	157800.000	7190.000	85560.000	13960.000
1980	175000.000	7300.000	89110.000	15090.000
1981	190620.000	7070.000	93540.000	16780.000
1982	203690.000	7070.000	96860.000	18570.000
1983	214930.000	7090.000	100530.000	20320.000
1984	226370.000	7320.000	106180.000	22860.000
1985	235360.000	7950.000	109060.000	22900.000
1986	243690.000	8350.000	110870.000	23930.000
1987	252300.000	8630.000	113980.000	24990.000
1988	263090.000	8290.000	116600.000	26940.000
1989	279450.000	8430.000	120690.000	29190.000
1990	300370.000	8620.000	123140.000	30710.000
1991	326960.000	8730.000	125690.000	32410.000
1992	341774.370	9065.903	133370.627	34072.832
1993	360314.257	9268.178	139639.711	35837.650
1994	378310.507	9458.806	146566.221	37647.051
1995	396079.299	9641.434	154068.064	39496.129
1996	415317.336	9821.877	162106.646	41381.292
1997	435882.654	10003.157	170701.553	43300.975
1998	458384.482	10187.567	179869.245	45253.672
1999	483162.897	10377.096	189627.613	47238.155
2000	509217.605	10569.470	200001.245	49253.080

Legend :

D \ Dimension : mill.DM
Consumption of fixed capital
DAN85_ST \ Dimension : mill.DM
Depreciation of fixed assets, public sector, in 1985 prices
DAU85_PR \ Dimension : mill.DM
Depreciation of fixed assets, equipment, private sector, in 1985 prices
DBA85_PR \ Dimension : mill.DM
Depreciation of fixed assets, construction, private sector, in 1985 prices

YEAR	KAP85_ST	KAPM85_ST	KAU85_PR	KBA85_PR
1959	440010.000	-	536540.000	1961040.000
1960	464460.000	452235.000	577420.000	2082360.000
1961	491380.000	477920.000	624460.000	2208190.000
1962	522380.000	506880.000	675170.000	2333760.000
1963	558480.000	540430.000	724120.000	2457050.000
1964	602620.000	580550.000	776770.000	2593700.000
1965	647040.000	624830.000	832640.000	2736780.000
1966	692020.000	669530.000	883680.000	2883810.000
1967	732080.000	712050.000	923680.000	3022770.000
1968	774790.000	753435.000	965690.000	3161930.000
1969	821190.000	797990.000	1021780.000	3306580.000
1970	874140.000	847665.000	1089750.000	3456740.000
1971	926930.000	900535.000	1158540.000	3621920.000
1972	977950.000	952440.000	1220110.000	3801090.000
1973	1028100.000	1003025.000	1277390.000	3980560.000
1974	1081440.000	1054770.000	1316680.000	4134580.000
1975	1133260.000	1107350.000	1352150.000	4272340.000
1976	1182950.000	1158105.000	1390440.000	4415520.000
1977	1230450.000	1206700.000	1432950.000	4563100.000
1978	1278850.000	1254650.000	1480450.000	4713700.000
1979	1328770.000	1303810.000	1535750.000	4873930.000
1980	1378550.000	1353660.000	1591020.000	5038170.000
1981	1423380.000	1400965.000	1635490.000	5193690.000
1982	1463590.000	1443485.000	1667160.000	5342440.000
1983	1500000.000	1481795.000	1703380.000	5496460.000
1984	1535320.000	1517660.000	1732340.000	5651520.000
1985	1570280.000	1552800.000	1770360.000	5794440.000
1986	1608340.000	1589310.000	1812470.000	5939610.000
1987	1646130.000	1627235.000	1858750.000	6084160.000
1988	1684390.000	1665260.000	1913460.000	6233040.000
1989	1724400.000	1704395.000	1979380.000	6387880.000
1990	1764990.000	1744695.000	2067540.000	6552120.000
1991	1806410.000	1785700.000	2173030.000	6723390.000
1992	1858615.076	1836174.798	2290660.211	6886276.385
1993	1900971.205	1879793.141	2408902.797	7033634.405
1994	1941257.280	1921114.243	2530310.862	7173463.205
1995	1981179.626	1961218.453	2656521.951	7308032.826
1996	2023029.459	2002104.542	2790612.781	7440993.937
1997	2066348.394	2044688.926	2932635.994	7572401.036
1998	2111373.607	2088861.000	3082884.029	7702717.731
1999	2158447.883	2134910.745	3241988.987	7831683.764
2000	2205240.353	2181844.118	3406712.308	7957520.028

Legend :

KAP85_ST \ Dimension : mill.DM
Stock of capital, public sector, in 1985 prices (end of year)
KAPM85_ST \ Dimension : mill.DM
Stock of capital, public sector, in 1985 prices (average of year)
KAU85_PR \ Dimension : mill.DM
Stock of capital, equipment, private sector, in 1985 prices (end of year)
KBA85_PR \ Dimension : mill.DM
Stock of capital, construction, private sector, in 1985 prices (end of year)

YEAR	KAUMA85_PR	KBAM85_PR	KAUM85_PR	KAP85
1959	-	-	-	2937590.000
1960	492927.300	2021700.000	556980.000	3124240.000
1961	525822.500	2145275.000	600940.000	3324030.000
1962	567288.495	2270975.000	649815.000	3531310.000
1963	601694.700	2395405.000	699645.000	3739650.000
1964	658140.265	2525375.000	750445.000	3973090.000
1965	708140.400	2665240.000	804705.000	4216460.000
1966	733726.800	2810295.000	858160.000	4459510.000
1967	709388.800	2953290.000	903680.000	4678530.000
1968	802982.250	3092350.000	944685.000	4902410.000
1969	892374.030	3234255.000	993735.000	5149550.000
1970	957578.855	3381660.000	1055765.000	5420630.000
1971	983626.875	3539330.000	1124145.000	5707390.000
1972	1018062.200	3711505.000	1189325.000	5999150.000
1973	1082666.250	3890825.000	1248750.000	6286050.000
1974	1059677.595	4057570.000	1297035.000	6532700.000
1975	1028833.965	4203460.000	1334415.000	6757750.000
1976	1099778.590	4343930.000	1371295.000	6988910.000
1977	1169589.308	4489310.000	1411695.000	7226500.000
1978	1187210.500	4638400.000	1456700.000	7473000.000
1979	1277813.130	4793815.000	1508100.000	7738450.000
1980	1287916.563	4956050.000	1563385.000	8007740.000
1981	1274148.799	5115930.000	1613255.000	8252560.000
1982	1261282.035	5268065.000	1651325.000	8473190.000
1983	1320409.045	5419450.000	1685270.000	8699840.000
1984	1385454.090	5573990.000	1717860.000	8919180.000
1985	1475162.105	5722980.000	1751350.000	9135080.000
1986	1516432.798	5867025.000	1791415.000	9360420.000
1987	1547419.230	6011885.000	1835610.000	9589040.000
1988	1635818.867	6158600.000	1886105.000	9830890.000
1989	1733870.936	6310460.000	1946420.000	10091660.000
1990	1814638.928	6470000.000	2023460.000	10384650.000
1991	1855249.375	6637755.000	2120285.000	10702830.000
1992	1889614.437	6805481.403	2233586.805	11035551.672
1993	1950318.649	6959955.395	2349781.504	11343508.408
1994	2049773.669	7103548.805	2469606.830	11645031.347
1995	2165502.699	7240748.015	2593416.406	11945734.403
1996	2274178.750	7374513.382	2723567.366	12254636.177
1997	2403764.485	7506697.487	2861624.387	12571385.424
1998	2526518.410	7637559.383	3007760.012	12896975.367
1999	2624822.302	7767200.747	3162436.508	13232120.634
2000	2759211.037	7894601.896	3324350.647	13569472.689

Legend :

KAUMA85_PR \ Dimension : mill.DM
Utilized stock of capital, equipment, pr. sector, in 1985 pr. (average of year)
KBAM85_PR \ Dimension : mill.DM
Stock of capital, construction, private sector, in 1985 prices (average of year)
KAUM85_PR \ Dimension : mill.DM
Stock of capital, equipment, private sector, in 1985 prices (average of year)
KAP85 \ Dimension : mill.DM
Stock of capital, in 1985 prices (end of year)

YEAR	MIAU85	M	MD85	KAPAM85
1960	4230.000	52750.000	25340.000	2966862.300
1961	5080.000	56070.000	28000.000	3149017.500
1962	5690.000	61960.000	31290.000	3345143.495
1963	5230.000	66420.000	31650.000	3537529.700
1964	5990.000	73960.000	34650.000	3764065.265
1965	8000.000	86860.000	37150.000	3998210.400
1966	8330.000	91000.000	39510.000	4213551.800
1967	8220.000	89070.000	41430.000	4374728.800
1968	8880.000	100470.000	42410.000	4648767.250
1969	11790.000	119760.000	48490.000	4924619.030
1970	15310.000	138800.000	59880.000	5186903.855
1971	16820.000	152880.000	64870.000	5423491.875
1972	17590.000	163730.000	68110.000	5682007.200
1973	16430.000	185570.000	74690.000	5976516.250
1974	15690.000	232380.000	72490.000	6172017.595
1975	17980.000	238430.000	74340.000	6339643.965
1976	19950.000	277800.000	78240.000	6601813.590
1977	22110.000	295610.000	81320.000	6865599.308
1978	25260.000	302960.000	84300.000	7080260.500
1979	27770.000	359930.000	88940.000	7375438.130
1980	28980.000	422150.000	89730.000	7597626.563
1981	29000.000	464750.000	90580.000	7791043.799
1982	27240.000	477340.000	92040.000	7972832.035
1983	30650.000	481570.000	90700.000	8221654.045
1984	33230.000	530130.000	90460.000	8477104.090
1985	38570.000	569470.000	92000.000	8750942.105
1986	41410.000	526300.000	90550.000	8972767.798
1987	45030.000	525040.000	92230.000	9186539.230
1988	50250.000	566140.000	93900.000	9459678.867
1989	60580.000	643490.000	96740.000	9748725.936
1990	73050.000	718680.000	100630.000	10029333.928
1991	89950.000	827210.000	108320.000	10278704.375
1992	71927.666	870007.000	110842.711	10531270.638
1993	63771.018	915332.000	113484.992	10790067.184
1994	68696.772	961387.000	115619.724	11074436.716
1995	70054.342	1008347.000	117572.492	11367469.168
1996	73344.329	1057918.000	120009.500	11650796.675
1997	75970.548	1110083.000	122812.912	11955150.898
1998	78298.331	1165589.000	126033.010	12252938.793
1999	80635.867	1224964.000	129607.192	12526933.794
2000	83133.669	1287383.000	133195.172	12835657.051

Legend :

MIAU85 \ Dimension : mill.DM
Imports of equipment in 1985 prices
M \ Dimension : mill.DM
Imports (including incomes from assets and business)
MD85 \ Dimension : mill.DM
Imports of services in 1985 prices
KAPAM85 \ Dimension : mill.DM
Utilized stock of capital, in 1985 prices (average of year)

YEAR	MR%D85	CPR	M85	CST85
1960	98380.000	171840.000	127950.000	159190.000
1961	105970.000	188330.000	139050.000	169050.000
1962	116290.000	204790.000	153270.000	185270.000
1963	123570.000	216790.000	160450.000	196740.000
1964	134730.000	233500.000	175370.000	200170.000
1965	154930.000	257620.000	200080.000	209960.000
1966	157600.000	275060.000	205440.000	216500.000
1967	154730.000	282630.000	204380.000	224410.000
1968	178910.000	300740.000	230200.000	225400.000
1969	208480.000	330900.000	268760.000	235320.000
1970	237980.000	368850.000	313170.000	245510.000
1971	257770.000	408980.000	339460.000	258070.000
1972	271350.000	451960.000	357050.000	268770.000
1973	282570.000	495590.000	373690.000	282210.000
1974	291850.000	533640.000	380030.000	293440.000
1975	288660.000	583450.000	380980.000	304740.000
1976	321310.000	631870.000	419500.000	309470.000
1977	334470.000	682130.000	437900.000	313690.000
1978	346920.000	725940.000	456480.000	325890.000
1979	384170.000	781310.000	500880.000	336920.000
1980	404390.000	837020.000	523100.000	345660.000
1981	396470.000	883520.000	516050.000	351960.000
1982	396470.000	916100.000	515750.000	348790.000
1983	394940.000	959280.000	516290.000	349540.000
1984	419110.000	1001200.000	542800.000	358310.000
1985	438900.000	1036530.000	569470.000	365720.000
1986	457110.000	1066430.000	589070.000	375040.000
1987	476700.000	1108020.000	613960.000	380850.000
1988	505220.000	1153690.000	649630.000	389100.000
1989	546880.000	1220950.000	704360.000	382670.000
1990	612960.000	1321210.000	787900.000	391750.000
1991	685880.000	1420650.000	884150.000	393600.000
1992	723486.406	1505426.231	906256.783	419463.716
1993	686265.060	1551287.625	863521.070	429156.200
1994	696236.186	1598627.334	880552.682	437952.166
1995	709037.254	1659043.508	896664.088	446207.520
1996	738076.240	1739554.710	931430.069	454611.937
1997	768897.634	1831412.087	967681.094	463367.695
1998	801675.814	1934034.634	1006007.154	472462.987
1999	836542.118	2052909.468	1046785.176	481867.275
2000	872904.030	2162899.881	1089232.871	491611.122

Legend :

MR%D85 \ Dimension : mill.DM
Imports without capital goods and services in 1985 prices
CPR \ Dimension : mill.DM
Private consumption
M85 \ Dimension : mill.DM
Imports (including incomes from assets and business) in 1985 prices
CST85 \ Dimension : mill.DM
Government consumption in 1985 prices

YEAR	CST	C	C85	CPR85
1960	40450.000	212290.000	604050.000	444860.000
1961	45780.000	234110.000	640920.000	471870.000
1962	52830.000	257620.000	683750.000	498480.000
1963	59390.000	276180.000	709070.000	512330.000
1964	62100.000	295600.000	739860.000	539690.000
1965	69650.000	327270.000	786660.000	576700.000
1966	75450.000	350510.000	811080.000	594580.000
1967	80050.000	362680.000	825820.000	601410.000
1968	82730.000	383470.000	855460.000	630060.000
1969	93120.000	424020.000	915610.000	680290.000
1970	106470.000	475320.000	977430.000	731920.000
1971	126760.000	535740.000	1030780.000	772710.000
1972	141040.000	593000.000	1077410.000	808640.000
1973	163090.000	658680.000	1115250.000	833040.000
1974	190110.000	723750.000	1131040.000	837600.000
1975	210080.000	793530.000	1168560.000	863820.000
1976	221860.000	853730.000	1206790.000	897320.000
1977	235130.000	917260.000	1251490.000	937800.000
1978	253090.000	979030.000	1297370.000	971480.000
1979	273540.000	1054850.000	1339980.000	1003060.000
1980	298020.000	1135040.000	1361230.000	1015570.000
1981	318390.000	1201910.000	1359880.000	1007920.000
1982	326440.000	1242540.000	1341340.000	992550.000
1983	336440.000	1295720.000	1355460.000	1005920.000
1984	350440.000	1351640.000	1379990.000	1021680.000
1985	365720.000	1402250.000	1402250.000	1036530.000
1986	382550.000	1448980.000	1447050.000	1072010.000
1987	397280.000	1505300.000	1487730.000	1106880.000
1988	412380.000	1566070.000	1526100.000	1137000.000
1989	418820.000	1639770.000	1550040.000	1167370.000
1990	444350.000	1765560.000	1622430.000	1230680.000
1991	468070.000	1888720.000	1668230.000	1274630.000
1992	510836.676	2016262.907	1723840.842	1304377.126
1993	544394.390	2095682.015	1732033.334	1302877.134
1994	571018.097	2169645.431	1746311.096	1308358.930
1995	595285.900	2254329.408	1772609.944	1326402.424
1996	629210.578	2368765.288	1807314.468	1352702.531
1997	661268.138	2492680.225	1847435.205	1384067.510
1998	699997.472	2634032.106	1888611.335	1416148.347
1999	744605.907	2797515.375	1932309.622	1450442.346
2000	784275.681	2947175.563	1970310.855	1478699.733

Legend :

CST \ Dimension : mill.DM
Government consumption
C \ Dimension : mill.DM
Consumption
C85 \ Dimension : mill.DM
Consumption in 1985 prices
CPR85 \ Dimension : mill.DM
Private consumption in 1985 prices

YEAR	CST_BSP	IAN_ST	CPR_BSP	DIAU_PR
1960	0.134	9720.000	0.567	-
1961	0.138	11440.000	0.568	4060.000
1962	0.147	14280.000	0.568	3470.000
1963	0.155	17110.000	0.567	480.000
1964	0.148	20880.000	0.557	3500.000
1965	0.152	20860.000	0.562	3960.000
1966	0.155	21200.000	0.564	650.000
1967	0.162	18870.000	0.573	-2850.000
1968	0.155	20680.000	0.564	2130.000
1969	0.156	23730.000	0.554	10240.000
1970	0.158	31090.000	0.546	11820.000
1971	0.169	33670.000	0.545	6300.000
1972	0.171	33850.000	0.548	-140.000
1973	0.178	35130.000	0.539	2150.000
1974	0.193	40030.000	0.543	-3370.000
1975	0.204	39730.000	0.568	5720.000
1976	0.197	39290.000	0.562	8160.000
1977	0.197	39040.000	0.571	8840.000
1978	0.196	42350.000	0.563	9980.000
1979	0.196	47910.000	0.561	12290.000
1980	0.202	52740.000	0.567	7760.000
1981	0.207	49700.000	0.574	480.000
1982	0.205	45440.000	0.576	-2920.000
1983	0.201	42180.000	0.573	11350.000
1984	0.199	42160.000	0.568	1730.000
1985	0.199	42910.000	0.565	15060.000
1986	0.198	47290.000	0.551	7250.000
1987	0.198	47990.000	0.553	8010.000
1988	0.196	48910.000	0.547	12940.000
1989	0.186	52370.000	0.543	20110.000
1990	0.182	56030.000	0.542	29720.000
1991	0.178	60870.000	0.540	27070.000
1992	0.183	67141.692	0.539	23820.898
1993	0.190	66431.784	0.541	24042.762
1994	0.193	65880.034	0.540	23433.864
1995	0.194	67375.942	0.541	26115.083
1996	0.194	72555.669	0.538	33021.431
1997	0.194	77417.658	0.537	35427.025
1998	0.194	83177.315	0.536	39298.183
1999	0.194	90174.186	0.535	44512.708
2000	0.194	93482.177	0.535	42046.175

Legend :

CST_BSP \ Dimension : no dimension
Share of government consumption to GNP
IAN_ST \ Dimension : mill.DM
Gross fixed capital formation, public sector
CPR_BSP \ Dimension : no dimension
Share of private consumption to GNP
DIAU_PR \ Dimension : mill.DM
First difference of gross fixed capital formation, equipment, private sector

YEAR	IAN85_ST	IAU85_PR	IAU_PR	IBA_PR
1960	26680.000	62410.000	26230.000	37630.000
1961	29530.000	69640.000	30290.000	41730.000
1962	34080.000	74670.000	33760.000	44840.000
1963	39310.000	74570.000	34240.000	46360.000
1964	47660.000	80450.000	37740.000	53080.000
1965	48300.000	86450.000	41700.000	57340.000
1966	48630.000	84940.000	42350.000	60620.000
1967	44420.000	77570.000	39500.000	55810.000
1968	47260.000	83360.000	41630.000	57080.000
1969	51240.000	101230.000	51870.000	63300.000
1970	57840.000	116950.000	63690.000	77270.000
1971	58060.000	121700.000	69990.000	92450.000
1972	56450.000	118270.000	69850.000	105470.000
1973	55960.000	117260.000	72000.000	112130.000
1974	59810.000	103690.000	68630.000	104050.000
1975	58250.000	103900.000	74350.000	95330.000
1976	56190.000	111180.000	82510.000	103850.000
1977	53860.000	120020.000	91350.000	112040.000
1978	55110.000	129260.000	101330.000	121220.000
1979	57110.000	140860.000	113620.000	139760.000
1980	57080.000	144380.000	121380.000	157960.000
1981	51900.000	138010.000	121860.000	159730.000
1982	47280.000	128530.000	118940.000	159070.000
1983	43500.000	136750.000	130290.000	168340.000
1984	42640.000	135140.000	132020.000	176490.000
1985	42910.000	147080.000	147080.000	165820.000
1986	46410.000	152980.000	154330.000	171860.000
1987	46420.000	160260.000	162340.000	175450.000
1988	46550.000	171310.000	175280.000	185710.000
1989	48440.000	186610.000	195390.000	200760.000
1990	49210.000	211300.000	225110.000	225670.000
1991	50150.000	231180.000	252180.000	252020.000
1992	53946.457	247517.439	290578.735	246709.132
1993	51624.308	257882.297	314621.496	237416.781
1994	49744.881	267974.285	338055.361	235082.810
1995	49563.780	280279.154	364170.444	235251.232
1996	51671.709	296197.476	397191.875	245057.482
1997	53322.091	312724.766	432618.900	253766.908
1998	55212.780	330117.280	471917.083	265606.070
1999	57451.373	348732.571	516429.791	278944.067
2000	57361.941	364724.566	558475.966	286490.575

Legend :

IAN85_ST \ Dimension : mill.DM
Gross fixed capital formation, public sector, in 1985 prices
IAU85_PR \ Dimension : mill.DM
Gross fixed capital formation, equipment, private sector, in 1985 prices
IAU_PR \ Dimension : mill.DM
Gross fixed capital formation, equipment, private sector
IBA_PR \ Dimension : mill.DM
Gross fixed capital formation, construction, private sector

YEAR	IANST_BSP	IAN85	IAN	IBA85_PR
1960	0.032	218840.000	73580.000	129750.000
1961	0.035	233300.000	83460.000	134130.000
1962	0.040	242390.000	92880.000	133640.000
1963	0.045	245390.000	97710.000	131510.000
1964	0.050	272940.000	111700.000	144830.000
1965	0.046	285960.000	119900.000	151210.000
1966	0.044	289290.000	124170.000	155720.000
1967	0.038	269270.000	114180.000	147280.000
1968	0.039	278330.000	119390.000	147710.000
1969	0.040	305780.000	138900.000	153310.000
1970	0.046	334040.000	172050.000	159250.000
1971	0.045	354140.000	196110.000	174380.000
1972	0.041	363460.000	209170.000	188740.000
1973	0.038	362460.000	219260.000	189240.000
1974	0.041	327240.000	212710.000	163740.000
1975	0.039	310340.000	209410.000	148190.000
1976	0.035	321730.000	225650.000	154360.000
1977	0.033	333920.000	242430.000	160040.000
1978	0.033	348260.000	264900.000	163890.000
1979	0.034	372160.000	301290.000	174190.000
1980	0.036	380790.000	332080.000	179330.000
1981	0.032	362210.000	331290.000	172300.000
1982	0.029	343130.000	323450.000	167320.000
1983	0.025	354590.000	340810.000	174340.000
1984	0.024	355700.000	350670.000	177920.000
1985	0.023	355810.000	355810.000	165820.000
1986	0.024	368490.000	373480.000	169100.000
1987	0.024	376220.000	385780.000	169540.000
1988	0.023	393680.000	409900.000	175820.000
1989	0.023	419080.000	448520.000	184030.000
1990	0.023	455460.000	506810.000	194950.000
1991	0.023	485010.000	565070.000	203680.000
1992	0.024	497126.693	604429.559	195662.796
1993	0.023	492702.275	618470.061	183195.670
1994	0.022	495195.017	639018.204	177475.851
1995	0.022	503908.684	666797.618	174065.750
1996	0.022	522211.589	714805.027	174342.404
1997	0.023	540754.932	763803.466	174708.074
1998	0.023	560900.427	820700.468	175570.366
1999	0.023	582388.131	885548.044	176204.188
2000	0.023	597175.851	938448.719	175089.344

Legend :

IANST_BSP \ Dimension : no dimension
Share of gross fixed capital formation (public sector) to GNP
IAN85 \ Dimension : mill.DM
Gross fixed capital formation in 1985 prices
IAN \ Dimension : mill.DM
Gross fixed capital formation
IBA85_PR \ Dimension : mill.DM
Gross fixed capital formation, construction, private sector, in 1985 prices

YEAR	IBAPR_BSP	OUT_ST	IAUPR_BSP	IN_ST
1960	0.124	105680.000	0.087	114890.000
1961	0.126	122080.000	0.091	131330.000
1962	0.124	136830.000	0.094	142010.000
1963	0.121	148300.000	0.090	151710.000
1964	0.127	161880.000	0.090	164890.000
1965	0.125	179550.000	0.091	176790.000
1966	0.124	191950.000	0.087	191080.000
1967	0.113	204840.000	0.080	197840.000
1968	0.107	222520.000	0.078	218210.000
1969	0.106	245120.000	0.087	251640.000
1970	0.114	276170.000	0.094	277520.000
1971	0.123	317430.000	0.093	316210.000
1972	0.128	356640.000	0.085	352260.000
1973	0.122	404560.000	0.078	415600.000
1974	0.106	465630.000	0.070	452910.000
1975	0.093	537220.000	0.072	479360.000
1976	0.092	575190.000	0.073	536930.000
1977	0.094	611280.000	0.076	582280.000
1978	0.094	652920.000	0.079	621620.000
1979	0.100	703020.000	0.082	667260.000
1980	0.107	759680.000	0.082	717000.000
1981	0.104	808560.000	0.079	752010.000
1982	0.100	842260.000	0.075	789560.000
1983	0.101	857740.000	0.078	815140.000
1984	0.100	890090.000	0.075	856110.000
1985	0.090	918400.000	0.080	897310.000
1986	0.089	955590.000	0.080	930190.000
1987	0.088	995240.000	0.081	957400.000
1988	0.088	1040200.000	0.083	994960.000
1989	0.089	1072080.000	0.087	1074830.000
1990	0.093	1173010.000	0.092	1123580.000
1991	0.096	1357820.000	0.096	1264210.000
1992	0.088	1421065.131	0.104	1332206.964
1993	0.083	1479255.395	0.110	1383323.629
1994	0.079	1534215.878	0.114	1440992.109
1995	0.077	1601734.064	0.119	1511301.226
1996	0.076	1665579.736	0.123	1588846.195
1997	0.074	1739962.900	0.127	1676143.577
1998	0.074	1824543.441	0.131	1777568.793
1999	0.073	1918743.001	0.135	1900797.596
2000	0.071	2006462.816	0.138	1997886.150

Legend :

IBAPR_BSP \ Dimension : no dimension
Share of gross fixed capital formation (construction, private sector) to GNP
OUT_ST \ Dimension : mill.DM
Total government expenditures
IAUPR_BSP \ Dimension : no dimension
Share of gross fixed capital formation (equipment, private sector) to GNP
IN_ST \ Dimension : mill.DM
Total government receipts

YEAR	FS_ST	TDIR	TD_HH	TIND
1960	9210.000	27990.000	19890.000	41780.000
1961	9250.000	33780.000	24450.000	46190.000
1962	5180.000	37830.000	27970.000	50060.000
1963	3410.000	40480.000	30800.000	52790.000
1964	3010.000	44470.000	34300.000	57480.000
1965	-2760.000	45650.000	35350.000	62190.000
1966	-870.000	49390.000	39420.000	65500.000
1967	-7000.000	49390.000	39820.000	67990.000
1968	-4310.000	54860.000	43610.000	74940.000
1969	6520.000	63880.000	50020.000	88280.000
1970	1350.000	72840.000	60440.000	89050.000
1971	-1220.000	84960.000	72870.000	98690.000
1972	-4380.000	91070.000	78570.000	110180.000
1973	11040.000	115810.000	99450.000	121070.000
1974	-12720.000	128380.000	112170.000	125040.000
1975	-57860.000	123820.000	108580.000	130280.000
1976	-38260.000	143830.000	124280.000	141920.000
1977	-29000.000	164650.000	138750.000	152520.000
1978	-31300.000	167490.000	141180.000	167560.000
1979	-35760.000	175510.000	146290.000	183160.000
1980	-42680.000	187750.000	160210.000	193470.000
1981	-56550.000	188110.000	161180.000	198290.000
1982	-52700.000	193180.000	164730.000	201680.000
1983	-42600.000	200360.000	169070.000	214390.000
1984	-33980.000	213020.000	177220.000	226130.000
1985	-21090.000	229640.000	188980.000	230310.000
1986	-25400.000	237040.000	196270.000	236170.000
1987	-37840.000	245940.000	209430.000	245500.000
1988	-45240.000	255410.000	214670.000	257110.000
1989	2750.000	281760.000	236340.000	278330.000
1990	-49430.000	271010.000	228560.000	302170.000
1991	-93610.000	316100.000	271480.000	342140.000
1992	-88858.167	316429.416	267896.683	354614.836
1993	-95931.767	328533.657	278225.172	372756.939
1994	-93223.769	341784.388	289531.954	385009.622
1995	-90432.838	358351.370	303668.477	397427.124
1996	-76733.541	376246.126	318937.983	411181.199
1997	-63819.323	398376.907	337822.067	425162.583
1998	-46974.648	424624.841	360219.299	441027.232
1999	-17945.405	456016.562	387005.697	457819.182
2000	-8576.666	484312.424	411150.414	474961.009

Legend :

FS_ST \ Dimension : mill.DM
Balance of government budget
TDIR \ Dimension : mill.DM
Direct taxes
TD_HH \ Dimension : mill.DM
Direct taxes, private households
TIND \ Dimension : mill.DM
Indirect taxes

YEAR	TD_KEST	TD_KOST	TD_LOST%P	TI_GEW
1960	846.000	6560.000	7910.000	6780.000
1961	980.000	7520.000	10180.000	7430.000
1962	1130.000	7820.000	11830.000	7980.000
1963	1138.000	7710.000	13310.000	8470.000
1964	1252.000	8040.000	15680.000	9100.000
1965	1351.000	8170.000	15880.000	9350.000
1966	1456.000	7710.000	18790.000	10090.000
1967	1469.000	7080.000	19110.000	10010.000
1968	1539.000	8560.000	21740.000	10540.000
1969	1715.000	10950.000	26760.000	14220.000
1970	2021.000	9250.000	36300.000	10730.000
1971	2074.000	8120.000	45890.000	12320.000
1972	2189.000	8530.000	48230.000	14850.000
1973	2024.000	12120.000	62680.000	17770.000
1974	2574.000	11740.000	73340.000	18770.000
1975	2246.000	10850.000	71870.000	17900.000
1976	2313.000	14580.000	81760.000	20110.000
1977	3381.000	19690.000	91260.000	23030.000
1978	3366.000	21180.000	92690.000	24000.000
1979	3809.000	23930.000	97700.000	25060.000
1980	4175.000	22260.000	112360.000	27090.000
1981	4630.000	21380.000	116720.000	26040.000
1982	4703.000	22680.000	122240.000	26100.000
1983	4709.000	25580.000	127350.000	26190.000
1984	5591.000	30300.000	135450.000	28330.000
1985	6206.000	34970.000	145520.000	30760.000
1986	8121.000	34030.000	150010.000	31980.000
1987	7880.000	29160.000	162360.000	31440.000
1988	8731.000	32030.000	165480.000	34460.000
1989	12648.000	35980.000	179170.000	36700.000
1990	10832.000	32190.000	173630.000	38790.000
1991	11381.000	34110.000	207050.000	40750.000
1992	12639.182	34722.681	189067.553	43802.083
1993	12749.458	34840.292	196143.907	43963.442
1994	12929.251	34324.485	204642.653	45057.782
1995	12955.105	33981.928	216133.057	45040.149
1996	13239.655	32632.732	232234.020	46179.288
1997	13483.522	32257.778	251551.696	46875.282
1998	13790.623	32489.249	274228.542	47954.153
1999	13892.502	32545.093	302339.047	48193.502
2000	14363.143	33412.544	326079.619	50124.273

Legend :

TD_KEST \ Dimension : mill.DM
Capital yields tax
TD_KOST \ Dimension : mill.DM
Corporate income tax
TD_LOST%P \ Dimension : mill.DM
Payroll tax (without that on pensions)
TI_GEW \ Dimension : mill.DM
Tax paid for carrying on a trade

YEAR	SUB	TI_UST	T	TI_MIN
1960	2520.000	-	69770.000	2664.000
1961	2660.000	17860.000	79970.000	3325.000
1962	2900.000	19210.000	87890.000	3699.000
1963	3480.000	20040.000	93270.000	4139.000
1964	4090.000	21930.000	101950.000	6071.000
1965	5750.000	24220.000	107840.000	7428.000
1966	5650.000	25070.000	114890.000	8016.000
1967	5550.000	24720.000	117380.000	9423.000
1968	12980.000	30990.000	129800.000	9875.000
1969	11620.000	37620.000	152160.000	10601.000
1970	11780.000	39910.000	161890.000	11512.000
1971	12610.000	45040.000	183650.000	12417.000
1972	15780.000	49380.000	201250.000	14227.000
1973	18650.000	52260.000	236880.000	16589.000
1974	18860.000	54430.000	253420.000	16052.000
1975	20390.000	57310.000	254100.000	17121.000
1976	22130.000	61810.000	285750.000	18121.000
1977	24630.000	65700.000	317170.000	19184.000
1978	29700.000	76240.000	335050.000	20463.000
1979	31160.000	87020.000	358670.000	21140.000
1980	30650.000	96570.000	381220.000	21351.000
1981	29120.000	100730.000	386400.000	22180.000
1982	29250.000	101170.000	394860.000	22835.000
1983	31720.000	109230.000	414750.000	23338.000
1984	36330.000	115900.000	439150.000	24033.000
1985	37940.000	116660.000	459950.000	24521.000
1986	41310.000	117880.000	473210.000	25644.000
1987	44800.000	125110.000	491440.000	26136.000
1988	47740.000	130100.000	512520.000	27032.000
1989	46780.000	137530.000	560090.000	32965.000
1990	48740.000	154950.000	573180.000	34621.000
1991	46650.000	175970.000	658240.000	43519.000
1992	54579.711	174093.252	671044.251	36719.501
1993	57667.409	185977.278	701290.596	37816.218
1994	60538.589	190755.985	726794.010	38945.856
1995	63353.906	196515.071	755778.494	40109.404
1996	66203.572	205037.470	787427.325	41307.880
1997	69200.564	214121.992	823539.490	42542.333
1998	72466.611	224595.685	865652.073	43813.844
1999	76089.099	236722.015	913835.744	45123.526
2000	79885.948	247389.568	959273.433	46472.525

Legend :

SUB \ Dimension : mill.DM
Subsidies
TI_UST \ Dimension : mill.DM
Turnover tax
T \ Dimension : mill.DM
Total taxes
TI_MIN \ Dimension : mill.DM
Petroleum tax

YEAR	GEW_BUV	BST_KST	GSV_BLG	TSB
1960	-	6426.000	30387.760	104660.000
1961	13123.960	6721.800	32862.960	118960.000
1962	13716.310	6359.700	38885.000	131050.000
1963	14127.750	6726.900	41725.000	139640.000
1964	15844.920	7517.400	45952.500	150910.000
1965	17031.840	8165.100	51188.760	162810.000
1966	17625.360	7803.000	55143.880	175660.000
1967	17981.550	7308.300	55344.060	180120.000
1968	20753.255	9562.500	61678.750	198820.000
1969	22480.105	11668.800	72585.800	231040.000
1970	24021.040	7945.800	81593.500	257270.000
1971	25382.500	8374.200	92270.350	292830.000
1972	28648.500	12352.200	103887.850	326020.000
1973	31605.650	13749.600	125032.960	384490.000
1974	31073.040	14417.700	138892.720	420470.000
1975	32702.840	15611.100	150279.600	439680.000
1976	37911.555	19507.500	170443.870	494500.000
1977	39549.650	22204.000	184012.560	537930.000
1978	44297.500	27714.400	196062.120	570990.000
1979	47030.750	29288.000	210484.960	615250.000
1980	45490.500	27938.400	229884.480	659870.000
1981	45592.695	30744.000	247715.370	684290.000
1982	47502.375	28974.400	259909.600	709700.000
1983	56653.170	40398.400	271319.580	737920.000
1984	63148.800	44688.000	278616.710	779050.000
1985	67704.080	44592.800	295158.120	815510.000
1986	75041.770	45813.600	310327.020	847770.000
1987	76341.350	50080.800	324960.360	882460.000
1988	84374.960	55748.000	340644.330	920620.000
1989	93434.010	57226.400	356418.790	986080.000
1990	103297.740	51790.000	379913.900	1030770.000
1991	107362.440	63475.000	419408.450	1152960.000
1992	125340.938	66117.218	439218.619	1177010.833
1993	126040.575	65513.859	455594.544	1226811.162
1994	130785.512	63771.206	477868.529	1278911.252
1995	130709.061	63450.507	508350.860	1344293.742
1996	135648.244	59808.159	550408.779	1426162.631
1997	138665.999	60562.374	597382.735	1518364.940
1998	143343.868	61798.231	651917.864	1625596.230
1999	144381.659	61642.903	721102.016	1756390.551
2000	152753.277	64216.293	768467.916	1858386.394

Legend :

GEW_BUV \ Dimension : mill.DM
Tax base, tax paid for carrying on a trade
BST_KST \ Dimension : mill.DM
Tax base of corporate income tax
GSV_BLG \ Dimension : mill.DM
Imputed contributions to social security
TSB \ Dimension : mill.DM
Taxes and social contributions

YEAR	BMG_UST	ZINS_GK	ZINS_ST	GEW_LSST
1960	268760.000	2190.000	2190.000	-
1961	298020.000	2210.000	2210.000	2269.510
1962	329120.000	2410.000	2410.000	2479.308
1963	350220.000	2650.000	2650.000	2606.978
1964	381460.000	2900.000	2900.000	2867.436
1965	417770.000	3230.000	3230.000	3185.078
1966	441920.000	4120.000	4120.000	3417.613
1967	442100.000	5190.000	5190.000	3412.157
1968	466230.000	5380.000	5380.000	3635.555
1969	521600.000	5840.000	5840.000	4067.938
1970	598880.000	6550.000	6550.000	4778.608
1971	673820.000	7340.000	7340.000	5424.956
1972	736990.000	8430.000	8430.000	6372.918
1973	802710.000	10170.000	10170.000	7234.768
1974	849000.000	12150.000	12150.000	7926.848
1975	908120.000	14170.000	14180.000	8366.681
1976	979930.000	17440.000	17450.000	9005.447
1977	1053640.000	20410.000	20410.000	9651.292
1978	1130840.000	21520.000	21530.000	9935.941
1979	1234960.000	24090.000	24100.000	11121.496
1980	1336370.000	28530.000	28550.000	0.000
1981	1394770.000	35390.000	35470.000	0.000
1982	1423430.000	44010.000	44030.000	0.000
1983	1489600.000	50080.000	50090.000	0.000
1984	1553220.000	52700.000	52720.000	0.000
1985	1603730.000	55250.000	55270.000	0.000
1986	1660890.000	57160.000	57180.000	0.000
1987	1722660.000	57750.000	57780.000	0.000
1988	1803540.000	59780.000	59810.000	0.000
1989	1911440.000	60430.000	60460.000	0.000
1990	2084930.000	63490.000	63520.000	0.000
1991	2252570.000	71860.000	71900.000	0.000
1992	2411423.666	70307.972	70352.972	0.000
1993	2496512.524	75134.547	75184.547	0.000
1994	2582318.501	81049.140	81099.140	0.000
1995	2685728.087	88252.124	88307.124	0.000
1996	2838755.417	94542.308	94597.308	0.000
1997	3001876.198	100261.157	100316.157	0.000
1998	3189940.782	106066.335	106121.335	0.000
1999	3407679.955	111606.599	111666.599	0.000
2000	3599225.478	116577.615	116637.615	0.000

Legend :

BMG_UST \ Dimension : mill.DM
Tax base of turnover tax
ZINS_GK \ Dimension : mill.DM
Interest on government debt, government
ZINS_ST \ Dimension : mill.DM
Interest on debts of the public sector
GEW_LSST \ Dimension : mill.DM
Tax base, payroll tax

YEAR	SB_UH	SB_ST	SB_AG	SB_PR
1960	3690.000	31210.000	19850.000	34890.000
1961	4600.000	34420.000	22370.000	38990.000
1962	5070.000	38120.000	24590.000	43160.000
1963	5250.000	41160.000	26250.000	46370.000
1964	5170.000	43830.000	27360.000	48960.000
1965	6510.000	48520.000	31000.000	54970.000
1966	7020.000	53820.000	34100.000	60770.000
1967	6360.000	56420.000	33950.000	62740.000
1968	6840.000	62200.000	37630.000	69020.000
1969	7490.000	71430.000	42970.000	78880.000
1970	10540.000	84940.000	52740.000	95380.000
1971	10830.000	98440.000	60550.000	109180.000
1972	12400.000	112480.000	69130.000	124770.000
1973	14330.000	133480.000	81860.000	147610.000
1974	17660.000	149560.000	92960.000	167050.000
1975	18500.000	167260.000	100870.000	185580.000
1976	20970.000	187970.000	112860.000	208750.000
1977	20780.000	200230.000	120110.000	220760.000
1978	23540.000	212660.000	129420.000	235940.000
1979	26830.000	230040.000	140900.000	256580.000
1980	30520.000	248490.000	154360.000	278650.000
1981	29590.000	268640.000	162090.000	297890.000
1982	30870.000	284250.000	169490.000	314840.000
1983	33090.000	290340.000	176020.000	323170.000
1984	35580.000	304580.000	185400.000	339900.000
1985	35680.000	320110.000	192630.000	355560.000
1986	37380.000	337400.000	202860.000	374560.000
1987	40650.000	350550.000	211890.000	391020.000
1988	41750.000	366520.000	220510.000	408100.000
1989	43010.000	383150.000	229080.000	425990.000
1990	48530.000	410560.000	247550.000	457590.000
1991	50300.000	449320.000	267470.000	494720.000
1992	53203.869	457762.713	277785.610	505966.582
1993	55187.534	475333.032	289461.804	525520.566
1994	57885.649	499231.593	301445.645	552117.242
1995	61578.065	531937.183	315823.646	588515.248
1996	66672.667	577062.639	334708.522	638735.305
1997	72362.763	627462.687	357408.008	694825.450
1998	78968.767	685975.390	384202.214	759944.156
1999	87349.250	760205.557	417128.460	842554.807
2000	93086.824	811026.137	447449.916	899112.961

Legend :

SB_UH \ Dimension : mill.DM
Social contributions to the private sector
SB_ST \ Dimension : mill.DM
Social contributions to the public sector
SB_AG \ Dimension : mill.DM
Contributions, paid by employers to public social insurance (consolidated)
SB_PR \ Dimension : mill.DM
Social contributions of private households

YEAR	SL_HH_ST	TR_HH_EMP	SL_ZU_ST	SL_ST
1960	36400.000	44420.000	6750.000	37960.000
1961	39560.000	48640.000	6990.000	41410.000
1962	43120.000	53350.000	7050.000	45170.000
1963	46230.000	57390.000	6940.000	48100.000
1964	50510.000	62630.000	8510.000	52340.000
1965	56780.000	70380.000	10220.000	58740.000
1966	62010.000	77090.000	10050.000	63870.000
1967	69490.000	85550.000	15110.000	71530.000
1968	72880.000	90340.000	13040.000	75240.000
1969	78710.000	98120.000	9540.000	80970.000
1970	85720.000	108470.000	3230.000	88170.000
1971	96660.000	122360.000	680.000	99120.000
1972	110720.000	139810.000	980.000	113460.000
1973	124080.000	156460.000	-6360.000	127120.000
1974	143960.000	179150.000	-2140.000	147420.000
1975	180700.000	219280.000	17310.000	184570.000
1976	194660.000	237050.000	10700.000	198670.000
1977	206720.000	252290.000	10770.000	211000.000
1978	216730.000	266070.000	8540.000	221200.000
1979	230280.000	284590.000	4820.000	234860.000
1980	244530.000	304150.000	830.000	249320.000
1981	265520.000	330050.000	2020.000	270660.000
1982	281800.000	349200.000	2870.000	287120.000
1983	285480.000	355990.000	550.000	290890.000
1984	288960.000	364030.000	-9780.000	294800.000
1985	295770.000	375560.000	-18680.000	301430.000
1986	306790.000	392360.000	-24770.000	312630.000
1987	321880.000	412890.000	-22520.000	328030.000
1988	336460.000	433310.000	-23690.000	342830.000
1989	349680.000	453310.000	-24410.000	358740.000
1990	368050.000	480490.000	-35840.000	374720.000
1991	416740.000	513100.000	-25610.000	423710.000
1992	440547.100	536597.300	-10008.633	447754.080
1993	454425.249	557092.931	-13455.767	461877.266
1994	469203.132	578389.528	-22323.075	476908.518
1995	495423.320	611444.292	-28546.494	503390.689
1996	519016.719	646403.469	-49807.660	527254.979
1997	546477.722	683377.540	-72466.604	554996.083
1998	575706.386	722483.433	-101461.019	584514.371
1999	606808.769	763844.900	-144289.332	615916.225
2000	639897.295	807592.917	-161711.732	649314.405

Legend :

SL_HH_ST \ Dimension : mill.DM
Social contributions from the public sector to the private households
TR_HH_EMP \ Dimension : mill.DM
Transfer income of private households from other sectors
SL_ZU_ST \ Dimension : mill.DM
Balance of the goverment social contributions
SL_ST \ Dimension : mill.DM
Social contributions of the government (government and social insurance)

YEAR	TR_HH_GEL	TR%T	PBSP	TR_HH_R
1960	59480.000	-15060.000	35.241	4700.000
1961	68910.000	-20270.000	36.970	5470.000
1962	77550.000	-24200.000	38.453	6420.000
1963	84420.000	-27030.000	39.666	7250.000
1964	91660.000	-29030.000	40.881	8400.000
1965	100200.000	-29820.000	42.414	9880.000
1966	111580.000	-34490.000	43.866	11390.000
1967	114470.000	-28920.000	44.542	11910.000
1968	125600.000	-35260.000	45.538	12970.000
1969	144110.000	-45990.000	47.452	15210.000
1970	174880.000	-66410.000	51.081	19060.000
1971	204160.000	-81800.000	55.051	22110.000
1972	228620.000	-88810.000	57.977	25280.000
1973	274660.000	-118200.000	61.619	27600.000
1974	308760.000	-129610.000	65.936	29540.000
1975	325620.000	-106340.000	69.769	31460.000
1976	367410.000	-130360.000	72.284	34380.000
1977	395060.000	-142770.000	74.988	35550.000
1978	415780.000	-149710.000	78.174	38660.000
1979	444240.000	-159650.000	81.229	41370.000
1980	483700.000	-179550.000	85.212	44840.000
1981	507780.000	-177730.000	88.702	48710.000
1982	530380.000	-181180.000	92.648	50810.000
1983	545210.000	-189220.000	95.842	52970.000
1984	573910.000	-209880.000	97.852	56790.000
1985	603300.000	-227740.000	100.000	58760.000
1986	631990.000	-239630.000	103.292	61160.000
1987	663640.000	-250750.000	105.294	63190.000
1988	690000.000	-256690.000	106.907	67230.000
1989	733740.000	-280430.000	109.696	71410.000
1990	765450.000	-284960.000	113.457	79300.000
1991	852970.000	-339870.000	118.161	86770.000
1992	862649.333	-326052.033	122.709	88786.068
1993	896745.847	-339652.917	126.594	93000.109
1994	938768.431	-360378.903	129.608	97119.236
1995	993410.219	-381965.927	132.338	101226.494
1996	1063472.375	-417068.906	137.068	105799.086
1997	1143422.471	-460044.931	141.244	110774.954
1998	1236476.096	-513992.664	146.491	116312.641
1999	1352052.113	-588207.214	152.576	122491.609
2000	1439271.521	-631678.604	157.377	129008.145

Legend :

TR_HH_GEL \ Dimension : mill.DM
Transfer payments of private households to other sectors
TR%T \ Dimension : mill.DM
Transfer income without direct taxes, paid transfers and social contributions
PBSP \ Dimension : index
Price, gross national product
TR_HH_R \ Dimension : mill.DM
Other transfer payments of private households

YEAR	PIAN_ST	PCST	PMD_PBSP	PCPR
1960	36.432	25.410	1.093	38.628
1961	38.740	27.081	1.065	39.911
1962	41.901	28.515	1.052	41.083
1963	43.526	30.187	1.054	42.315
1964	43.810	31.024	1.059	43.266
1965	43.188	33.173	1.052	44.671
1966	43.595	34.850	1.050	46.261
1967	42.481	35.671	1.027	46.995
1968	43.758	36.704	1.024	47.732
1969	46.312	39.572	0.971	48.641
1970	53.752	43.367	0.920	50.395
1971	57.992	49.119	0.881	52.928
1972	59.965	52.476	0.852	55.891
1973	62.777	57.790	0.834	59.492
1974	66.929	64.787	0.889	63.711
1975	68.206	68.938	0.892	67.543
1976	69.924	71.690	0.886	70.418
1977	72.484	74.956	0.874	72.737
1978	76.846	77.661	0.875	74.725
1979	83.891	81.188	0.899	77.893
1980	92.397	86.218	0.941	82.419
1981	95.761	90.462	0.995	87.658
1982	96.108	93.592	0.968	92.298
1983	96.966	96.252	0.959	95.363
1984	98.874	97.804	0.991	97.996
1985	100.000	100.000	1.000	100.000
1986	101.896	102.003	0.962	99.480
1987	103.382	104.314	0.955	100.103
1988	105.070	105.983	0.979	101.468
1989	108.113	109.447	0.999	104.590
1990	113.859	113.427	1.001	107.356
1991	121.376	118.920	0.995	111.456
1992	124.460	121.783	0.982	115.413
1993	128.683	126.852	0.976	119.066
1994	132.436	130.384	0.977	122.186
1995	135.938	133.410	0.981	125.078
1996	140.417	138.406	0.971	128.598
1997	145.189	142.709	0.966	132.321
1998	150.649	148.159	0.954	136.570
1999	156.957	154.525	0.939	141.537
2000	162.969	159.532	0.933	146.270

Legend :

PIAN_ST \ Dimension : index
Price index, gross fixed capital formation, public sector
PCST \ Dimension : index
Price index, government consumption
PMD_PBSP \ Dimension : no dimension
Relative prices, price of imported services to price of GNP
PCPR \ Dimension : index
Price index, private consumption

YEAR	PIBA_PR	BLG_EH85	M1	PIAU_PR
1960	29.002	8.107	47909.667	42.029
1961	31.112	8.615	52381.250	43.495
1962	33.553	9.168	58129.500	45.212
1963	35.252	9.625	62351.917	45.917
1964	36.650	10.071	67632.500	46.911
1965	37.921	10.688	73647.833	48.236
1966	38.929	11.195	76857.333	49.859
1967	37.894	11.634	79468.583	50.922
1968	38.643	12.147	85461.167	49.940
1969	41.289	12.865	92421.667	51.240
1970	48.521	13.902	98351.250	54.459
1971	53.016	14.524	110108.083	57.510
1972	55.881	15.227	125136.167	59.060
1973	59.253	16.186	132291.417	61.402
1974	63.546	17.070	140277.583	66.188
1975	64.330	17.476	159656.750	71.559
1976	67.278	17.707	176177.500	74.213
1977	70.008	18.570	190849.750	76.112
1978	73.964	18.922	216255.750	78.392
1979	80.234	19.470	232378.000	80.662
1980	88.083	19.959	238023.667	84.070
1981	92.705	20.289	240760.083	88.298
1982	95.069	20.125	249335.500	92.539
1983	96.558	20.161	275097.917	95.276
1984	99.196	20.431	284061.667	97.691
1985	100.000	20.866	296553.667	100.000
1986	101.632	21.063	325851.000	100.883
1987	103.486	21.460	355319.917	101.298
1988	105.625	21.730	389936.750	102.317
1989	109.091	22.082	414322.167	104.705
1990	115.758	22.847	433063.500	106.536
1991	123.733	23.674	447180.917	109.084
1992	126.089	23.836	476656.770	117.397
1993	129.597	24.193	498553.832	122.002
1994	132.459	24.799	521349.303	126.152
1995	135.151	25.770	544544.700	129.931
1996	140.561	26.556	572776.194	134.097
1997	145.252	27.417	604639.769	138.339
1998	151.282	28.243	640120.157	142.954
1999	158.307	29.428	681118.616	148.088
2000	163.625	29.775	725549.078	153.123

Legend :

PIBA_PR \ Dimension : index
Price index, gross fixed capital formation, construction, private sector
BLG_EH85 \ Dimension : DM/hour
Gross wage per hour in 1985 prices
M1 \ Dimension : mill.DM
Monetary supply M1
PIAU_PR \ Dimension : index
Price index, gross fixed capital formation, equipment, private sector

YEAR	BUV	BUA_EH85	BUA	BLG
1960	95720.000	9.399	144390.000	124540.000
1961	97940.000	9.988	162810.000	140440.000
1962	101980.000	10.618	180130.000	155540.000
1963	104650.000	11.139	193150.000	166900.000
1964	116080.000	11.570	211170.000	183810.000
1965	124320.000	12.319	234130.000	203130.000
1966	127720.000	12.946	252060.000	217960.000
1967	128900.000	13.447	251840.000	217890.000
1968	147710.000	14.111	270380.000	232750.000
1969	158870.000	14.982	304070.000	261100.000
1970	169760.000	16.283	360640.000	307900.000
1971	177500.000	17.049	408740.000	348190.000
1972	190990.000	17.972	452480.000	383350.000
1973	205900.000	19.248	514500.000	432640.000
1974	201120.000	20.406	568620.000	475660.000
1975	206980.000	21.053	593590.000	492720.000
1976	237690.000	21.494	640550.000	527690.000
1977	245650.000	22.497	688050.000	567940.000
1978	272600.000	22.969	734550.000	605130.000
1979	289420.000	23.667	794580.000	653680.000
1980	275700.000	24.301	863880.000	709520.000
1981	273830.000	24.710	905980.000	743890.000
1982	280250.000	24.587	933930.000	764440.000
1983	324660.000	24.726	953440.000	777420.000
1984	358800.000	25.149	988330.000	802930.000
1985	380360.000	25.687	1026410.000	833780.000
1986	418060.000	25.937	1079490.000	876630.000
1987	425300.000	26.441	1124700.000	912810.000
1988	466160.000	26.780	1169380.000	948870.000
1989	516210.000	27.177	1221890.000	992810.000
1990	567570.000	28.132	1317730.000	1070180.000
1991	586680.000	29.158	1422070.000	1154600.000
1992	677518.584	29.367	1474949.876	1197164.266
1993	670428.591	29.889	1518966.365	1229504.561
1994	681174.544	30.653	1578292.132	1276846.487
1995	677249.019	31.822	1660669.302	1344845.656
1996	699217.750	32.721	1776401.757	1441693.235
1997	709288.996	33.742	1906648.364	1549240.356
1998	725791.737	34.726	2058133.560	1673931.347
1999	723717.587	36.124	2250371.717	1833243.257
2000	758080.780	36.662	2381767.382	1934317.466

Legend :

BUV \ Dimension : mill.DM
Gross income from entrepreneurial activity and property
BUA_EH85 \ Dimension : DM/hour
Total labour cost per hour in 1985 prices
BUA \ Dimension : mill.DM
Gross income of employees
BLG \ Dimension : mill.DM
Gross wages and salaries, total

YEAR	X	X@	BESCH	BESVOL
1960	60680.000	-	20257.000	43591.038
1961	63200.000	-	20730.000	44092.710
1962	66260.000	-	21032.000	44118.826
1963	72030.000	-	21261.000	43716.868
1964	79860.000	-	21484.000	44645.900
1965	87190.000	-	21757.000	44810.717
1966	98420.000	-	21765.000	44385.365
1967	106410.000	-	21054.000	42046.943
1968	120210.000	-	21183.000	42077.911
1969	137340.000	-	21752.000	42770.958
1970	152930.000	-	22246.000	43359.679
1971	166960.000	-	22605.000	43548.533
1972	181860.000	-	22841.000	43425.309
1973	214050.000	-	23222.000	43378.696
1974	275910.000	-	23036.000	42261.846
1975	269550.000	-	22467.000	40411.393
1976	306540.000	-	22512.000	41228.477
1977	324530.000	-	22686.000	40784.891
1978	341200.000	-	22961.000	40909.614
1979	374590.000	-	23472.000	41331.845
1980	420660.000	-	23897.000	41719.383
1981	481700.000	-	23907.000	41335.203
1982	517690.000	-	23639.000	40999.482
1983	522240.000	-	23293.000	40233.999
1984	585800.000	-	23351.000	40161.385
1985	644660.000	-	23559.000	39958.420
1986	637020.000	-	23910.000	40293.132
1987	637520.000	-	24141.000	40397.549
1988	687870.000	-	24365.000	40845.486
1989	788290.000	-	24750.000	40986.000
1990	882280.000	60900.000	25471.000	41285.944
1991	1013230.000	60400.000	25948.000	41275.484
1992	1057392.000	70836.541	26070.000	40929.900
1993	1066479.000	81265.459	25900.000	40145.000
1994	1114972.000	92297.090	25965.000	39726.450
1995	1155291.000	103626.025	26115.000	39433.650
1996	1210262.000	119807.194	26265.000	39607.620
1997	1261381.000	135907.470	26565.000	40006.890
1998	1321727.000	154227.722	26865.000	40458.690
1999	1380883.000	175071.148	27165.000	40828.995
2000	1445900.000	197336.428	27465.000	41279.895

Legend :

X \ Dimension : mill.DM
Exports (including incomes from assets and business)
X@ \ Dimension : mill.DM
Exports (including incomes from assets and business)
BESCH \ Dimension : thousands
Wage and salary earners
BESVOL \ Dimension : mill.hours
Total man hours

YEAR	NSPF@	BSP@	BSP85@	QSP@
1990	203200.000	229200.000	229200.000	342500.000
1991	172800.000	195400.000	164063.810	418900.000
1992	205554.565	238398.353	172723.013	492337.513
1993	243854.376	292373.744	186974.344	563641.480
1994	269697.757	324684.955	199545.309	596343.954
1995	303539.642	365263.770	219539.887	630924.256
1996	339123.544	407881.746	242085.215	670701.538
1997	386211.408	463721.675	266117.291	726892.539
1998	442947.569	533945.232	294351.332	800673.614
1999	530046.789	639230.074	319345.007	913477.736
2000	622760.940	752002.082	359858.472	1037258.996

Legend :

NSPF@ \ Dimension : mill.DM
Net national income at factor cost
BSP@ \ Dimension : mill.DM
Gross national product
BSP85@ \ Dimension : mill.DM
Gross national product in 1985 prices
QSP@ \ Dimension : mill.DM
Total supply

YEAR	NSPF_HH@	GUMER_U@	QSP85@	YVPE@
1990	196530.000	6850.000	342500.000	162400.000
1991	169786.000	-2257.000	378967.658	199900.000
1992	206403.887	-3524.198	410716.602	235978.576
1993	242374.629	-1309.431	441208.398	259428.325
1994	265991.868	-1280.763	449153.886	272046.543
1995	293322.286	-566.137	458850.633	287375.328
1996	329825.329	-1153.707	474194.831	301155.452
1997	377839.937	-1752.690	493979.708	322740.866
1998	433676.634	-1977.657	520765.683	350151.510
1999	498840.046	1607.532	547577.505	382962.648
2000	585149.415	3129.268	592598.219	430109.328

Legend :

NSPF_HH@ \ Dimension : mill.DM
Net national income at factor cost, households
GUMER_U@ \ Dimension : mill.DM
Undistributed profits of companies with a legal entity
QSP85@ \ Dimension : mill.DM
Total supply in 1985 prices
YVPE@ \ Dimension : mill.DM
Personal disposable income, private households

YEAR	DAN85_ST@	DAU85_PR@	D@	DBA85_PR@
1990	2817.600	10262.100	25000.000	4145.300
1991	2667.000	21611.200	26900.000	4011.300
1992	2589.721	29371.862	29449.036	3837.300
1993	2557.391	34364.788	32909.231	3677.121
1994	2550.917	37178.771	36553.325	3529.456
1995	2559.183	38242.341	40571.110	3392.472
1996	2576.024	37907.081	44953.633	3265.161
1997	2599.005	36469.858	49992.421	3147.171
1998	2627.289	34195.163	55960.545	3038.786
1999	2661.577	31311.909	63637.494	2940.795
2000	2701.809	28025.697	72933.198	2854.332

Legend :

DAN85_ST@ \ Dimension : mill.DM
Depreciation of fixed assets, public sector, in 1985 prices
DAU85_PR@ \ Dimension : mill.DM
Depreciation of fixed assets, equipment, private sector, in 1985 prices
D@ \ Dimension : mill.DM
Consumption of fixed capital
DBA85_PR@ \ Dimension : mill.DM
Depreciation of fixed assets, construction, private sector, in 1985 prices

YEAR	KAP85_ST@	KAPM85_ST@	KAU85_PR@	KBA85_PR@
1990	178903.760	172312.560	215270.180	677122.740
1991	191382.560	185143.160	231965.480	699432.040
1992	203517.129	197453.378	254193.143	718935.881
1993	214379.086	208948.108	277947.335	736459.672
1994	223340.407	218859.747	300774.680	751015.699
1995	231121.599	227231.003	323305.734	764080.954
1996	238341.816	234731.708	346572.115	776841.226
1997	245994.708	242168.262	372290.459	790470.165
1998	254550.755	250272.731	401578.223	805920.452
1999	264825.093	259687.924	435860.501	823864.121
2000	276482.305	270653.699	476064.922	844831.049

Legend :

KAP85_ST@ \ Dimension : mill.DM
Stock of capital, public sector, in 1985 prices (end of year)
KAPM85_ST@ \ Dimension : mill.DM
Stock of capital, public sector, in 1985 prices (average of year)
KAU85_PR@ \ Dimension : mill.DM
Stock of capital, equipment, private sector, in 1985 prices (end of year)
KBA85_PR@ \ Dimension : mill.DM
Stock of capital, construction, private sector, in 1985 prices (end of year)

YEAR	KAP85@	KBAM85_PR@	KAUM85_PR@	KAUMA85PR@
1990	1071296.680	654068.040	207632.280	41526.456
1991	1122780.040	688277.390	223617.830	40251.094
1992	1176646.153	709174.109	243086.763	54694.522
1993	1228786.093	727697.777	266070.239	66517.560
1994	1275130.786	743737.686	289361.007	86808.302
1995	1318508.287	757548.327	312040.207	109214.072
1996	1361755.157	770461.090	334938.925	133975.570
1997	1408755.332	783655.695	359431.287	179715.644
1998	1462049.429	798195.308	386934.341	232160.605
1999	1524549.714	814892.286	418719.362	293103.553
2000	1597378.275	834347.585	455962.712	364770.169

Legend :

KAP85@ \ Dimension : mill.DM
Stock of capital in 1985 prices (end of year)
KBAM85_PR@ \ Dimension : mill.DM
Stock of capital, construction, private sector, in 1985 prices (average of year)
KAUM85_PR@ \ Dimension : mill.DM
Stock of capital, equipment, private sector, in 1985 prices (average of year)
KAUMA85PR@ \ Dimension : mill.DM
Utilized stock of capital, equipment, pr. sector, in 1985 pr. (average of year)

YEAR	MIAU85@	MD85@	KAPAM85@	M@
1990	10498.000	14687.000	867907.056	113300.000
1991	19913.000	27858.000	913671.759	223500.000
1992	21387.637	36903.774	961322.009	253939.160
1993	25242.188	42759.343	1003163.444	271267.736
1994	27122.109	44932.746	1049405.734	271658.999
1995	29962.207	44698.013	1093993.402	265660.487
1996	32929.260	42909.547	1139168.367	262819.792
1997	35816.949	40684.377	1205539.601	263170.864
1998	38782.410	38499.801	1280628.644	266728.382
1999	41437.496	37439.522	1367683.763	274247.662
2000	44815.887	36480.145	1469771.452	285256.914

Legend :

MIAU85@ \ Dimension : mill.DM
Imports of equipment in 1985 prices
MD85@ \ Dimension : mill.DM
Imports of services in 1985 prices
KAPAM85@ \ Dimension : mill.DM
Utilized stock of capital in 1985 prices (average of year)
M@ \ Dimension : mill.DM
Imports (including incomes from assets and business)

YEAR	CST85@	CPR@	MR%D85@	M85@
1990	71000.000	159400.000	88115.000	113300.000
1991	67927.600	186700.000	167132.846	214903.846
1992	66577.460	219086.667	179702.179	237993.590
1993	66775.602	244357.294	186232.523	254234.054
1994	67982.072	258695.589	177553.722	249608.577
1995	70328.208	270242.968	164650.526	239310.746
1996	74089.448	279361.272	156270.809	232109.616
1997	79579.427	292142.721	151361.090	227862.417
1998	87257.410	309214.671	149132.141	226414.352
1999	97548.529	330538.832	149355.479	228232.498
2000	111438.304	359965.179	151443.715	232739.747

Legend :

CST85@ \ Dimension : mill.DM
Government consumption in 1985 prices
CPR@ \ Dimension : mill.DM
Private consumption
MR%D85@ \ Dimension : mill.DM
Imports without capital goods and services in 1985 prices
M85@ \ Dimension : mill.DM
Imports (including incomes from assets and business) in 1985 prices

YEAR	CST@	CPR85@	C85@	C@
1990	71000.000	159400.000	230400.000	230400.000
1991	86200.000	165514.184	233441.784	272900.000
1992	97105.743	170188.986	236766.446	316192.410
1993	109596.475	170858.882	237634.484	353953.769
1994	117043.338	169018.933	237001.005	375738.928
1995	123939.968	170400.718	240728.926	394182.936
1996	133058.431	173296.665	247386.112	412419.703
1997	149512.411	178027.446	257606.873	441655.132
1998	172894.362	184131.869	271389.280	482109.032
1999	216908.153	186568.437	284116.965	547446.985
2000	261991.162	194189.912	305628.215	621956.341

Legend :

CST@ \ Dimension : mill.DM
Government consumption
CPR85@ \ Dimension : mill.DM
Private consumption in 1985 prices
C85@ \ Dimension : mill.DM
Consumption in 1985 prices
C@ \ Dimension : mill.DM
Consumption

YEAR	CPR_BSP@	CST_BSP@	IAN_ST@	DIAU_PR@
1990	0.696	0.310	16000.000	4521.830
1991	0.956	0.441	16100.000	20100.000
1992	0.919	0.407	17669.746	18529.789
1993	0.836	0.375	18374.619	15563.184
1994	0.797	0.360	17298.647	10148.921
1995	0.740	0.339	16583.640	7433.640
1996	0.685	0.326	16488.529	5593.755
1997	0.630	0.322	18187.702	6407.136
1998	0.579	0.324	21027.157	7120.545
1999	0.517	0.339	26568.812	11309.347
2000	0.479	0.348	31830.622	12440.225

Legend :

CPR_BSP@ \ Dimension : no dimension
Share of private consumption to GNP
CST_BSP@ \ Dimension : no dimension
Share of government consumption to GNP
IAN_ST@ \ Dimension : mill.DM
Gross fixed capital formation, public sector
DIAU_PR@ \ Dimension : mill.DM
First difference of gross fixed capital formation, equipment, private sector

YEAR	IAU85_PR@	IAU_PR@	IAN85_ST@	IBA_PR@
1990	17900.000	17900.000	16000.000	27200.000
1991	38306.500	38000.000	15145.800	28900.000
1992	51584.621	56569.387	14717.222	30769.429
1993	58118.980	72132.571	13419.348	32415.062
1994	60006.116	82281.492	11512.238	28727.797
1995	60773.395	89715.133	10340.375	26816.522
1996	61173.463	95308.888	9796.241	26677.225
1997	62188.202	101716.024	10251.897	29426.212
1998	63482.926	108836.569	11183.336	34473.134
1999	65594.188	120145.915	12935.915	44244.876
2000	68230.118	132586.140	14359.021	53549.465

Legend :

IAU85_PR@ \ Dimension : mill.DM
Gross fixed capital formation, equipment, private sector, in 1985 prices
IAU_PR@ \ Dimension : mill.DM
Gross fixed capital formation, equipment, private sector
IAN85_ST@ \ Dimension : mill.DM
Gross fixed capital formation, public sector, in 1985 prices
IBA_PR@ \ Dimension : mill.DM
Gross fixed capital formation, construction, private sector

YEAR	IAN85@	IAN@	IBA85_PR@	IANST_BSP@
1990	61100.000	61100.000	27200.000	0.070
1991	79772.900	83000.000	26320.600	0.082
1992	89662.687	105008.562	23360.844	0.074
1993	92739.239	122922.251	21200.912	0.063
1994	89603.836	128307.936	18085.483	0.053
1995	87571.497	133115.295	16457.727	0.045
1996	86995.135	138474.641	16025.432	0.040
1997	89216.209	149329.937	16776.110	0.039
1998	93155.335	164336.860	18489.073	0.039
1999	99414.566	190959.603	20884.464	0.042
2000	106410.399	217966.227	23821.260	0.042

Legend :

IAN85@ \ Dimension : mill.DM
Gross fixed capital formation in 1985 prices
IAN@ \ Dimension : mill.DM
Gross fixed capital formation
IBA85_PR@ \ Dimension : mill.DM
Gross fixed capital formation, construction, private sector, in 1985 prices
IANST_BSP@ \ Dimension : no dimension
Share of gross fixed capital formation the (public sector) to GNP

YEAR	IBAPR_BSP@	IN_ST@	IAUPR_BSP@	OUT_ST@
1990	0.119	148222.000	0.078	160894.000
1991	0.148	241400.000	0.195	236900.000
1992	0.129	277314.312	0.237	255205.442
1993	0.111	300846.166	0.247	276044.091
1994	0.088	317447.326	0.253	291948.186
1995	0.073	336253.694	0.246	310391.580
1996	0.065	342376.094	0.234	330908.374
1997	0.063	363845.169	0.219	359520.041
1998	0.065	392857.188	0.204	395534.656
1999	0.069	429453.064	0.188	454442.058
2000	0.071	474097.585	0.176	513545.686

Legend :

IBAPR_BSP@ \ Dimension : no dimension
Share of gross fixed capital formation (construction, private sector) to GNP
IN_ST@ \ Dimension : mill.DM
Total government receipts
IAUPR_BSP@ \ Dimension : no dimension
Share of gross fixed capital formation (equipment, private sector) to GNP
OUT_ST@ \ Dimension : mill.DM
Total government expenditures

YEAR	FS_ST@	TDIR@	TD_HH@	TIND@
1990	-12672.000	15325.000	12921.000	27375.000
1991	4500.000	11700.000	9865.000	20900.000
1992	22108.870	18361.570	15504.584	28155.056
1993	24802.075	23142.772	19522.804	40534.818
1994	25499.140	27727.832	23350.447	43687.540
1995	25862.114	32813.875	27573.614	46865.735
1996	11467.720	38771.959	32496.877	49795.402
1997	4325.129	46177.597	38594.722	53727.442
1998	-2677.469	54865.604	45703.343	61567.098
1999	-24988.995	65521.821	54376.498	72610.255
2000	-39448.100	78124.457	64552.253	83826.231

Legend :

FS_ST@ \ Dimension : mill.DM
Balance of government budget
TDIR@ \ Dimension : mill.DM
Direct taxes
TD_HH@ \ Dimension : mill.DM
Direct taxes, private households
TIND@ \ Dimension : mill.DM
Indirect taxes

YEAR	TDLOST%P@	TI_GEW@	TD_KEST@	TD_KOST@
1990	8600.000	0.000	0.000	0.000
1991	9600.000	550.000	30.000	330.000
1992	13720.717	333.728	47.014	373.839
1993	17622.467	1010.668	227.681	861.624
1994	21529.464	1164.402	322.748	1223.070
1995	25846.862	1532.565	439.485	1642.350
1996	31244.665	1603.315	479.702	1918.156
1997	38150.061	1727.867	500.959	2140.669
1998	46232.260	2030.882	560.832	2417.308
1999	55345.937	3474.528	942.431	3295.490
2000	66359.670	4528.858	1343.938	4185.987

Legend :

TDLOST%P@ \ Dimension : mill.DM
Payroll tax (without that on pensions)
TI_GEW@ \ Dimension : mill.DM
Tax paid for carrying on a trade
TD_KEST@ \ Dimension : mill.DM
Capital yields tax
TD_KOST@ \ Dimension : mill.DM
Corporate income tax

YEAR	TI_UST@	SUB@	T@	TI_MIN@
1990	11000.000	26375.000	42700.000	4900.000
1991	8350.000	25200.000	32600.000	3747.000
1992	14666.896	24760.304	46516.626	4241.192
1993	25402.631	24924.682	63677.591	4762.617
1994	27383.557	25253.667	71415.372	5312.734
1995	29121.897	25712.717	79679.610	5893.083
1996	30852.702	25990.833	88567.361	6505.287
1997	33472.717	26209.595	99905.039	7151.053
1998	39759.437	26529.980	116432.702	7832.185
1999	48043.325	27064.464	138132.077	8550.578
2000	56820.225	27518.287	161950.688	9308.233

Legend :

TI_UST@ \ Dimension : mill.DM
Turnover tax
SUB@ \ Dimension : mill.DM
Subsidies
T@ \ Dimension : mill.DM
Total taxes
TI_MIN@ \ Dimension : mill.DM
Petroleum tax

YEAR	BST_KST@	TSB@	GSV_BLG@	GEW_BUV@
1990	3425.000	99275.000	50836.000	6297.200
1991	-1128.500	105580.000	55105.025	-2086.200
1992	-1762.099	133179.887	67614.980	-3350.410
1993	-654.716	158401.405	75346.647	-765.584
1994	-614.766	174763.246	83550.235	-474.909
1995	-271.746	193439.145	93250.891	718.067
1996	-507.631	216538.453	106133.855	592.033
1997	-771.184	246553.187	122756.552	667.678
1998	-870.169	284275.227	141487.436	1483.206
1999	707.314	329743.914	162374.758	7208.002
2000	1376.878	383812.048	188689.084	11205.722

Legend :

BST_KST@ \ Dimension : mill.DM
Tax base of corporate income tax
TSB@ \ Dimension : mill.DM
Taxes and social contributions
GSV_BLG@ \ Dimension : mill.DM
Imputed contributions to social security
GEW_BUV@ \ Dimension : mill.DM
Tax base, tax paid for carrying on a trade

YEAR	GEW_LSST@	ZINS_GK@	BMG_UST@	ZINS_ST@
1990	0.000	3998.800	261793.884	4000.000
1991	0.000	4698.600	319834.265	4700.000
1992	0.000	6123.676	381528.663	6125.276
1993	0.000	8532.694	433236.481	8534.694
1994	-0.000	12431.313	456043.371	12434.313
1995	0.000	18682.126	474494.389	18686.126
1996	-0.000	24088.261	492810.117	24092.761
1997	-0.000	28249.529	527092.420	28254.029
1998	0.000	31361.011	576163.977	31366.011
1999	-0.000	33522.120	661096.482	33527.120
2000	-0.000	34860.453	754881.451	34866.453

Legend :

GEW_LSST@ \ Dimension : mill.DM
Tax base, payroll tax
ZINS_GK@ \ Dimension : mill.DM
Interest on government debt, government
BMG_UST@ \ Dimension : mill.DM
Tax base of turnover tax
ZINS_ST@ \ Dimension : mill.DM
Interest on debts of the public sector

YEAR	SB_UH@	SB_ST@	SB_PR@	SB_AG@
1990	5538.000	51163.000	56575.000	25300.000
1991	7144.000	66000.000	72980.000	32500.000
1992	8565.576	78297.686	86663.262	39368.880
1993	9455.239	85468.575	94723.815	44590.028
1994	10402.068	93145.806	103347.874	48928.196
1995	11530.242	102429.293	113759.535	53123.222
1996	13043.897	115127.194	127971.092	58073.971
1997	15010.558	131837.590	146648.148	64441.807
1998	17232.590	150809.935	167842.525	72139.974
1999	19715.838	172095.999	191611.837	81114.347
2000	22856.475	199204.885	221861.360	92198.435

Legend :

SB_UH@ \ Dimension : mill.DM
Social contributions to the private sector
SB_ST@ \ Dimension : mill.DM
Social contributions to the public sector
SB_PR@ \ Dimension : mill.DM
Social contributions of private households
SB_AG@ \ Dimension : mill.DM
Contributions, paid by employers to public social insurance (consolidated)

YEAR	TR_HH_EMP@	SL_ZU_ST@	SL_HH_ST@	SL_ST@
1990	30589.000	-29707.000	21071.000	21456.000
1991	115599.000	9160.000	100172.000	75160.000
1992	125893.215	229.686	109733.540	78527.372
1993	129731.799	-3422.803	112804.549	82045.772
1994	134163.144	-7423.828	116431.754	85721.978
1995	138796.027	-12866.219	120222.183	89563.074
1996	139439.624	-21550.732	119983.181	93576.463
1997	142503.528	-34067.712	122122.424	97769.878
1998	145797.771	-48658.535	124447.933	102151.400
1999	149332.841	-65366.524	126968.090	106729.475
2000	153119.706	-87691.959	129691.655	111512.926

Legend :

TR_HH_EMP@ \ Dimension : mill.DM
Transfer income of private households from other sectors
SL_ZU_ST@ \ Dimension : mill.DM
Balance of the government social contributions
SL_HH_ST@ \ Dimension : mill.DM
Social contributions to the East-German private households, total
SL_ST@ \ Dimension : mill.DM
Social contributions of the government (goverment and social insurance)

YEAR	TR%T@	TR_HH_GEL@	PBSP@	TR_HH_R@
1990	-38907.000	69496.000	100.000	0.000
1991	24306.000	91293.000	119.100	8448.000
1992	9574.688	116318.527	138.024	14150.681
1993	-2946.304	132678.103	156.371	18431.484
1994	-13945.325	148108.469	162.712	21410.148
1995	-25946.958	164742.985	166.377	23409.836
1996	-45669.877	185109.501	168.487	24641.531
1997	-68099.071	210602.599	174.255	25359.729
1998	-93525.125	239322.895	181.397	25777.027
1999	-122877.398	272210.239	200.169	26221.904
2000	-160040.086	313159.793	208.972	26746.179

Legend :

TR%T@ \ Dimension : mill.DM
Transfer income without direct taxes, paid transfers and social contributions
TR_HH_GEL@ \ Dimension : mill.DM
Transfer payments of private households to other sectors
PBSP@ \ Dimension : index
Price index, gross national product
TR_HH_R@ \ Dimension : mill.DM
Other transfer payments of private households

YEAR	PCST@	PCPR@	PMD_PBSP@	PIAN_ST@
1990	100.000	100.000	1.000	100.000
1991	126.900	112.800	0.861	106.300
1992	145.854	128.731	0.762	120.062
1993	164.127	143.017	0.690	136.926
1994	172.168	153.057	0.680	150.263
1995	176.231	158.593	0.682	160.378
1996	179.592	161.204	0.691	168.315
1997	187.878	164.100	0.685	177.408
1998	198.143	167.931	0.675	188.022
1999	222.359	177.168	0.627	205.388
2000	235.100	185.368	0.616	221.677

Legend :

PCST@ \ Dimension : index
Price index, government consumption
PCPR@ \ Dimension : index
Price index, private consumption
PMD_PBSP@ \ Dimension : index
Relative prices, price of imported services to price of GNP
PIAN_ST@ \ Dimension : index
Price index, gross fixed capital formation, public sector

YEAR	PIBA_PR@	PIAU_PR@	M1@	BLG_EH85@
1990	100.000	100.000	70480.857	9.619
1991	109.800	99.200	100349.667	10.719
1992	131.714	109.663	126752.097	13.343
1993	152.895	124.112	148455.013	13.978
1994	158.845	137.122	159125.312	15.002
1995	162.942	147.622	168403.926	16.434
1996	166.468	155.801	176316.449	18.218
1997	175.405	163.562	184818.281	19.777
1998	186.451	171.442	194549.081	21.282
1999	211.855	183.165	205322.295	21.574
2000	224.797	194.322	215850.745	23.122

Legend :

PIBA_PR@ \ Dimension : index
Price index, gross fixed capital formation, construction, private sector
PIAU_PR@ \ Dimension : index
Price index, gross fixed capital formation, equipment, private sector
M1@ \ Dimension : mill.DM
Money supply M1
BLG_EH85@ \ Dimension : DM/hour
Gross wage per hour in 1985 prices

YEAR	BLG@	BUA@	BUV@	BUA_EH85@
1990	143200.000	168500.000	34600.000	11.318
1991	151700.000	184200.000	-11400.000	13.015
1992	184296.007	223664.887	-18110.323	16.193
1993	203336.601	247926.629	-4072.253	17.043
1994	223243.043	272171.239	-2473.482	18.289
1995	246695.866	299819.088	3720.553	19.973
1996	277997.857	336071.828	3051.716	22.024
1997	318354.371	382796.177	3415.230	23.780
1998	363297.691	435437.666	7509.903	25.508
1999	412802.105	493916.452	36130.337	25.813
2000	474950.980	567149.415	55611.525	27.610

Legend :

BLG@ \ Dimension : mill.DM
Gross wages and salaries, total
BUA@ \ Dimension : mill.DM
Gross income of employees
BUV@ \ Dimension : mill.DM
Gross income from entrepreneurial activity and property
BUA_EH85@ \ Dimension : DM/hour
Total labour cost per hour in 1985 prices

YEAR	M_R	M_O	BESCH@	BESVOL@
1990	701199.050	17480.950	8631.000	14887.612
1991	788210.000	39000.000	6979.000	11883.143
1992	815170.459	54836.541	5955.000	10007.378
1993	855066.541	60265.459	5610.000	9303.063
1994	894089.910	67297.090	5590.000	9145.799
1995	932720.975	75626.025	5590.000	9022.260
1996	970110.806	87807.194	5770.000	9056.592
1997	1010175.530	99907.470	5970.000	9237.978
1998	1051361.278	114227.722	6170.000	9410.484
1999	1093892.852	131071.148	6360.000	9559.080
2000	1138046.572	149336.428	6540.000	9829.620

Legend :

M_R \ Dimension : mill.DM
Imports of West Germany from the rest of the world without imports from East Germany
M_O \ Dimension : mill.DM
Imports, West Germany from East Germany
BESCH@ \ Dimension : thousands
Wage and salary earners
BESVOL@ \ Dimension : mill.hours
Total man hours

YEAR	X_W@	M_R@	M_W@	X_O
1990	17480.950	29198.800	84101.200	84101.200
1991	39000.000	20800.000	202600.000	202600.000
1992	54836.541	17547.196	236391.964	236391.964
1993	60265.459	19588.243	251679.493	251679.493
1994	67297.090	24449.310	247209.689	247209.689
1995	75626.025	34535.863	231124.623	231124.623
1996	87807.194	36794.771	226025.021	226025.021
1997	99907.470	50002.464	213168.400	213168.400
1998	114227.722	61347.528	205380.854	205380.854
1999	131071.148	82274.299	191973.363	191973.363
2000	149336.428	105545.058	179711.856	179711.856

Legend :

X_W@ \ Dimension : mill.DM
Exports from East Germany to West Germany
M_R@ \ Dimension : mill.DM
Imports of East Germany from the rest of the world without imports from West Germany
M_W@ \ Dimension : mill.DM
Imports of East Germany from West Germany
X_O \ Dimension : mill.DM
Exports from West Germany to East Germany

3.5.2 Exogenous variables

General remarks:
- Variables for East Germany with @ at the end of symbol

YEAR	BUV_HH	BUA_EH	BLG_ST	BEI_GSV
1960	81960.000	3.312	17110.000	24.400
1961	83350.000	3.692	19550.000	23.400
1962	88330.000	4.083	21380.000	25.000
1963	90200.000	4.418	23670.000	25.000
1964	100270.000	4.730	25840.000	25.000
1965	107430.000	5.225	29400.000	25.200
1966	111890.000	5.679	32760.000	25.300
1967	114870.000	5.990	34760.000	25.400
1968	128840.000	6.426	36630.000	26.500
1969	136310.000	7.109	41320.000	27.800
1970	155310.000	8.317	48490.000	26.500
1971	163080.000	9.386	58030.000	26.500
1972	171090.000	10.420	65180.000	27.100
1973	184250.000	11.861	75230.000	28.900
1974	181110.000	13.455	87460.000	29.200
1975	187110.000	14.689	94820.000	30.500
1976	212570.000	15.537	99450.000	32.300
1977	222160.000	16.870	106050.000	32.400
1978	239200.000	17.955	113090.000	32.400
1979	255270.000	19.224	121180.000	32.200
1980	250800.000	20.707	130750.000	32.400
1981	250270.000	21.918	138430.000	33.300
1982	260810.000	22.779	142560.000	34.000
1983	289740.000	23.697	146930.000	34.900
1984	317470.000	24.609	149090.000	34.700
1985	338930.000	25.687	154330.000	35.400
1986	377480.000	26.791	161570.000	35.400
1987	384090.000	27.841	168420.000	35.600
1988	424700.000	28.629	172430.000	35.900
1989	462490.000	29.812	176850.000	35.900
1990	515220.000	31.917	187440.000	35.500
1991	524750.000	34.453	201220.000	36.325
1992	545740.000	36.036	209268.800	36.688
1993	567569.600	37.837	217639.552	37.055
1994	590272.384	39.729	226345.134	37.426
1995	613883.279	42.113	235398.940	37.800
1996	638438.611	44.850	244814.897	38.178
1997	663976.155	47.658	254607.493	38.560
1998	690535.201	50.870	264791.793	38.945
1999	718156.609	55.117	275383.465	39.335
2000	746882.874	57.698	286398.803	39.728

Legend :

BUV_HH \ Dimension : mill.DM
Gross income from entrepreneurial activity and property, private households
BUA_EH \ Dimension : DM/hour
Total labour cost per hour
BLG_ST \ Dimension : mill.DM
Gross wages and salaries, public sector
BEI_GSV \ Dimension : p.c.
Rate of social insurance payment (total)

YEAR	CAPIFO	ET	GEW_SATZ	EH
1960	88.500	26247.000	-	2151.900
1961	87.500	26591.000	268.000	2127.000
1962	87.300	26690.000	269.000	2097.700
1963	86.000	26744.000	270.000	2056.200
1964	87.700	26753.000	273.000	2078.100
1965	88.000	26887.000	274.000	2059.600
1966	85.500	26801.000	276.000	2039.300
1967	78.500	25950.000	279.000	1997.100
1968	85.000	25968.000	281.000	1986.400
1969	89.800	26356.000	283.000	1966.300
1970	90.700	26668.000	283.000	1949.100
1971	87.500	26772.000	286.000	1926.500
1972	85.600	26875.000	300.000	1901.200
1973	86.700	27160.000	307.000	1868.000
1974	81.700	26829.000	309.000	1834.600
1975	77.100	26110.000	316.000	1798.700
1976	80.200	25974.000	319.000	1831.400
1977	82.850	26008.000	322.000	1797.800
1978	81.500	26219.000	325.000	1781.700
1979	84.730	26652.000	325.000	1760.900
1980	82.380	27059.000	330.000	1745.800
1981	78.980	27033.000	333.000	1729.000
1982	76.380	26725.000	339.000	1734.400
1983	78.350	26347.000	349.000	1727.300
1984	80.650	26393.000	352.000	1719.900
1985	84.230	26593.000	356.000	1696.100
1986	84.650	26960.000	359.000	1685.200
1987	84.300	27157.000	359.000	1673.400
1988	86.730	27366.000	362.000	1676.400
1989	89.080	27761.000	362.000	1656.000
1990	89.680	28495.000	364.000	1620.900
1991	87.500	28989.000	366.000	1590.700
1992	84.600	29120.000	370.000	1570.000
1993	83.000	28935.000	376.000	1550.000
1994	83.000	29000.000	384.000	1530.000
1995	83.500	29150.000	386.000	1510.000
1996	83.500	29300.000	388.000	1508.000
1997	84.000	29600.000	391.000	1506.000
1998	84.000	29900.000	395.000	1506.000
1999	83.000	30200.000	399.000	1503.000
2000	83.000	30500.000	403.000	1503.000

Legend :

CAPIFO \ Dimension : p.c.
Degree of capacity utilization in the manufacturing sector
ET \ Dimension : thousands
Workers (on the basis of resident status)
GEW_SATZ \ Dimension : p.c.
Rate of tax from yield of manufacturing, average
EH \ Dimension : hour/ET
Annual average working hours

YEAR	IVOR	KST_SATZ	IN_SONS	GUOER_N
1960	9200.000	51.000	9650.000	22420.000
1961	6700.000	51.000	12230.000	17710.000
1962	5700.000	51.000	11170.000	18920.000
1963	2600.000	51.000	12020.000	14390.000
1964	6400.000	51.000	13570.000	17670.000
1965	10700.000	51.000	14610.000	16590.000
1966	5300.000	51.000	15950.000	16560.000
1967	-500.000	51.000	17260.000	17770.000
1968	11100.000	51.000	18760.000	18140.000
1969	17300.000	51.000	20110.000	10430.000
1970	14200.000	51.000	21930.000	18230.000
1971	4470.000	51.000	24850.000	13190.000
1972	4300.000	51.000	29850.000	2130.000
1973	12380.000	51.000	34440.000	-820.000
1974	3710.000	51.000	39170.000	-11390.000
1975	-6360.000	51.000	48150.000	-19540.000
1976	15680.000	51.000	52580.000	-12350.000
1977	6990.000	56.000	53910.000	-16100.000
1978	7230.000	56.000	61190.000	-8980.000
1979	23000.000	56.000	63430.000	-13840.000
1980	11770.000	56.000	70540.000	-38470.000
1981	-10550.000	56.000	76210.000	-60530.000
1982	-16040.000	56.000	80250.000	-54640.000
1983	-1500.000	56.000	79320.000	-40570.000
1984	5320.000	56.000	80370.000	-51680.000
1985	1250.000	56.000	82510.000	-50180.000
1986	2920.000	56.000	85700.000	-16290.000
1987	-560.000	56.000	88370.000	-27020.000
1988	10300.000	56.000	96030.000	-3930.000
1989	16010.000	56.000	100140.000	-9780.000
1990	3130.000	50.000	105210.000	-4750.000
1991	-8610.000	50.000	122970.000	-59820.000
1992	-13800.000	50.000	160000.000	-35000.000
1993	-500.000	50.000	167200.000	-30000.000
1994	0.000	48.000	174724.000	-25000.000
1995	0.000	48.000	182586.580	-20000.000
1996	0.000	44.000	182586.580	-20000.000
1997	0.000	44.000	182586.580	-20000.000
1998	0.000	44.000	182586.580	-20000.000
1999	0.000	44.000	182586.580	-20000.000
2000	0.000	44.000	182586.580	-20000.000

Legend :

IVOR \ Dimension : mill.DM
Changes in stocks
KST_SATZ \ Dimension : p.c.
Corporate income tax rate
IN_SONS \ Dimension : mill.DM
Other government receipts
GUOER_N \ Dimension : mill.DM
Undistributed profits of enterprises without a legal entity

YEAR	MWST_SATZ	OUT_SONS	LSST_SATZ	PIAU
1960	0.000	12840.000	-	42.143
1961	0.000	18580.000	808.000	43.573
1962	0.000	19240.000	797.000	45.241
1963	0.000	17570.000	781.000	45.940
1964	0.000	19570.000	780.000	46.913
1965	0.000	21320.000	784.000	48.210
1966	0.000	21660.000	784.000	49.808
1967	0.000	23650.000	783.000	50.867
1968	10.500	25510.000	781.000	49.925
1969	11.000	29840.000	779.000	51.253
1970	11.000	32110.000	776.000	54.473
1971	11.000	37930.000	779.000	57.512
1972	11.000	44080.000	837.000	59.042
1973	11.000	50400.000	844.000	61.380
1974	11.000	57060.000	844.000	66.118
1975	11.000	68270.000	861.000	71.402
1976	11.000	75790.000	869.000	74.047
1977	11.000	81070.000	868.000	75.970
1978	12.000	85050.000	839.000	78.270
1979	12.500	91450.000	873.000	80.568
1980	13.000	100400.000	0.000	84.028
1981	13.000	105220.000	0.000	88.240
1982	13.000	109980.000	0.000	92.529
1983	13.500	106420.000	0.000	95.277
1984	14.000	113640.000	0.000	97.699
1985	14.000	115130.000	0.000	100.000
1986	14.000	114630.000	0.000	100.884
1987	14.000	119360.000	0.000	101.303
1988	14.000	128530.000	0.000	102.350
1989	14.000	134910.000	0.000	104.768
1990	14.000	140980.000	0.000	106.523
1991	14.000	181180.000	0.000	109.155
1992	14.000	140000.000	0.000	111.400
1993	15.000	144900.000	0.000	113.100
1994	15.000	149971.500	0.000	115.362
1995	15.000	155220.503	0.000	117.669
1996	15.000	163757.630	0.000	120.023
1997	15.000	172764.300	0.000	122.423
1998	15.000	182266.336	0.000	124.872
1999	15.000	192290.985	0.000	127.369
2000	15.000	202866.989	0.000	129.916

Legend :

MWST_SATZ \ Dimension : p.c.
Upper tax rate, value added tax
OUT_SONS \ Dimension : mill.DM
Other public consumption expenditures
LSST_SATZ \ Dimension : p.c.
Average payroll tax rate
PIAU \ Dimension : index
Price index, gross fixed capital formation, equipment

YEAR	PMD	R_WPUM	PM	PMIAU
1960	38.516	6.300	41.227	41.227
1961	39.357	5.900	40.324	40.324
1962	40.460	6.000	40.425	40.425
1963	41.801	6.100	41.396	41.396
1964	43.290	6.200	42.174	42.174
1965	44.603	6.800	43.413	43.413
1966	46.039	7.800	44.295	44.295
1967	45.764	7.000	43.581	43.581
1968	46.616	6.700	43.645	43.645
1969	46.071	7.000	44.560	44.560
1970	47.011	8.200	44.321	44.321
1971	48.482	8.200	45.036	45.036
1972	49.420	8.200	45.856	45.856
1973	51.413	9.500	49.659	49.659
1974	58.601	10.600	61.148	61.148
1975	62.228	8.700	62.583	62.583
1976	64.059	8.000	66.222	66.222
1977	65.507	6.400	67.506	67.506
1978	68.410	6.100	66.369	66.369
1979	73.016	7.600	71.860	71.860
1980	80.207	8.600	80.702	80.702
1981	88.242	10.600	90.059	90.059
1982	89.689	9.100	92.553	92.553
1983	91.863	8.000	93.275	93.275
1984	96.960	7.800	97.666	97.666
1985	100.000	6.900	100.000	100.000
1986	99.326	6.000	89.344	89.344
1987	100.575	5.800	85.517	85.517
1988	104.739	6.000	87.148	87.148
1989	109.541	7.100	91.358	91.358
1990	113.525	8.900	91.215	91.215
1991	117.605	8.700	93.560	93.560
1992	120.545	8.300	96.000	96.000
1993	123.559	8.000	106.000	106.000
1994	126.648	7.800	109.180	109.180
1995	129.814	7.700	112.455	112.455
1996	133.059	7.600	113.580	113.580
1997	136.386	7.500	114.716	114.716
1998	139.795	7.500	115.863	115.863
1999	143.290	7.400	117.022	117.022
2000	146.873	7.200	118.192	118.192

Legend :

PMD \ Dimension : index
Price index, imports of services
R_WPUM \ Dimension : p.c.
Average yield on circulating bearer bonds
PM \ Dimension : index
Price index, imports
PMIAU \ Dimension : index
Price index, imports of equipment

YEAR	SELB	SL_HA_ST	SB_EA	SL_HH_H
1960	5990.000	36400.000	-10.000	290.000
1961	5861.000	39560.000	-30.000	330.000
1962	5658.000	43120.000	-30.000	370.000
1963	5483.000	46230.000	-40.000	390.000
1964	5269.000	50510.000	-40.000	420.000
1965	5130.000	56780.000	-60.000	460.000
1966	5036.000	62010.000	-70.000	500.000
1967	4896.000	69490.000	-40.000	500.000
1968	4785.000	72880.000	-20.000	530.000
1969	4604.000	78710.000	-40.000	600.000
1970	4422.000	85720.000	-100.000	690.000
1971	4167.000	96660.000	-90.000	790.000
1972	4034.000	110720.000	-110.000	880.000
1973	3938.000	124080.000	-200.000	990.000
1974	3793.000	143960.000	-170.000	1080.000
1975	3643.000	180700.000	-180.000	1130.000
1976	3462.000	194660.000	-190.000	1230.000
1977	3322.000	206720.000	-250.000	1320.000
1978	3258.000	216730.000	-260.000	1400.000
1979	3180.000	230280.000	-290.000	1470.000
1980	3162.000	244530.000	-360.000	1580.000
1981	3126.000	265520.000	-340.000	1760.000
1982	3086.000	281800.000	-280.000	1820.000
1983	3054.000	285480.000	-260.000	1930.000
1984	3042.000	288960.000	-260.000	2020.000
1985	3034.000	295770.000	-230.000	2130.000
1986	3050.000	306790.000	-220.000	2260.000
1987	3016.000	321880.000	-180.000	2380.000
1988	3001.000	336460.000	-170.000	2510.000
1989	3011.000	349680.000	-170.000	2650.000
1990	3024.000	368050.000	-1500.000	2810.000
1991	3041.000	390380.000	-4900.000	3010.000
1992	3050.000	407947.100	-5000.000	3145.450
1993	3035.000	422225.249	-5000.000	3286.995
1994	3035.000	437003.132	-5000.000	3434.910
1995	3035.000	463223.320	-5000.000	3589.481
1996	3035.000	491016.719	-5000.000	3751.008
1997	3035.000	520477.722	-5000.000	3919.803
1998	3035.000	551706.386	-5000.000	4096.194
1999	3035.000	584808.769	-5000.000	4280.523
2000	3035.000	619897.295	-5000.000	4473.146

Legend :

SELB \ Dimension : thousands
Self employed persons and unpaid family members
SL_HA_ST \ Dimension : mill.DM
Social contributions of the public sector to the private households in West Germany
SB_EA \ Dimension : mill.DM
Balance of social contribution of foreign commuters
SL_HH_H \ Dimension : mill.DM
Social contributions to private households from private households

YEAR	SL_W_ST	SL_W	SL_U	SL_HN_ST
1960	1560.000	20.000	3430.000	0.000
1961	1850.000	20.000	3810.000	0.000
1962	2050.000	30.000	4230.000	0.000
1963	1870.000	40.000	4620.000	0.000
1964	1830.000	60.000	4930.000	0.000
1965	1960.000	60.000	5370.000	0.000
1966	1860.000	70.000	5770.000	0.000
1967	2040.000	90.000	5990.000	0.000
1968	2360.000	100.000	6260.000	0.000
1969	2260.000	130.000	7070.000	0.000
1970	2450.000	140.000	7910.000	0.000
1971	2460.000	160.000	8710.000	0.000
1972	2740.000	190.000	9450.000	0.000
1973	3040.000	170.000	10790.000	0.000
1974	3460.000	220.000	12170.000	0.000
1975	3870.000	240.000	13520.000	0.000
1976	4010.000	260.000	14790.000	0.000
1977	4280.000	300.000	15860.000	0.000
1978	4470.000	310.000	16590.000	0.000
1979	4580.000	270.000	17770.000	0.000
1980	4790.000	280.000	19330.000	0.000
1981	5140.000	300.000	20540.000	0.000
1982	5320.000	330.000	21410.000	0.000
1983	5410.000	350.000	22220.000	0.000
1984	5840.000	370.000	23030.000	0.000
1985	5660.000	410.000	25080.000	0.000
1986	5840.000	410.000	27470.000	0.000
1987	6150.000	460.000	29340.000	0.000
1988	6370.000	450.000	31030.000	0.000
1989	9060.000	560.000	32880.000	0.000
1990	6670.000	810.000	34860.000	0.000
1991	6970.000	660.000	36830.000	26360.000
1992	7206.980	686.400	38487.350	32600.000
1993	7452.017	713.856	40219.281	32200.000
1994	7705.386	742.410	42029.148	32200.000
1995	7967.369	772.107	43920.460	32200.000
1996	8238.260	802.991	45896.881	28000.000
1997	8518.360	835.111	47962.240	26000.000
1998	8807.985	868.515	50120.541	24000.000
1999	9107.456	903.256	52375.966	22000.000
2000	9417.110	939.386	54732.884	20000.000

Legend :

SL_W_ST \ Dimension : mill.DM
Social contributions of the government to the rest of the world
SL_W \ Dimension : mill.DM
Social contributions from the rest of the world to private households
SL_U \ Dimension : mill.DM
Social contributions from enterprises with own legal entity to private households
SL_HN_ST \ Dimension : mill.DM
Social contributions of the West German government to the East German households

YEAR	TI_SONS	TVS_GK	TD_SONS	TR_SONS
1960	-	52759.000	12674.000	4280.000
1961	17575.000	57093.000	15100.000	4920.000
1962	19171.000	60365.000	17050.000	5600.000
1963	20141.000	67084.000	18322.000	6110.000
1964	20379.000	73796.000	19498.000	6710.000
1965	21192.000	83667.000	20249.000	7710.000
1966	22324.000	93048.000	21434.000	8740.000
1967	23837.000	108174.000	21731.000	9480.000
1968	23535.000	117117.000	23021.000	10570.000
1969	25839.000	117904.000	24455.000	11610.000
1970	26898.000	125890.000	25269.000	14010.000
1971	28913.000	140399.000	28876.000	16040.000
1972	31723.000	156033.000	32121.000	18570.000
1973	34451.000	167754.000	38986.000	20430.000
1974	35788.000	192383.000	40726.000	21720.000
1975	37949.000	256389.000	38854.000	23690.000
1976	41879.000	296650.000	45177.000	26110.000
1977	44606.000	328484.000	50319.000	28090.000
1978	46857.000	370811.000	50254.000	31040.000
1979	49940.000	413935.000	50071.000	34800.000
1980	48459.000	468612.000	48955.000	38430.000
1981	49340.000	545617.000	45380.000	41930.000
1982	51575.000	614820.000	43557.000	43840.000
1983	55632.000	671708.000	42721.000	46010.000
1984	57867.000	717522.000	41679.000	49650.000
1985	58369.000	760192.000	42944.000	52170.000
1986	60666.000	800967.000	44879.000	55430.000
1987	62814.000	848816.000	46540.000	58830.000
1988	65518.000	903015.000	49169.000	62860.000
1989	71135.000	928837.000	53962.000	67540.000
1990	73809.000	991079.000	54358.000	73960.000
1991	81901.000	1099361.000	63559.000	82220.000
1992	100000.000	1207494.720	80000.000	86331.000
1993	105000.000	1326264.529	84800.000	90647.550
1994	110250.000	1456716.598	89888.000	95179.928
1995	115762.500	1600000.000	95281.280	99938.924
1996	118656.563	1673023.284	98139.718	104935.870
1997	121622.977	1749379.318	101083.910	110182.664
1998	124663.551	1829220.208	104116.427	115691.797
1999	127780.140	1912705.000	107239.920	121476.387
2000	130974.643	2000000.000	110457.118	127550.206

Legend :

TI_SONS \ Dimension : mill.DM
Other indirect taxes
TVS_GK \ Dimension : mill.DM
National debt at the end of the year
TD_SONS \ Dimension : mill.DM
Other direct taxes
TR_SONS \ Dimension : mill.DM
Other transfer incomes of the private households

YEAR	VOL_MIN	X_R	YUVST	ZINS_GSV
1960	-	-	4260.000	0.000
1961	460.000	-	4710.000	0.000
1962	516.000	-	4830.000	0.000
1963	563.000	-	5260.000	0.000
1964	636.000	-	5540.000	0.000
1965	692.000	-	5820.000	0.000
1966	762.000	-	6420.000	0.000
1967	783.000	-	6780.000	0.000
1968	838.000	-	7450.000	0.000
1969	903.000	-	7940.000	0.000
1970	993.000	-	8760.000	0.000
1971	1080.000	-	9270.000	0.000
1972	1136.000	-	8680.000	0.000
1973	1181.000	-	10800.000	0.000
1974	1129.000	-	10760.000	0.000
1975	1216.000	-	9850.000	10.000
1976	1281.000	-	10630.000	10.000
1977	1361.000	-	10970.000	0.000
1978	1436.000	-	12720.000	10.000
1979	1485.000	-	15120.000	10.000
1980	1506.000	-	16750.000	20.000
1981	1448.000	-	20760.000	80.000
1982	1475.000	-	30200.000	20.000
1983	1506.000	-	30730.000	10.000
1984	1550.000	-	32010.000	20.000
1985	1546.000	-	34740.000	20.000
1986	1630.000	-	33880.000	20.000
1987	1689.000	-	27040.000	30.000
1988	1752.000	-	19890.000	30.000
1989	1778.000	-	31450.000	30.000
1990	1861.000	798178.800	34630.000	30.000
1991	1916.830	810630.000	33680.000	40.000
1992	1974.335	821000.000	43400.000	45.000
1993	2033.566	814800.000	39500.000	50.000
1994	2094.575	867762.000	40242.506	50.000
1995	2157.415	924166.530	40998.968	55.000
1996	2222.142	984237.354	41769.651	55.000
1997	2288.812	1048212.782	42554.821	55.000
1998	2357.483	1116346.613	43354.749	55.000
1999	2428.216	1188909.143	44169.715	60.000
2000	2501.072	1266188.238	45000.000	60.000

Legend :

VOL_MIN \ Dimension : Petajoule
Consumption of gasoline and diesel
X_R \ Dimension : mill.DM
Exports from West Germany to the rest of the world without exports to East Germany
YUVST \ Dimension : mill.DM
Gross income of the government from property and entrepreneurial activity
ZINS_GSV \ Dimension : mill.DM
Interest on public debt, social insurance

YEAR	ZINS_HH_KR	ZU_NL_ST
1960	910.000	0.000
1961	1090.000	0.000
1962	1240.000	0.000
1963	1350.000	0.000
1964	1570.000	0.000
1965	1710.000	0.000
1966	1770.000	0.000
1967	1890.000	0.000
1968	1950.000	0.000
1969	2420.000	0.000
1970	3340.000	0.000
1971	3930.000	0.000
1972	4570.000	0.000
1973	5940.000	0.000
1974	6870.000	0.000
1975	6410.000	0.000
1976	6310.000	0.000
1977	6720.000	0.000
1978	7280.000	0.000
1979	9170.000	0.000
1980	13190.000	0.000
1981	16630.000	0.000
1982	18470.000	0.000
1983	17860.000	0.000
1984	17760.000	0.000
1985	17670.000	0.000
1986	17930.000	0.000
1987	17480.000	0.000
1988	18170.000	0.000
1989	19460.000	0.000
1990	22340.000	45410.000
1991	26800.000	105440.000
1992	32400.000	130400.000
1993	36000.000	128800.000
1994	40000.000	128800.000
1995	44000.000	128800.000
1996	48000.000	112000.000
1997	52000.000	104000.000
1998	56000.000	96000.000
1999	60000.000	88000.000
2000	64000.000	80000.000

Legend :

ZINS_HH_KR \ Dimension : mill.DM
Interest on consumers' debts, private households
ZU_NL_ST \ Dimension : mill.DM
Payments of the West German government to the East German government

YEAR	BLG_ST@	BETA	BEI_GSV@	ALPHA
1990	29706.116	0.742	35.500	0.024
1991	36065.735	0.907	36.325	0.047
1992	39672.309	0.931	36.688	0.063
1993	43639.539	0.928	37.055	0.066
1994	48003.493	0.910	37.426	0.070
1995	52803.843	0.870	37.800	0.075
1996	58084.227	0.860	38.178	0.083
1997	63892.650	0.810	38.560	0.090
1998	70281.915	0.770	38.945	0.098
1999	77310.106	0.700	39.335	0.107
2000	85041.117	0.630	39.728	0.116

Legend :

BLG_ST@ \ Dimension : mill.DM
Gross wages and salaries, public sector
BETA \ Dimension : no dimension
Share of imports from West Germany to total East German imports
BEI_GSV@ \ Dimension : p.c.
Rate of social insurance payment (total)
ALPHA \ Dimension : no dimension
Share of West German imports from East Germany to total imports

YEAR	BUA_EH@	EH@	BUV_HH@	CAPIFO@
1990	11.318	1724.900	31000.000	20.000
1991	15.501	1702.700	-10214.000	18.000
1992	22.350	1680.500	-11961.000	22.500
1993	26.650	1658.300	448.000	25.000
1994	29.759	1636.100	820.629	30.000
1995	33.231	1614.000	1503.198	35.000
1996	37.108	1569.600	2753.501	40.000
1997	41.437	1547.400	5043.760	50.000
1998	46.272	1525.200	9238.969	60.000
1999	51.670	1503.000	16923.594	70.000
2000	57.698	1503.000	31000.000	80.000

Legend :

BUA_EH@ \ Dimension : DM/hour
Total labour cost per hour
EH@ \ Dimension : hour/ET
Annual average working hours
BUV_HH@ \ Dimension : mill.DM
Gross income from entrepreneurial activity and property, private households
CAPIFO@ \ Dimension : p.c.
Degree of capacity utilization in the manufacturing sector

YEAR	GEW_SATZ@	IN_SONS@	GUOER_N@	ET@
1990	364.000	8749.000	-4778.000	8948.000
1991	366.000	35060.000	-5809.000	7469.000
1992	370.000	20000.000	-20000.000	6535.000
1993	376.000	20900.000	-20000.000	6240.000
1994	384.000	21840.500	-20000.000	6240.000
1995	386.000	22823.323	-20000.000	6240.000
1996	388.000	23850.372	-17000.000	6440.000
1997	391.000	24923.639	-13000.000	6640.000
1998	395.000	26045.202	-10000.000	6840.000
1999	399.000	27217.237	-7000.000	7040.000
2000	403.000	28442.012	-5000.000	7240.000

Legend :

GEW_SATZ@ \ Dimension : p.c.
Rate of tax from yield of manufacturing, average
IN_SONS@ \ Dimension : mill.DM
Other government receipts
GUOER_N@ \ Dimension : mill.DM
Undistributed profits of enterprises without a legal entity
ET@ \ Dimension : thousands
Workers (on the basis of resident status)

YEAR	IVOR@	MWST_SATZ@	KST_SATZ@	LSST_SATZ@
1990	-9900.000	14.000	50.000	0.000
1991	2600.000	14.000	50.000	0.000
1992	300.000	14.000	50.000	0.000
1993	5500.000	15.000	50.000	0.000
1994	0.000	15.000	48.000	0.000
1995	0.000	15.000	48.000	0.000
1996	0.000	15.000	44.000	0.000
1997	0.000	15.000	44.000	0.000
1998	0.000	15.000	44.000	0.000
1999	0.000	15.000	44.000	0.000
2000	0.000	15.000	44.000	0.000

Legend :

IVOR@ \ Dimension : mill.DM
Changes in stocks
MWST_SATZ@ \ Dimension : p.c.
Upper tax rate, value added tax
KST_SATZ@ \ Dimension : p.c.
Corporate income tax rate
LSST_SATZ@ \ Dimension : p.c.
Average payroll tax rate

YEAR	PIAU@	PM@	PMD@	OUT_SONS@
1990	100.000	100.000	100.000	22063.000
1991	99.200	104.000	102.560	29540.000
1992	100.400	106.700	105.186	31017.000
1993	102.400	106.700	107.878	32567.850
1994	104.448	108.834	110.640	34196.243
1995	106.537	111.011	113.472	35906.055
1996	108.668	113.231	116.377	37701.357
1997	110.841	115.496	119.357	39586.425
1998	113.058	117.805	122.412	41565.746
1999	115.319	120.162	125.546	43644.034
2000	117.625	122.565	128.760	45826.236

Legend :

PIAU@ \ Dimension : index
Price index, gross fixed capital formation, equipment
PM@ \ Dimension : index
Price index, imports
PMD@ \ Dimension : index
Price index, imports of services
OUT_SONS@ \ Dimension : mill.DM
Other public consumption expenditures

YEAR	SB_EA@	R_WPUM@	SELB@	PMIAU@
1990	-126.000	8.900	317.000	100.000
1991	-164.000	8.700	490.000	104.000
1992	-200.000	8.300	580.000	106.700
1993	-200.000	8.000	630.000	106.700
1994	-200.000	7.800	650.000	108.834
1995	-200.000	7.700	650.000	111.011
1996	-200.000	7.600	670.000	113.231
1997	-200.000	7.500	670.000	115.496
1998	-200.000	7.500	670.000	117.805
1999	-200.000	7.400	680.000	120.162
2000	-200.000	7.200	700.000	122.565

Legend :

SB_EA@ \ Dimension : mill.DM
Balance of social contribution of foreign commuters
R_WPUM@ \ Dimension : p.c.
Avarage yield on circulating bearer bonds
SELB@ \ Dimension : thousands
Self employed persons and unpaid family members
PMIAU@ \ Dimension : index
Price index, imports of equipment

YEAR	SL_W@	SL_U@	SL_HN_ST@	SL_HH_H@
1990	34.000	1981.000	21071.000	160.000
1991	118.000	6940.000	73812.000	559.000
1992	122.720	7252.300	77133.540	584.155
1993	127.629	7578.654	80604.549	610.442
1994	132.734	7919.693	84231.754	637.912
1995	138.043	8276.079	88022.183	666.618
1996	143.565	8648.503	91983.181	696.616
1997	149.308	9037.685	96122.424	727.963
1998	155.280	9444.381	100447.933	760.722
1999	161.491	9869.378	104968.090	794.954
2000	167.951	10313.500	109691.655	830.727

Legend :

SL_W@ \ Dimension : mill.DM
Social contributions from the rest of the world to private households
SL_U@ \ Dimension : mill.DM
Social contributions from enterprises with own legal entity to priv. households
SL_HN_ST@ \ Dimension : mill.DM
Social contributions of the East German government to the East German households
SL_HH_H@ \ Dimension : mill.DM
Social contributions to private households from private households

YEAR	TR_SONS@	SL_W_ST@	TI_SONS@	TD_SONS@
1990	7343.000	385.000	11475.000	6725.000
1991	7810.000	1348.000	8253.000	1740.000
1992	8200.500	1393.832	8913.240	4220.000
1993	8610.525	1441.222	9358.902	4431.000
1994	9041.051	1490.224	9826.847	4652.550
1995	9493.104	1540.891	10318.189	4885.178
1996	9967.759	1593.282	10834.099	5129.436
1997	10466.147	1647.453	11375.804	5385.908
1998	10989.454	1703.467	11944.594	5655.204
1999	11538.927	1761.385	12541.824	5937.964
2000	12115.873	1821.272	13168.915	6234.862

Legend :

TR_SONS@ \ Dimension : mill.DM
Other transfer incomes of the private households
SL_W_ST@ \ Dimension : mill.DM
Social contributions of the government to the rest of the world
TI_SONS@ \ Dimension : mill.DM
Other direct taxes
TD_SONS@ \ Dimension : mill.DM
Other direct taxes

YEAR	X_R@	YUVST@	VOL_MIN@	TVS_GK@
1990	43419.050	200.000	486.520	62411.000
1991	21400.000	2300.000	512.590	71864.000
1992	16000.000	2100.000	540.065	110382.071
1993	21000.000	2000.000	569.012	169545.274
1994	25000.000	2245.649	599.511	260419.104
1995	28000.000	2521.469	631.645	400000.000
1996	32000.000	2831.166	665.501	418255.821
1997	36000.000	3178.902	701.172	437344.830
1998	40000.000	3569.348	738.755	457305.052
1999	44000.000	4007.751	778.352	478176.251
2000	48000.000	4500.000	820.072	500000.000

Legend :

X_R@ \ Dimension : mill.DM
Exports from East Germany to the rest of the world without exports to West Germany
YUVST@ \ Dimension : mill.DM
Gross income of the government from property and entrepreneurial activity
VOL_MIN@ \ Dimension : Petajoule
Consumption of gasoline and diesel
TVS_GK@ \ Dimension : mill.DM
National debt in the end of the year

YEAR	ZINSHHKR@	ZINS_GSV@
1990	2970.000	1.200
1991	4200.000	1.400
1992	5300.000	1.600
1993	6000.000	2.000
1994	7000.000	3.000
1995	8000.000	4.000
1996	9000.000	4.500
1997	10000.000	4.500
1998	11000.000	5.000
1999	12000.000	5.000
2000	13000.000	6.000

Legend :

ZINSHHKR@ \ Dimension : mill.DM
Interest on consumers' debts, private households
ZINS_GSV@ \ Dimension : mill.DM
Interest on public debt, social incurance

3.6 Tables (growth rates)

3.6.1 Endogenous variables

General remarks:
- Variables for East Germany with @ at the end of the symbol
- <G1> for growth rates

YEAR	<G1> QSP	<G1> BSP	<G1> BSP85	<G1> NSPF
1978	6.783	7.845	3.450	7.867
1979	10.134	8.097	4.032	7.630
1980	8.315	5.998	1.043	5.127
1981	5.517	4.210	0.110	3.530
1982	3.158	3.293	-1.106	2.913
1983	4.335	5.370	1.858	5.264
1984	6.312	5.228	3.066	5.401
1985	4.820	4.038	1.804	4.427
1986	2.431	5.538	2.175	6.453
1987	2.666	3.455	1.488	3.502
1988	5.779	5.242	3.653	5.519
1989	8.169	6.694	3.981	6.271
1990	9.168	8.448	4.853	8.469
1991	9.520	7.876	3.582	6.548
1992	5.953	6.198	2.262	7.155
1993	3.162	2.524	-0.622	1.716
1994	3.796	3.402	0.996	3.201
1995	3.894	3.572	1.436	3.472
1996	5.333	5.471	1.831	5.890
1997	5.218	5.311	2.197	5.668
1998	5.724	5.960	2.164	6.422
1999	6.019	6.317	2.077	6.831
2000	5.284	5.344	2.131	5.573

YEAR	<G1> QSP85	<G1> GUMER_U	<G1> NSPF_HH	<G1> YVPE
1978	3.621	24.817	6.971	6.297
1979	5.266	5.678	7.678	8.372
1980	1.810	-4.608	5.843	7.324
1981	-0.228	10.042	3.462	6.457
1982	-0.866	-5.756	3.216	2.671
1983	1.453	39.428	4.170	2.566
1984	3.537	10.618	5.119	4.938
1985	2.523	-0.213	4.630	3.564
1986	2.475	2.738	6.780	3.896
1987	2.143	9.314	3.632	4.268
1988	4.180	11.316	5.673	4.384
1989	5.082	2.652	5.648	5.375
1990	6.645	1.360	8.751	9.764
1991	5.897	22.562	6.043	7.160
1992	2.329	4.163	3.556	3.492
1993	-1.788	-0.913	3.131	2.572
1994	1.266	1.396	3.805	3.004
1995	1.546	-0.503	4.791	4.205
1996	2.402	2.829	6.110	5.415
1997	2.677	1.261	6.413	5.524
1998	2.679	2.041	6.910	5.778
1999	2.650	-0.251	8.017	6.442
2000	2.696	4.175	5.368	4.813

YEAR	<G1> D	<G1> DAN85_ST	<G1> DAU85_PR	<G1> DBA85_PR
1978	7.746	5.503	5.483	6.661
1979	9.287	7.154	4.648	5.041
1980	10.900	1.530	4.149	8.095
1981	8.926	-3.151	4.971	11.199
1982	6.857	0.000	3.549	10.667
1983	5.518	0.283	3.789	9.424
1984	5.323	3.244	5.620	12.500
1985	3.971	8.607	2.712	0.175
1986	3.539	5.031	1.660	4.498
1987	3.533	3.353	2.805	4.430
1988	4.277	-3.940	2.299	7.803
1989	6.218	1.689	3.508	8.352
1990	7.486	2.254	2.030	5.207
1991	8.852	1.276	2.071	5.536
1992	4.531	3.848	6.111	5.131
1993	5.425	2.231	4.700	5.180
1994	4.995	2.057	4.960	5.049
1995	4.697	1.931	5.118	4.912
1996	4.857	1.872	5.218	4.773
1997	4.952	1.846	5.302	4.639
1998	5.162	1.844	5.371	4.510
1999	5.406	1.860	5.425	4.385
2000	5.393	1.854	5.471	4.265

YEAR	<G1> KAP85_ST	<G1> KAPM85_ST	<G1> KAU85_PR	<G1> KBA85_PR
1978	3.934	3.974	3.315	3.300
1979	3.904	3.918	3.735	3.399
1980	3.746	3.823	3.599	3.370
1981	3.252	3.495	2.795	3.087
1982	2.825	3.035	1.936	2.864
1983	2.488	2.654	2.173	2.883
1984	2.355	2.420	1.700	2.821
1985	2.277	2.315	2.195	2.529
1986	2.424	2.351	2.379	2.505
1987	2.350	2.386	2.553	2.434
1988	2.324	2.337	2.943	2.447
1989	2.375	2.350	3.445	2.484
1990	2.354	2.364	4.454	2.571
1991	2.347	2.350	5.102	2.614
1992	2.890	2.827	5.413	2.423
1993	2.279	2.376	5.162	2.140
1994	2.119	2.198	5.040	1.988
1995	2.057	2.088	4.988	1.876
1996	2.112	2.085	5.048	1.819
1997	2.141	2.127	5.089	1.766
1998	2.179	2.160	5.123	1.721
1999	2.230	2.205	5.161	1.674
2000	2.168	2.198	5.081	1.607

YEAR	<G1> KAUMA85_PR	<G1> KBAM85_PR	<G1> KAUM85_PR	<G1> KAP85
1978	1.507	3.321	3.188	3.411
1979	7.632	3.351	3.529	3.552
1980	0.791	3.384	3.666	3.480
1981	-1.069	3.226	3.190	3.057
1982	-1.010	2.974	2.360	2.673
1983	4.688	2.874	2.056	2.675
1984	4.926	2.852	1.934	2.521
1985	6.475	2.673	1.950	2.421
1986	2.798	2.517	2.288	2.467
1987	2.043	2.469	2.467	2.442
1988	5.713	2.440	2.751	2.522
1989	5.994	2.466	3.198	2.653
1990	4.658	2.528	3.958	2.903
1991	2.238	2.593	4.785	3.064
1992	1.852	2.527	5.344	3.109
1993	3.213	2.270	5.202	2.791
1994	5.099	2.063	5.099	2.658
1995	5.646	1.931	5.013	2.582
1996	5.019	1.847	5.019	2.586
1997	5.698	1.792	5.069	2.585
1998	5.107	1.743	5.107	2.590
1999	3.891	1.697	5.143	2.599
2000	5.120	1.640	5.120	2.549

YEAR	<G1> MIAU85	<G1> M	<G1> MD85	<G1> KAPAM85
1978	14.247	2.486	3.665	3.127
1979	9.937	18.804	5.504	4.169
1980	4.357	17.287	0.888	3.013
1981	0.069	10.091	0.947	2.546
1982	-6.069	2.709	1.612	2.333
1983	12.518	0.886	-1.456	3.121
1984	8.418	10.084	-0.265	3.107
1985	16.070	7.421	1.702	3.230
1986	7.363	-7.581	-1.576	2.535
1987	8.742	-0.239	1.855	2.382
1988	11.592	7.828	1.811	2.973
1989	20.557	13.663	3.024	3.056
1990	20.584	11.685	4.021	2.878
1991	23.135	15.101	7.642	2.486
1992	-20.036	5.174	2.329	2.457
1993	-11.340	5.210	2.384	2.457
1994	7.724	5.032	1.881	2.635
1995	1.976	4.885	1.689	2.646
1996	4.696	4.916	2.073	2.492
1997	3.581	4.931	2.336	2.612
1998	3.064	5.000	2.622	2.491
1999	2.985	5.094	2.836	2.236
2000	3.098	5.096	2.768	2.464

YEAR	<G1> MR%D85	<G1> M85	<G1> CPR	<G1> CST85
1978	3.722	4.243	6.423	3.889
1979	10.737	9.727	7.627	3.385
1980	5.263	4.436	7.130	2.594
1981	-1.959	-1.348	5.555	1.823
1982	0.000	-0.058	3.688	-0.901
1983	-0.386	0.105	4.713	0.215
1984	6.120	5.135	4.370	2.509
1985	4.722	4.913	3.529	2.068
1986	4.149	3.442	2.885	2.548
1987	4.286	4.225	3.900	1.549
1988	5.983	5.810	4.122	2.166
1989	8.246	8.425	5.830	-1.653
1990	12.083	11.860	8.212	2.373
1991	11.896	12.216	7.526	0.472
1992	5.483	2.500	5.967	6.571
1993	-5.145	-4.716	3.046	2.311
1994	1.453	1.972	3.052	2.050
1995	1.839	1.830	3.779	1.885
1996	4.096	3.877	4.853	1.884
1997	4.176	3.892	5.281	1.926
1998	4.263	3.961	5.603	1.963
1999	4.349	4.053	6.146	1.990
2000	4.347	4.055	5.358	2.022

YEAR	<G1> CST	<G1> C	<G1> C85	<G1> CPR85
1978	7.638	6.734	3.666	3.591
1979	8.080	7.744	3.284	3.251
1980	8.949	7.602	1.586	1.247
1981	6.835	5.891	-0.099	-0.753
1982	2.528	3.380	-1.363	-1.525
1983	3.063	4.280	1.053	1.347
1984	4.161	4.316	1.810	1.567
1985	4.360	3.744	1.613	1.453
1986	4.602	3.333	3.195	3.423
1987	3.850	3.887	2.811	3.253
1988	3.801	4.037	2.579	2.721
1989	1.562	4.706	1.569	2.671
1990	6.096	7.671	4.670	5.423
1991	5.338	6.976	2.823	3.571
1992	9.137	6.753	3.334	2.334
1993	6.569	3.939	0.475	-0.115
1994	4.891	3.529	0.824	0.421
1995	4.250	3.903	1.506	1.379
1996	5.699	5.076	1.958	1.983
1997	5.095	5.231	2.220	2.319
1998	5.857	5.671	2.229	2.318
1999	6.373	6.207	2.314	2.422
2000	5.328	5.350	1.967	1.948

YEAR	<G1> CPR_BSP	<G1> CST_BSP	<G1> IAN_ST	<G1> DIAU_PR
1978	-1.315	-0.203	8.478	12.896
1979	-0.426	0.000	13.129	23.146
1980	1.052	2.751	10.081	-36.859
1981	1.306	2.529	-5.764	-93.814
1982	0.383	-0.725	-8.571	-708.333
1983	-0.625	-2.192	-7.174	-488.699
1984	-0.821	-1.046	-0.047	-84.758
1985	-0.493	0.352	1.779	770.520
1986	-2.513	-0.903	10.207	-51.859
1987	0.436	0.354	1.480	10.483
1988	-1.067	-1.362	1.917	61.548
1989	-0.804	-4.806	7.074	55.410
1990	-0.221	-2.148	6.989	47.787
1991	-0.332	-2.360	8.638	-8.917
1992	-0.212	2.763	10.303	-12.003
1993	0.510	3.946	-1.057	0.931
1994	-0.338	1.440	-0.831	-2.533
1995	0.200	0.654	2.271	11.442
1996	-0.586	0.216	7.688	26.446
1997	-0.029	-0.205	6.701	7.285
1998	-0.336	-0.097	7.440	10.927
1999	-0.161	0.052	8.412	13.269
2000	0.013	-0.016	3.668	-5.541

YEAR	<G1> IAN85_ST	<G1> IAU85_PR	<G1> IAU_PR	<G1> IBA_PR
1978	2.321	7.699	10.925	8.194
1979	3.629	8.974	12.129	15.295
1980	-0.053	2.499	6.830	13.022
1981	-9.075	-4.412	0.395	1.121
1982	-8.902	-6.869	-2.396	-0.413
1983	-7.995	6.395	9.543	5.828
1984	-1.977	-1.177	1.328	4.841
1985	0.633	8.835	11.407	-6.046
1986	8.157	4.011	4.929	3.643
1987	0.022	4.759	5.190	2.089
1988	0.280	6.895	7.971	5.848
1989	4.060	8.931	11.473	8.104
1990	1.590	13.231	15.211	12.408
1991	1.910	9.408	12.025	11.676
1992	7.570	7.067	15.227	-2.107
1993	-4.305	4.188	8.274	-3.767
1994	-3.641	3.913	7.448	-0.983
1995	-0.364	4.592	7.725	0.072
1996	4.253	5.679	9.068	4.168
1997	3.194	5.580	8.919	3.554
1998	3.546	5.562	9.084	4.665
1999	4.054	5.639	9.432	5.022
2000	-0.156	4.586	8.142	2.705

YEAR	<G1> IAN	<G1> IAN85	<G1> IBA85_PR	<G1> IANST_BSP
1978	9.269	4.294	2.406	0.306
1979	13.737	6.863	6.285	4.878
1980	10.219	2.319	2.951	3.779
1981	-0.238	-4.879	-3.920	-9.524
1982	-2.367	-5.268	-2.890	-11.455
1983	5.367	3.340	4.196	-11.888
1984	2.893	0.313	2.053	-5.159
1985	1.466	0.031	-6.801	-2.092
1986	4.966	3.564	1.978	4.274
1987	3.293	2.098	0.260	-1.639
1988	6.252	4.641	3.704	-3.333
1989	9.422	6.452	4.670	0.431
1990	12.996	8.681	5.934	-1.288
1991	11.495	6.488	4.478	0.435
1992	6.965	2.498	-3.936	4.019
1993	2.323	-0.890	-6.372	-3.493
1994	3.322	0.506	-3.122	-4.093
1995	4.347	1.760	-1.921	-1.257
1996	7.200	3.632	0.159	2.102
1997	6.855	3.551	0.210	1.320
1998	7.449	3.725	0.494	1.397
1999	7.901	3.831	0.361	1.970
2000	5.974	2.539	-0.633	-1.591

YEAR	<G1> IAUPR_BSP	<G1> IBAPR_BSP	<G1> IN_ST	<G1> OUT_ST
1978	2.880	0.320	6.756	6.812
1979	3.690	6.702	7.342	7.673
1980	0.859	6.580	7.454	8.060
1981	-3.650	-2.993	4.883	6.434
1982	-5.556	-3.568	4.993	4.168
1983	4.011	0.500	3.240	1.838
1984	-3.728	-0.398	5.026	3.772
1985	7.076	-9.690	4.812	3.181
1986	-0.623	-1.770	3.664	4.049
1987	1.631	-1.351	2.925	4.149
1988	2.593	0.571	3.923	4.518
1989	4.573	1.362	8.027	3.065
1990	6.214	3.583	4.536	9.414
1991	3.792	3.568	12.516	15.755
1992	8.550	-7.838	5.379	4.658
1993	5.609	-6.135	3.837	4.095
1994	3.914	-4.240	4.169	3.715
1995	4.009	-3.380	4.879	4.401
1996	3.410	-1.235	5.131	3.986
1997	3.426	-1.669	5.494	4.466
1998	2.949	-1.221	6.051	4.861
1999	2.930	-1.219	6.932	5.163
2000	2.656	-2.505	5.108	4.572

YEAR	<G1> FS_ST	<G1> TDIR	<G1> TIND	<G1> TD_HH
1978	7.931	1.725	9.861	1.751
1979	14.249	4.788	9.310	3.619
1980	19.351	6.974	5.629	9.515
1981	32.498	0.192	2.491	0.605
1982	-6.808	2.695	1.710	2.203
1983	-19.165	3.717	6.302	2.635
1984	-20.235	6.319	5.476	4.820
1985	-37.934	7.802	1.848	6.636
1986	20.436	3.222	2.544	3.858
1987	48.976	3.755	3.951	6.705
1988	19.556	3.851	4.729	2.502
1989	-106.079	10.317	8.253	10.095
1990	-1897.455	-3.815	8.565	-3.292
1991	89.379	16.638	13.228	18.778
1992	-5.076	0.104	3.646	-1.320
1993	7.961	3.825	5.116	3.855
1994	-2.823	4.033	3.287	4.064
1995	-2.994	4.847	3.225	4.883
1996	-15.149	4.994	3.461	5.028
1997	-16.830	5.882	3.400	5.921
1998	-26.394	6.589	3.731	6.630
1999	-61.798	7.393	3.807	7.436
2000	-52.207	6.205	3.744	6.239

YEAR	<G1> TD_KEST	<G1> TD_KOST	<G1> TD_LOST%P	<G1> TI_GEW
1978	-0.444	7.567	1.567	4.212
1979	13.161	12.984	5.405	4.417
1980	9.609	-6.979	15.005	8.101
1981	10.898	-3.953	3.880	-3.876
1982	1.577	6.080	4.729	0.230
1983	0.128	12.787	4.180	0.345
1984	18.730	18.452	6.360	8.171
1985	11.000	15.413	7.434	8.577
1986	30.857	-2.688	3.085	3.966
1987	-2.968	-14.311	8.233	-1.689
1988	10.799	9.842	1.922	9.606
1989	44.863	12.332	8.273	6.500
1990	-14.358	-10.534	-3.092	5.695
1991	5.068	5.965	19.248	5.053
1992	11.055	1.796	-8.685	7.490
1993	0.872	0.339	3.743	0.368
1994	1.410	-1.480	4.333	2.489
1995	0.200	-0.998	5.615	-0.039
1996	2.196	-3.970	7.450	2.529
1997	1.842	-1.149	8.318	1.507
1998	2.278	0.718	9.015	2.302
1999	0.739	0.172	10.251	0.499
2000	3.388	2.665	7.852	4.006

YEAR	<G1> TI_MIN	<G1> TI_UST	<G1> T	<G1> SUB
1978	6.667	16.043	5.637	20.585
1979	3.308	14.140	7.050	4.916
1980	0.998	10.974	6.287	-1.637
1981	3.883	4.308	1.359	-4.992
1982	2.953	0.437	2.189	0.446
1983	2.203	7.967	5.037	8.444
1984	2.978	6.106	5.883	14.533
1985	2.031	0.656	4.736	4.432
1986	4.580	1.046	2.883	8.882
1987	1.919	6.133	3.852	8.448
1988	3.428	3.988	4.289	6.563
1989	21.948	5.711	9.282	-2.011
1990	5.024	12.666	2.337	4.190
1991	25.701	13.566	14.840	-4.288
1992	-15.624	-1.067	1.945	16.998
1993	2.987	6.826	4.507	5.657
1994	2.987	2.570	3.637	4.979
1995	2.988	3.019	3.988	4.650
1996	2.988	4.337	4.188	4.498
1997	2.988	4.431	4.586	4.527
1998	2.989	4.891	5.114	4.720
1999	2.989	5.399	5.566	4.999
2000	2.990	4.506	4.972	4.990

YEAR	<G1> GEW_BUV	<G1> GSV_BLG	<G1> BST_KST	<G1> TSB
1978	12.005	6.548	24.817	6.146
1979	6.170	7.356	5.678	7.751
1980	-3.275	9.217	-4.608	7.252
1981	0.225	7.756	10.042	3.701
1982	4.189	4.923	-5.756	3.713
1983	19.264	4.390	39.428	3.976
1984	11.466	2.689	10.618	5.574
1985	7.214	5.937	-0.213	4.680
1986	10.838	5.139	2.738	3.956
1987	1.732	4.715	9.314	4.092
1988	10.523	4.826	11.316	4.324
1989	10.737	4.631	2.652	7.110
1990	10.557	6.592	-9.500	4.532
1991	3.935	10.396	22.562	11.854
1992	16.746	4.723	4.163	2.086
1993	0.558	3.728	-0.913	4.231
1994	3.765	4.889	-2.660	4.247
1995	-0.058	6.379	-0.503	5.112
1996	3.779	8.273	-5.740	6.090
1997	2.225	8.534	1.261	6.465
1998	3.373	9.129	2.041	7.062
1999	0.724	10.612	-0.251	8.046
2000	5.798	6.569	4.175	5.807

YEAR	<G1> BMG_UST	<G1> GEW_LSST	<G1> ZINS_GK	<G1> ZINS_ST
1978	7.327	0.000	5.439	5.488
1979	9.207	0.000	11.942	11.937
1980	8.212	0.000	18.431	18.465
1981	4.370	0.000	24.045	24.238
1982	2.055	0.000	24.357	24.133
1983	4.649	0.000	13.792	13.763
1984	4.271	0.000	5.232	5.251
1985	3.252	0.000	4.839	4.837
1986	3.564	0.000	3.457	3.456
1987	3.719	0.000	1.032	1.049
1988	4.695	0.000	3.515	3.513
1989	5.983	0.000	1.087	1.087
1990	9.076	0.000	5.064	5.061
1991	8.041	0.000	13.183	13.193
1992	7.052	0.000	-2.160	-2.152
1993	3.529	0.000	6.865	6.868
1994	3.437	0.000	7.872	7.867
1995	4.005	0.000	8.887	8.888
1996	5.698	0.000	7.128	7.123
1997	5.746	0.000	6.049	6.045
1998	6.265	0.000	5.790	5.787
1999	6.826	0.000	5.223	5.225
2000	5.621	0.000	4.454	4.452

YEAR	<G1> SB_UH	<G1> SB_ST	<G1> SB_AG	<G1> SB_PR
1978	13.282	6.208	7.751	6.876
1979	13.976	8.173	8.870	8.748
1980	13.753	8.020	9.553	8.602
1981	-3.047	8.109	5.008	6.905
1982	4.326	5.811	4.565	5.690
1983	7.191	2.142	3.853	2.646
1984	7.525	4.905	5.329	5.177
1985	0.281	5.099	3.900	4.607
1986	4.765	5.401	5.311	5.344
1987	8.748	3.897	4.451	4.394
1988	2.706	4.556	4.068	4.368
1989	3.018	4.537	3.886	4.384
1990	12.834	7.154	8.063	7.418
1991	3.647	9.441	8.047	8.114
1992	5.773	1.879	3.857	2.273
1993	3.728	3.838	4.203	3.865
1994	4.889	5.028	4.140	5.061
1995	6.379	6.551	4.770	6.592
1996	8.273	8.483	5.980	8.533
1997	8.534	8.734	6.782	8.781
1998	9.129	9.325	7.497	9.372
1999	10.612	10.821	8.570	10.871
2000	6.569	6.685	7.269	6.713

YEAR	<G1> SL_HH_ST	<G1> SL_ST	<G1> SL_ZU_ST	<G1> TR_HH_EMP
1978	4.842	4.834	-20.706	5.462
1979	6.252	6.175	-43.560	6.961
1980	6.188	6.157	-82.780	6.873
1981	8.584	8.559	143.373	8.516
1982	6.131	6.081	42.079	5.802
1983	1.306	1.313	-80.836	1.944
1984	1.219	1.344	-1878.182	2.258
1985	2.357	2.249	91.002	3.167
1986	3.726	3.716	32.602	4.473
1987	4.919	4.926	-9.084	5.232
1988	4.530	4.512	5.195	4.946
1989	3.929	4.641	3.039	4.616
1990	5.253	4.454	46.825	5.996
1991	13.229	13.074	-28.544	6.787
1992	5.713	5.675	-60.919	4.579
1993	3.150	3.154	34.442	3.820
1994	3.252	3.254	65.900	3.823
1995	5.588	5.553	27.879	5.715
1996	4.762	4.741	74.479	5.717
1997	5.291	5.261	45.493	5.720
1998	5.349	5.319	40.011	5.722
1999	5.402	5.372	42.212	5.725
2000	5.453	5.423	12.075	5.727

YEAR	<G1> TR_HH_GEL	<G1> TR%T	<G1> TR_HH_R	<G1> PBSP
1978	5.245	4.861	8.748	4.249
1979	6.845	6.640	7.010	3.907
1980	8.883	12.465	8.388	4.904
1981	4.978	-1.014	8.631	4.096
1982	4.451	1.941	4.311	4.448
1983	2.796	4.438	4.251	3.448
1984	5.264	10.919	7.212	2.098
1985	5.121	8.510	3.469	2.195
1986	4.756	5.221	4.084	3.292
1987	5.008	4.640	3.319	1.938
1988	3.972	2.369	6.393	1.533
1989	6.339	9.249	6.217	2.609
1990	4.322	1.615	11.049	3.429
1991	11.434	19.269	9.420	4.146
1992	1.135	-4.066	2.323	3.849
1993	3.953	4.171	4.746	3.166
1994	4.686	6.102	4.429	2.381
1995	5.821	5.990	4.229	2.106
1996	7.053	9.190	4.517	3.574
1997	7.518	10.304	4.703	3.047
1998	8.138	11.727	4.999	3.715
1999	9.347	14.439	5.312	4.154
2000	6.451	7.390	5.320	3.146

YEAR	<G1> PIAN_ST	<G1> PCST	<G1> PCPR	<G1> PMD_PBSP
1978	6.018	3.609	2.733	0.172
1979	9.167	4.542	4.239	2.720
1980	10.139	6.195	5.811	4.717
1981	3.641	4.923	6.357	5.684
1982	0.363	3.460	5.293	-2.684
1983	0.892	2.842	3.322	-0.992
1984	1.969	1.612	2.760	3.380
1985	1.139	2.246	2.046	0.918
1986	1.896	2.003	-0.520	-3.840
1987	1.458	2.266	0.627	-0.666
1988	1.632	1.600	1.363	2.450
1989	2.896	3.268	3.077	2.095
1990	5.315	3.637	2.645	0.150
1991	6.602	4.843	3.819	-0.530
1992	2.541	2.408	3.551	-1.299
1993	3.393	4.162	3.165	-0.645
1994	2.916	2.784	2.620	0.116
1995	2.644	2.321	2.368	0.386
1996	3.295	3.745	2.814	-1.037
1997	3.399	3.109	2.895	-0.531
1998	3.761	3.819	3.211	-1.171
1999	4.188	4.297	3.637	-1.588
2000	3.830	3.240	3.344	-0.627

YEAR	<G1> PIAU_PR	<G1> PIBA_PR	<G1> M1	<G1> BLG_EH85
1978	2.996	5.652	13.312	1.894
1979	2.895	8.477	7.455	2.899
1980	4.225	9.783	2.430	2.507
1981	5.029	5.246	1.150	1.654
1982	4.803	2.551	3.562	-0.808
1983	2.958	1.566	10.332	0.179
1984	2.535	2.732	3.258	1.342
1985	2.363	0.810	4.398	2.128
1986	0.883	1.632	9.879	0.943
1987	0.412	1.824	9.044	1.883
1988	1.006	2.067	9.742	1.259
1989	2.334	3.281	6.254	1.621
1990	1.748	6.111	4.523	3.463
1991	2.392	6.890	3.260	3.620
1992	7.621	1.904	6.591	0.687
1993	3.922	2.783	4.594	1.496
1994	3.402	2.208	4.572	2.504
1995	2.996	2.032	4.449	3.919
1996	3.206	4.003	5.184	3.047
1997	3.163	3.337	5.563	3.242
1998	3.337	4.151	5.868	3.015
1999	3.591	4.644	6.405	4.196
2000	3.400	3.359	6.523	1.177

YEAR	<G1> BUA_EH85	<G1> BUV	<G1> BUA	<G1> BLG
1978	2.094	10.971	6.758	6.548
1979	3.041	6.170	8.172	8.023
1980	2.677	-4.741	8.722	8.542
1981	1.683	-0.678	4.873	4.844
1982	-0.497	2.345	3.085	2.763
1983	0.565	15.847	2.089	1.698
1984	1.713	10.516	3.659	3.281
1985	2.139	6.009	3.853	3.842
1986	0.974	9.912	5.171	5.139
1987	1.943	1.732	4.188	4.127
1988	1.280	9.607	3.973	3.950
1989	1.485	10.737	4.490	4.631
1990	3.511	9.949	7.844	7.793
1991	3.649	3.367	7.918	7.888
1992	0.717	15.483	3.719	3.686
1993	1.776	-1.046	2.984	2.701
1994	2.558	1.603	3.906	3.850
1995	3.814	-0.576	5.219	5.326
1996	2.824	3.244	6.969	7.201
1997	3.119	1.440	7.332	7.460
1998	2.917	2.327	7.945	8.049
1999	4.027	-0.286	9.340	9.517
2000	1.489	4.748	5.839	5.513

YEAR	<G1> BESCH	<G1> BESVOL	<G1> X	<G1> X@
1978	1.212	0.306	5.137	-
1979	2.226	1.032	9.786	-
1980	1.811	0.938	12.299	-
1981	0.042	-0.921	14.511	-
1982	-1.121	-0.812	7.471	-
1983	-1.464	-1.867	0.879	-
1984	0.249	-0.180	12.171	-
1985	0.891	-0.505	10.048	-
1986	1.490	0.838	-1.185	-
1987	0.966	0.259	0.078	-
1988	0.928	1.109	7.898	-
1989	1.580	0.344	14.599	-
1990	2.913	0.732	11.923	-
1991	1.873	-0.025	14.842	-0.821
1992	0.470	-0.837	4.359	17.279
1993	-0.652	-1.918	0.859	14.723
1994	0.251	-1.043	4.547	13.575
1995	0.578	-0.737	3.616	12.274
1996	0.574	0.441	4.758	15.615
1997	1.142	1.008	4.224	13.438
1998	1.129	1.129	4.784	13.480
1999	1.117	0.915	4.476	13.515
2000	1.104	1.104	4.708	12.718

YEAR	<G1> QSP@	<G1> BSP@	<G1> BSP85@	<G1> NSPF@
1991	22.307	-14.747	-28.419	-14.961
1992	17.531	22.005	5.278	18.955
1993	14.483	22.641	8.251	18.632
1994	5.802	11.051	6.723	10.598
1995	5.799	12.498	10.020	12.548
1996	6.305	11.668	10.269	11.723
1997	8.378	13.690	9.927	13.885
1998	10.150	15.143	10.610	14.690
1999	14.089	19.718	8.491	19.664
2000	13.551	17.642	12.686	17.492

YEAR	<G1> NSPF_HH@	<G1> GUMER_U@	<G1> QSP85@	<G1> YVPE@
1991	-13.608	-132.949	10.647	23.091
1992	21.567	56.145	8.378	18.048
1993	17.427	-62.845	7.424	9.937
1994	9.744	-2.189	1.801	4.864
1995	10.275	-55.797	2.159	5.635
1996	12.445	103.786	3.344	4.795
1997	14.558	51.918	4.172	7.168
1998	14.778	12.836	5.422	8.493
1999	15.026	-181.285	5.149	9.371
2000	17.302	94.663	8.222	12.311

YEAR	<G1> D@	<G1> DAN85_ST@	<G1> DAU85_P@	<G1> DBA85_PR@
1991	7.600	-5.345	110.592	-3.233
1992	9.476	-2.898	35.910	-4.338
1993	11.750	-1.248	16.999	-4.174
1994	11.073	-0.253	8.189	-4.016
1995	10.992	0.324	2.861	-3.881
1996	10.802	0.658	-0.877	-3.753
1997	11.209	0.892	-3.791	-3.614
1998	11.938	1.088	-6.237	-3.444
1999	13.719	1.305	-8.432	-3.225
2000	14.607	1.512	-10.495	-2.940

YEAR	<G1> KAP85_ST@	<G1> KAPM85_ST@	<G1> KAU85_PR@	<G1> KBA85_PR@
1991	6.975	7.446	7.756	3.295
1992	6.340	6.649	9.582	2.789
1993	5.337	5.821	9.345	2.437
1994	4.180	4.744	8.213	1.976
1995	3.484	3.825	7.491	1.740
1996	3.124	3.301	7.196	1.670
1997	3.211	3.168	7.421	1.754
1998	3.478	3.347	7.867	1.955
1999	4.036	3.762	8.537	2.226
2000	4.402	4.223	9.224	2.545

YEAR	<G1> KAP85@	<G1> KBAM85_PR@	<G1> KAUM85_PR@	<G1> KAUMA85PR@
1991	4.806	5.230	7.699	-3.071
1992	4.798	3.036	8.706	35.883
1993	4.431	2.612	9.455	21.616
1994	3.772	2.204	8.754	30.504
1995	3.402	1.857	7.838	25.811
1996	3.280	1.705	7.338	22.672
1997	3.451	1.713	7.312	34.141
1998	3.783	1.855	7.652	29.182
1999	4.275	2.092	8.215	26.250
2000	4.777	2.387	8.895	24.451

YEAR	<G1> MIAU85@	<G1> MD85@	<G1> KAPAM85@	<G1> M@
1991	89.684	89.678	5.273	97.264
1992	7.405	32.471	5.215	13.619
1993	18.022	15.867	4.352	6.824
1994	7.448	5.083	4.610	0.144
1995	10.472	-0.522	4.249	-2.208
1996	9.903	-4.001	4.129	-1.069
1997	8.769	-5.186	5.826	0.134
1998	8.279	-5.370	6.229	1.352
1999	6.846	-2.754	6.798	2.819
2000	8.153	-2.562	7.464	4.014

YEAR	<G1> CST85@	<G1> CPR@	<G1> MR%D85@	<G1> M85@
1991	-4.327	17.127	89.676	89.677
1992	-1.988	17.347	7.521	10.744
1993	0.298	11.535	3.634	6.824
1994	1.807	5.868	-4.660	-1.819
1995	3.451	4.464	-7.267	-4.126
1996	5.348	3.374	-5.089	-3.009
1997	7.410	4.575	-3.142	-1.830
1998	9.648	5.844	-1.473	-0.635
1999	11.794	6.896	0.150	0.803
2000	14.239	8.903	1.398	1.975

YEAR	<G1> CST@	<G1> CPR85@	<G1> C85@	<G1> C@
1991	21.408	3.836	1.320	18.446
1992	12.652	2.824	1.424	15.864
1993	12.863	0.394	0.367	11.943
1994	6.795	-1.077	-0.267	6.155
1995	5.892	0.818	1.573	4.909
1996	7.357	1.699	2.765	4.626
1997	12.366	2.730	4.132	7.089
1998	15.639	3.429	5.350	9.160
1999	25.457	1.323	4.690	13.553
2000	20.784	4.085	7.571	13.610

YEAR	<G1> CPR_BSP@	<G1> CST_BSP@	<G1> IAN_ST@	<G1> DIAU_PR@
1991	37.383	42.382	0.625	344.510
1992	-3.821	-7.657	9.750	-7.812
1993	-9.056	-7.973	3.989	-16.010
1994	-4.668	-3.833	-5.856	-34.789
1995	-7.142	-5.872	-4.133	-26.754
1996	-7.427	-3.860	-0.574	-24.751
1997	-8.017	-1.165	10.305	14.541
1998	-8.077	0.430	15.612	11.135
1999	-10.710	4.794	26.355	58.827
2000	-7.429	2.671	19.804	9.999

YEAR	<G1> IAU85_PR@	<G1> IAU_PR@	<G1> IAN85_ST@	<G1> IBA_PR@
1991	114.003	112.291	-5.339	6.250
1992	34.663	48.867	-2.830	6.469
1993	12.667	27.512	-8.819	5.348
1994	3.247	14.070	-14.212	-11.375
1995	1.279	9.034	-10.179	-6.653
1996	0.658	6.235	-5.262	-0.519
1997	1.659	6.722	4.651	10.305
1998	2.082	7.000	9.086	17.151
1999	3.326	10.391	15.671	28.346
2000	4.019	10.354	11.001	21.030

YEAR	<G1> IAN85@	<G1> IAN@	<G1> IBA85_PR@	<G1> IANST_BSP@
1991	30.561	35.843	-3.233	18.052
1992	12.397	26.516	-11.245	-10.050
1993	3.431	17.059	-9.246	-15.208
1994	-3.381	4.381	-14.695	-15.225
1995	-2.268	3.747	-9.000	-14.784
1996	-0.658	4.026	-2.627	-10.962
1997	2.553	7.839	4.684	-2.977
1998	4.415	10.050	10.211	0.407
1999	6.719	16.200	12.956	5.543
2000	7.037	14.143	14.062	1.838

YEAR	<G1> IBAPR_BSP@	<G1> IAUPR_BSP@	<G1> IN_ST@	<G1> OUT_ST@
1991	24.600	149.040	62.864	47.240
1992	-12.733	22.000	14.878	7.727
1993	-14.100	3.972	8.486	8.165
1994	-20.195	2.718	5.518	5.761
1995	-17.023	-3.079	5.924	6.317
1996	-10.914	-4.865	1.821	6.610
1997	-2.978	-6.129	6.271	8.646
1998	1.744	-7.072	7.974	10.017
1999	7.207	-7.791	9.315	14.893
2000	2.880	-6.195	10.396	13.006

YEAR	<G1> FS_ST@	<G1> TDIR@	<G1> TD_HH@	<G1> TIND@
1991	-135.511	-23.654	-23.651	-23.653
1992	391.308	56.936	57.168	34.713
1993	12.182	26.039	25.916	43.970
1994	2.811	19.812	19.606	7.778
1995	1.423	18.343	18.086	7.275
1996	-55.658	18.157	17.855	6.251
1997	-62.284	19.100	18.764	7.896
1998	-161.905	18.814	18.419	14.592
1999	833.307	19.422	18.977	17.937
2000	57.862	19.234	18.714	15.447

YEAR	<G1> TDLOST%P@	<G1> TI_GEW@	<G1> TD_KOST@	<G1> TD_KEST@
1991	11.628	-	-	-
1992	42.924	-39.322	13.284	56.713
1993	28.437	202.842	130.480	384.283
1994	22.171	15.211	41.949	41.755
1995	20.053	31.618	34.281	36.169
1996	20.884	4.616	16.793	9.151
1997	22.101	7.768	11.600	4.431
1998	21.185	17.537	12.923	11.952
1999	19.713	71.085	36.329	68.042
2000	19.900	30.345	27.022	42.603

YEAR	<G1> TI_UST@	<G1> SUB@	<G1> T@	<G1> TI_MIN@
1991	-24.091	-4.455	-23.653	-23.531
1992	75.651	-1.745	42.689	13.189
1993	73.197	0.664	36.892	12.294
1994	7.798	1.320	12.151	11.551
1995	6.348	1.818	11.572	10.924
1996	5.943	1.082	11.154	10.389
1997	8.492	0.842	12.801	9.927
1998	18.782	1.222	16.543	9.525
1999	20.835	2.015	18.637	9.172
2000	18.269	1.677	17.243	8.861

YEAR	<G1> BST_KST@	<G1> TSB@	<G1> GSV_BLG@	<G1> GEW_BUV@
1991	-132.949	6.351	8.398	-133.129
1992	56.145	26.141	22.702	60.599
1993	-62.845	18.938	11.435	-77.150
1994	-6.102	10.329	10.888	-37.968
1995	-55.797	10.686	11.611	-251.201
1996	86.804	11.941	13.815	-17.552
1997	51.918	13.861	15.662	12.777
1998	12.836	15.300	15.259	122.144
1999	-181.285	15.995	14.763	385.975
2000	94.663	16.397	16.206	55.462

YEAR	<G1> GEW_LSST@	<G1> BMG_UST@	<G1> ZINS_GK@	<G1> ZINS_ST@
1991	0.000	22.170	17.500	17.500
1992	0.000	19.289	30.330	30.325
1993	0.000	13.553	39.339	39.336
1994	0.000	5.264	45.690	45.691
1995	0.000	4.046	50.283	50.279
1996	0.000	3.860	28.937	28.934
1997	0.000	6.956	17.275	17.272
1998	0.000	9.310	11.014	11.014
1999	0.000	14.741	6.891	6.890
2000	0.000	14.186	3.992	3.995

YEAR	<G1> SB_UH@	<G1> SB_ST@	<G1> SB_PR@	<G1> SB_AG@
1991	29.000	28.999	28.997	28.458
1992	19.899	18.633	18.749	21.135
1993	10.387	9.158	9.301	13.262
1994	10.014	8.983	9.104	9.729
1995	10.846	9.967	10.074	8.574
1996	13.128	12.397	12.493	9.319
1997	15.077	14.515	14.595	10.965
1998	14.803	14.391	14.453	11.946
1999	14.410	14.114	14.162	12.440
2000	15.930	15.752	15.787	13.665

YEAR	<G1> TR_HH_EMP@	<G1> SL_ZU_ST@	<G1> SL_HH_ST@	<G1> SL_ST@
1991	277.910	-130.834	375.402	250.298
1992	8.905	-97.493	9.545	4.480
1993	3.049	-1590.209	2.799	4.480
1994	3.416	116.893	3.215	4.481
1995	3.453	73.310	3.255	4.481
1996	0.464	67.499	-0.199	4.481
1997	2.197	58.081	1.783	4.481
1998	2.312	42.829	1.904	4.481
1999	2.425	34.337	2.025	4.482
2000	2.536	34.154	2.145	4.482

YEAR	<G1> TR%T@	<G1> TR_HH_GEL@	<G1> TR_HH_R@	<G1> PBSP@
1991	-162.472	31.364	-	19.100
1992	-60.608	27.412	67.503	15.889
1993	-130.772	14.064	30.252	13.293
1994	373.316	11.630	16.161	4.055
1995	86.062	11.231	9.340	2.252
1996	76.012	12.363	5.261	1.268
1997	49.112	13.772	2.915	3.423
1998	37.337	13.637	1.646	4.099
1999	31.384	13.742	1.726	10.348
2000	30.244	15.043	1.999	4.398

YEAR	<G1> PCST@	<G1> PCPR@	<G1> PMD_PBSP@	<G1> PIAN_ST@
1991	26.900	12.800	-13.890	6.300
1992	14.936	14.124	-11.499	12.946
1993	12.528	11.097	-9.474	14.047
1994	4.900	7.020	-1.437	9.740
1995	2.360	3.617	0.301	6.731
1996	1.907	1.647	1.276	4.949
1997	4.614	1.796	-0.835	5.403
1998	5.463	2.335	-1.478	5.983
1999	12.222	5.500	-7.058	9.236
2000	5.730	4.628	-1.760	7.931

YEAR	<G1> PIBA_PR@	<G1> PIAU_PR@	<G1> M1@	<G1> BLG_EH85@
1991	9.800	-0.800	42.379	11.436
1992	19.958	10.548	26.310	24.480
1993	16.081	13.175	17.122	4.759
1994	3.891	10.482	7.188	7.325
1995	2.579	7.658	5.831	9.551
1996	2.164	5.540	4.699	10.856
1997	5.369	4.981	4.822	8.552
1998	6.297	4.818	5.265	7.614
1999	13.625	6.838	5.538	1.370
2000	6.109	6.091	5.128	7.176

YEAR	<G1> BLG@	<G1> BUA@	<G1> BUV@	<G1> BUA_EH85@
1991	5.936	9.318	-132.948	14.993
1992	21.487	21.425	58.862	24.417
1993	10.332	10.847	-77.514	5.249
1994	9.790	9.779	-39.260	7.315
1995	10.506	10.158	-250.418	9.207
1996	12.688	12.092	-17.977	10.268
1997	14.517	13.903	11.912	7.970
1998	14.117	13.752	119.894	7.270
1999	13.626	13.430	381.103	1.195
2000	15.055	14.827	53.919	6.963

YEAR	<G1> BESCH@	<G1> BESVOL@	<G1> M_R	<G1> M_O
1991	-19.140	-20.181	12.409	123.100
1992	-14.673	-15.785	3.420	40.607
1993	-5.793	-7.038	4.894	9.900
1994	-0.357	-1.690	4.564	11.668
1995	0.000	-1.351	4.321	12.376
1996	3.220	0.381	4.009	16.107
1997	3.466	2.003	4.130	13.781
1998	3.350	1.867	4.077	14.334
1999	3.079	1.579	4.045	14.745
2000	2.830	2.830	4.036	13.935

YEAR	<G1> X_W@	<G1> M_R@	<G1> M_W@	<G1> X_O
1991	123.100	-28.764	140.900	140.900
1992	40.607	-15.638	16.679	16.679
1993	9.900	11.632	6.467	6.467
1994	11.668	24.816	-1.776	-1.776
1995	12.376	41.255	-6.507	-6.507
1996	16.107	6.541	-2.206	-2.206
1997	13.781	35.896	-5.688	-5.688
1998	14.334	22.689	-3.653	-3.653
1999	14.745	34.112	-6.528	-6.528
2000	13.935	28.284	-6.387	-6.387

3.6.2 Exogenous variables

General remarks:
- Variables for East Germany with @ at the end of symbol
- <G1> for growth rates

YEAR	<G1> BUV_HH	<G1> BUA_EH	<G1> BLG_ST	<G1> BEI_GSV
1978	7.670	6.433	6.638	0.000
1979	6.718	7.068	7.154	-0.617
1980	-1.751	7.712	7.897	0.621
1981	-0.211	5.848	5.874	2.778
1982	4.211	3.929	2.983	2.102
1983	11.092	4.031	3.065	2.647
1984	9.571	3.847	1.470	-0.573
1985	6.760	4.381	3.515	2.017
1986	11.374	4.298	4.691	0.000
1987	1.751	3.919	4.240	0.565
1988	10.573	2.833	2.381	0.843
1989	8.898	4.132	2.563	0.000
1990	11.401	7.060	5.988	-1.114
1991	1.850	7.945	7.352	2.324
1992	4.000	4.594	4.000	1.000
1993	4.000	4.998	4.000	1.000
1994	4.000	5.000	4.000	1.000
1995	4.000	6.001	4.000	1.000
1996	4.000	6.499	4.000	1.000
1997	4.000	6.261	4.000	1.000
1998	4.000	6.740	4.000	1.000
1999	4.000	8.349	4.000	1.000
2000	4.000	4.683	4.000	1.000

YEAR	<G1> CAPIFO	<G1> ET	<G1> EH	<G1> GEW_SATZ
1978	-1.629	0.811	-0.896	0.932
1979	3.963	1.651	-1.167	0.000
1980	-2.774	1.527	-0.858	1.538
1981	-4.127	-0.096	-0.962	0.909
1982	-3.292	-1.139	0.312	1.802
1983	2.579	-1.414	-0.409	2.950
1984	2.936	0.175	-0.428	0.860
1985	4.439	0.758	-1.384	1.136
1986	0.499	1.380	-0.643	0.843
1987	-0.413	0.731	-0.700	0.000
1988	2.883	0.770	0.179	0.836
1989	2.710	1.443	-1.217	0.000
1990	0.674	2.644	-2.120	0.552
1991	-2.431	1.734	-1.863	0.549
1992	-3.314	0.452	-1.301	1.093
1993	-1.891	-0.635	-1.274	1.622
1994	0.000	0.225	-1.290	2.128
1995	0.602	0.517	-1.307	0.521
1996	0.000	0.515	-0.132	0.518
1997	0.599	1.024	-0.133	0.773
1998	0.000	1.014	0.000	1.023
1999	-1.190	1.003	-0.199	1.013
2000	0.000	0.993	0.000	1.003

YEAR	<G1> IVOR	<G1> KST_SATZ	<G1> IN_SONS	<G1> GUOER_N
1978	3.433	0.000	13.504	-44.224
1979	218.119	0.000	3.661	54.120
1980	-48.826	0.000	11.209	177.962
1981	-189.635	0.000	8.038	57.343
1982	52.038	0.000	5.301	-9.731
1983	-90.648	0.000	-1.159	-25.750
1984	-454.667	0.000	1.324	27.385
1985	-76.504	0.000	2.663	-2.902
1986	133.600	0.000	3.866	-67.537
1987	-119.178	0.000	3.116	65.869
1988	-1939.286	0.000	8.668	-85.455
1989	55.437	0.000	4.280	148.855
1990	-80.450	-10.714	5.063	-51.431
1991	-375.080	0.000	16.881	1159.368
1992	60.279	0.000	30.113	-41.491
1993	-96.377	0.000	4.500	-14.286
1994	0.000	-4.000	4.500	-16.667
1995	0.000	0.000	4.500	-20.000
1996	0.000	-8.333	0.000	0.000
1997	0.000	0.000	0.000	0.000
1998	0.000	0.000	0.000	0.000
1999	0.000	0.000	0.000	0.000
2000	0.000	0.000	0.000	0.000

YEAR	<G1> MWST_SATZ	<G1> OUT_SONS	<G1> LSST_SATZ	<G1> PIAU
1978	9.091	4.909	-3.341	3.026
1979	4.167	7.525	4.052	2.937
1980	4.000	9.787	0.000	4.294
1981	0.000	4.801	0.000	5.013
1982	0.000	4.524	0.000	4.861
1983	3.846	-3.237	0.000	2.969
1984	3.704	6.784	0.000	2.542
1985	0.000	1.311	0.000	2.355
1986	0.000	-0.434	0.000	0.884
1987	0.000	4.126	0.000	0.416
1988	0.000	7.683	0.000	1.034
1989	0.000	4.964	0.000	2.362
1990	0.000	4.499	0.000	1.675
1991	0.000	28.515	0.000	2.471
1992	0.000	-22.729	0.000	2.056
1993	7.143	3.500	0.000	1.526
1994	0.000	3.500	0.000	2.000
1995	0.000	3.500	0.000	2.000
1996	0.000	5.500	0.000	2.000
1997	0.000	5.500	0.000	2.000
1998	0.000	5.500	0.000	2.000
1999	0.000	5.500	0.000	2.000
2000	0.000	5.500	0.000	2.000

YEAR	<G1> PMD	<G1> R_WPUM	<G1> PM	<G1> PMIAU
1978	4.433	-4.688	-1.685	-1.685
1979	6.732	24.590	8.273	8.273
1980	9.850	13.158	12.305	12.305
1981	10.018	23.256	11.595	11.595
1982	1.640	-14.151	2.769	2.769
1983	2.424	-12.088	0.781	0.781
1984	5.548	-2.500	4.707	4.707
1985	3.135	-11.538	2.390	2.390
1986	-0.674	-13.043	-10.656	-10.656
1987	1.257	-3.333	-4.284	-4.284
1988	4.141	3.448	1.907	1.907
1989	4.585	18.333	4.831	4.831
1990	3.637	25.352	-0.157	-0.157
1991	3.594	-2.247	2.571	2.571
1992	2.500	-4.598	2.608	2.608
1993	2.500	-3.614	10.417	10.417
1994	2.500	-2.500	3.000	3.000
1995	2.500	-1.282	3.000	3.000
1996	2.500	-1.299	1.000	1.000
1997	2.500	-1.316	1.000	1.000
1998	2.500	0.000	1.000	1.000
1999	2.500	-1.333	1.000	1.000
2000	2.500	-2.703	1.000	1.000

YEAR	<G1> SELB	<G1> SL_HA_ST	<G1> SB_EA	<G1> SL_HH_H
1978	-1.927	4.842	4.000	6.061
1979	-2.394	6.252	11.538	5.000
1980	-0.566	6.188	24.138	7.483
1981	-1.139	8.584	-5.556	11.392
1982	-1.280	6.131	-17.647	3.409
1983	-1.037	1.306	-7.143	6.044
1984	-0.393	1.219	-0.000	4.663
1985	-0.263	2.357	-11.538	5.446
1986	0.527	3.726	-4.348	6.103
1987	-1.115	4.919	-18.182	5.310
1988	-0.497	4.530	-5.556	5.462
1989	0.333	3.929	-0.000	5.578
1990	0.432	5.253	782.353	6.038
1991	0.562	6.067	226.667	7.117
1992	0.296	4.500	2.041	4.500
1993	-0.492	3.500	-0.000	4.500
1994	0.000	3.500	-0.000	4.500
1995	0.000	6.000	-0.000	4.500
1996	0.000	6.000	-0.000	4.500
1997	0.000	6.000	-0.000	4.500
1998	0.000	6.000	-0.000	4.500
1999	0.000	6.000	-0.000	4.500
2000	0.000	6.000	-0.000	4.500

YEAR	<G1> SL_W_ST	<G1> SL_W	<G1> SL_U	<G1> SL_HN_ST
1978	4.439	3.333	4.603	-
1979	2.461	-12.903	7.113	-
1980	4.585	3.704	8.779	-
1981	7.307	7.143	6.260	-
1982	3.502	10.000	4.236	-
1983	1.692	6.061	3.783	-
1984	7.948	5.714	3.645	-
1985	-3.082	10.811	8.901	-
1986	3.180	0.000	9.530	-
1987	5.308	12.195	6.807	-
1988	3.577	-2.174	5.760	-
1989	42.229	24.444	5.962	-
1990	-26.380	44.643	6.022	-
1991	4.498	-18.519	5.651	-
1992	3.400	4.000	4.500	23.672
1993	3.400	4.000	4.500	-1.227
1994	3.400	4.000	4.500	0.000
1995	3.400	4.000	4.500	0.000
1996	3.400	4.000	4.500	-13.043
1997	3.400	4.000	4.500	-7.143
1998	3.400	4.000	4.500	-7.692
1999	3.400	4.000	4.500	-8.333
2000	3.400	4.000	4.500	-9.091

YEAR	<G1> TI_SONS	<G1> TVS_GK	<G1> TD_SONS	<G1> TR_SONS
1978	5.046	12.886	-0.129	10.502
1979	6.580	11.630	-0.364	12.113
1980	-2.966	13.209	-2.229	10.431
1981	1.818	16.433	-7.303	9.107
1982	4.530	12.683	-4.017	4.555
1983	7.866	9.253	-1.919	4.950
1984	4.017	6.821	-2.439	7.911
1985	0.868	5.947	3.035	5.076
1986	3.935	5.364	4.506	6.249
1987	3.541	5.974	3.701	6.134
1988	4.305	6.385	5.649	6.850
1989	8.573	2.860	9.748	7.445
1990	3.759	6.701	0.734	9.505
1991	10.963	10.926	16.927	11.168
1992	22.099	9.836	25.867	5.000
1993	5.000	9.836	6.000	5.000
1994	5.000	9.836	6.000	5.000
1995	5.000	9.836	6.000	5.000
1996	2.500	4.564	3.000	5.000
1997	2.500	4.564	3.000	5.000
1998	2.500	4.564	3.000	5.000
1999	2.500	4.564	3.000	5.000
2000	2.500	4.564	3.000	5.000

YEAR	<G1> VOL_MIN	<G1> YUVST	<G1> ZINS_GSV	<G1> X_R
1978	5.511	15.953	-	-
1979	3.412	18.868	0.000	-
1980	1.414	10.780	100.000	-
1981	-3.851	23.940	300.000	-
1982	1.865	45.472	-75.000	-
1983	2.102	1.755	-50.000	-
1984	2.922	4.165	100.000	-
1985	-0.258	8.529	0.000	-
1986	5.433	-2.476	0.000	-
1987	3.620	-20.189	50.000	-
1988	3.730	-26.442	0.000	-
1989	1.484	58.120	0.000	-
1990	4.668	10.111	0.000	-
1991	3.000	-2.743	33.333	1.560
1992	3.000	28.860	12.500	1.279
1993	3.000	-8.986	11.111	-0.755
1994	3.000	1.880	0.000	6.500
1995	3.000	1.880	10.000	6.500
1996	3.000	1.880	0.000	6.500
1997	3.000	1.880	0.000	6.500
1998	3.000	1.880	0.000	6.500
1999	3.000	1.880	9.091	6.500
2000	3.000	1.880	0.000	6.500

YEAR	<G1> ZINS_HH_KR	<G1> ZU_NL_ST	<G1> ZINSHHKR@	<G1> ZINS_GSV@
1978	8.333	0.000	-	-
1979	25.962	0.000	-	-
1980	43.839	0.000	-	-
1981	26.080	0.000	-	-
1982	11.064	0.000	-	-
1983	-3.303	0.000	-	-
1984	-0.560	0.000	-	-
1985	-0.507	0.000	-	-
1986	1.471	0.000	-	-
1987	-2.510	0.000	-	-
1988	3.947	0.000	-	-
1989	7.100	0.000	-	-
1990	14.800	0.000	-	-
1991	19.964	132.196	41.414	16.667
1992	20.896	23.672	26.190	14.286
1993	11.111	-1.227	13.208	25.000
1994	11.111	0.000	16.667	50.000
1995	10.000	0.000	14.286	33.333
1996	9.091	-13.043	12.500	12.500
1997	8.333	-7.143	11.111	0.000
1998	7.692	-7.692	10.000	11.111
1999	7.143	-8.333	9.091	0.000
2000	6.667	-9.091	8.333	20.000

YEAR	<G1> ALPHA	<G1> BETA	<G1> BLG_ST@	<G1> BEI_GSV@
1991	94.239	22.174	21.408	2.324
1992	33.538	2.646	10.000	1.000
1993	4.458	-0.334	10.000	1.000
1994	6.318	-1.917	10.000	1.000
1995	7.143	-4.396	10.000	1.000
1996	10.667	-1.149	10.000	1.000
1997	8.434	-5.814	10.000	1.000
1998	8.889	-4.938	10.000	1.000
1999	9.184	-9.091	10.000	1.000
2000	8.411	-10.000	10.000	1.000

YEAR	<G1> BUA_EH@	<G1> EH@	<G1> BUV_HH@	<G1> CAPIFO@
1991	36.957	-1.287	-132.948	-10.000
1992	44.185	-1.304	17.104	25.000
1993	19.239	-1.321	-103.746	11.111
1994	11.667	-1.339	83.176	20.000
1995	11.667	-1.351	83.176	16.667
1996	11.667	-2.751	83.176	14.286
1997	11.667	-1.414	83.176	25.000
1998	11.667	-1.435	83.176	20.000
1999	11.667	-1.456	83.176	16.667
2000	11.667	0.000	83.176	14.286

YEAR	<G1> GEW_SATZ@	<G1> IN_SONS@	<G1> GUOER_N@	<G1> ET@
1991	0.549	300.732	21.578	-16.529
1992	1.093	-42.955	244.293	-12.505
1993	1.622	4.500	-0.000	-4.514
1994	2.128	4.500	-0.000	0.000
1995	0.521	4.500	-0.000	0.000
1996	0.518	4.500	-15.000	3.205
1997	0.773	4.500	-23.529	3.106
1998	1.023	4.500	-23.077	3.012
1999	1.013	4.500	-30.000	2.924
2000	1.003	4.500	-28.571	2.841

YEAR	<G1> IVOR@	<G1> MWST_SATZ@	<G1> KST_SATZ@	<G1> LSST_SATZ@
1991	-126.263	0.000	0.000	0.000
1992	-88.462	0.000	0.000	0.000
1993	1733.333	7.143	0.000	0.000
1994	0.000	0.000	-4.000	0.000
1995	0.000	0.000	0.000	0.000
1996	0.000	0.000	-8.333	0.000
1997	0.000	0.000	0.000	0.000
1998	0.000	0.000	0.000	0.000
1999	0.000	0.000	0.000	0.000
2000	0.000	0.000	0.000	0.000

YEAR	<G1> PIAU@	<G1> PM@	<G1> PMD@	<G1> OUT_SONS@
1991	-0.800	4.000	2.560	33.889
1992	1.210	2.596	2.560	5.000
1993	1.992	0.000	2.560	5.000
1994	2.000	2.000	2.560	5.000
1995	2.000	2.000	2.560	5.000
1996	2.000	2.000	2.560	5.000
1997	2.000	2.000	2.560	5.000
1998	2.000	2.000	2.560	5.000
1999	2.000	2.000	2.560	5.000
2000	2.000	2.000	2.560	5.000

YEAR	<G1> SB_EA@	<G1> R_WPUM@	<G1> SELB@	<G1> PMIAU@
1991	30.159	-2.247	54.574	4.000
1992	21.951	-4.598	18.367	2.596
1993	0.000	-3.614	8.621	0.000
1994	0.000	-2.500	3.175	2.000
1995	0.000	-1.282	0.000	2.000
1996	0.000	-1.299	3.077	2.000
1997	0.000	-1.316	0.000	2.000
1998	0.000	0.000	0.000	2.000
1999	0.000	-1.333	1.493	2.000
2000	0.000	-2.703	2.941	2.000

YEAR	<G1> SL_W@	<G1> SL_U@	<G1> SL_HN_ST@	<G1> SL_HH_H@
1991	247.059	250.328	250.301	249.375
1992	4.000	4.500	4.500	4.500
1993	4.000	4.500	4.500	4.500
1994	4.000	4.500	4.500	4.500
1995	4.000	4.500	4.500	4.500
1996	4.000	4.500	4.500	4.500
1997	4.000	4.500	4.500	4.500
1998	4.000	4.500	4.500	4.500
1999	4.000	4.500	4.500	4.500
2000	4.000	4.500	4.500	4.500

YEAR	<G1> TR_SONS@	<G1> SL_W_ST@	<G1> TI_SONS@	<G1> TD_SONS@
1991	6.360	250.130	-28.078	-74.126
1992	5.000	3.400	8.000	142.529
1993	5.000	3.400	5.000	5.000
1994	5.000	3.400	5.000	5.000
1995	5.000	3.400	5.000	5.000
1996	5.000	3.400	5.000	5.000
1997	5.000	3.400	5.000	5.000
1998	5.000	3.400	5.000	5.000
1999	5.000	3.400	5.000	5.000
2000	5.000	3.400	5.000	5.000

YEAR	<G1> X_R@	<G1> YUVST@	<G1> VOL_MIN@	<G1> TVS_GK@
1991	-50.713	1050.000	5.358	15.146
1992	-25.234	-8.696	5.360	53.599
1993	31.250	-4.762	5.360	53.599
1994	19.048	12.282	5.360	53.599
1995	12.000	12.282	5.360	53.599
1996	14.286	12.282	5.360	4.564
1997	12.500	12.282	5.360	4.564
1998	11.111	12.282	5.360	4.564
1999	10.000	12.282	5.360	4.564
2000	9.091	12.282	5.360	4.564

3.7 Selected Graphs

3.7.1 Endogenous variables

3.7.2 Exogenous variables

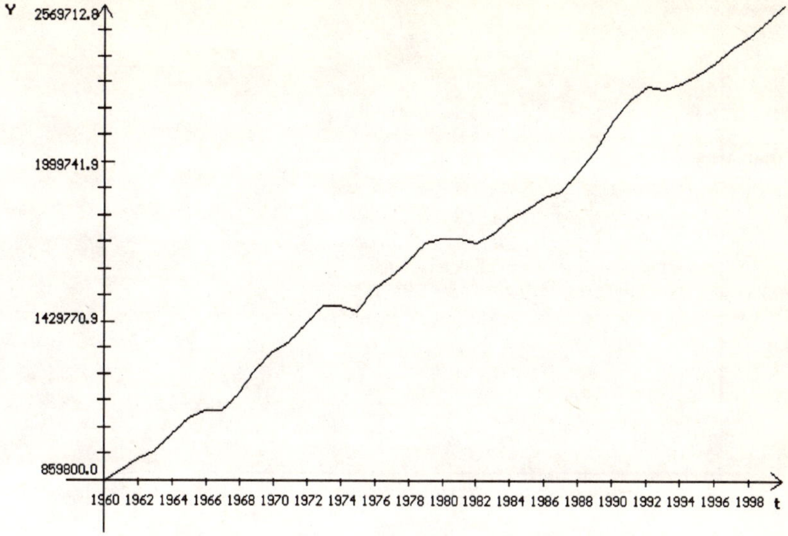

Figure 1 BSP85 Gross national product in 1985 prices

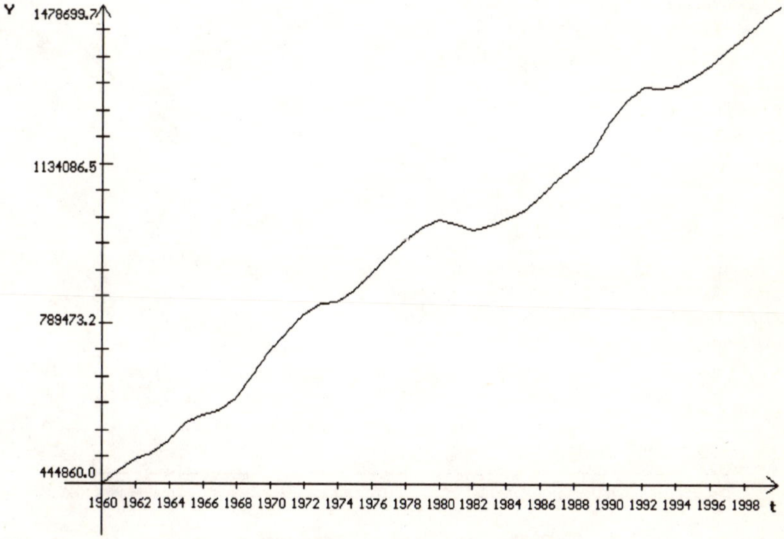

Figure 2 CPR85 Private consumption in 1985 prices

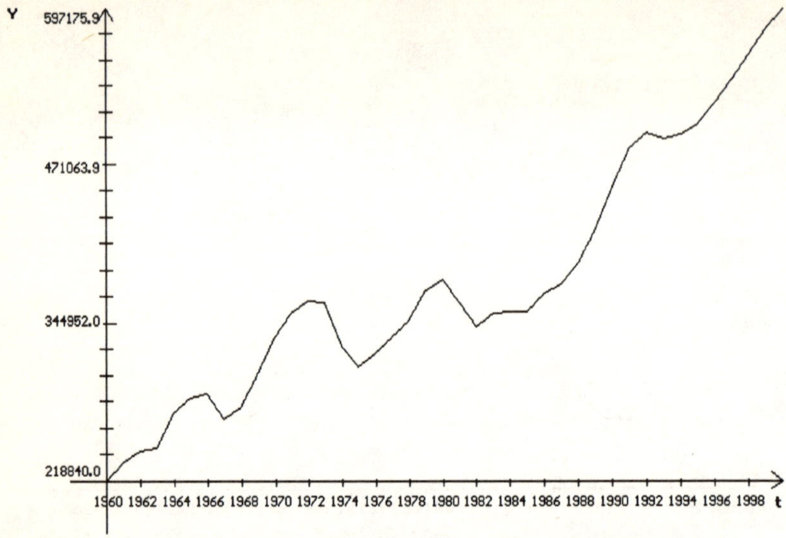

Figure 3 IAN85 Gross fixed capital formation in 1985 prices

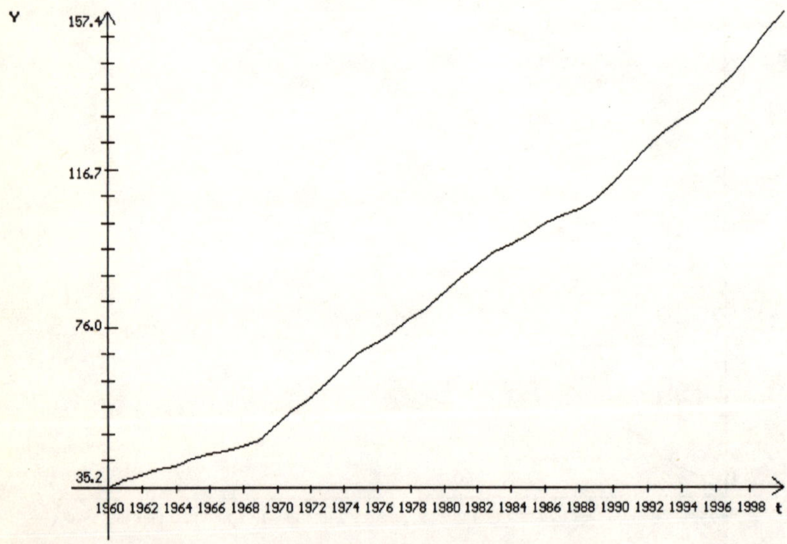

Figure 4 PBSP Price index, gross national product

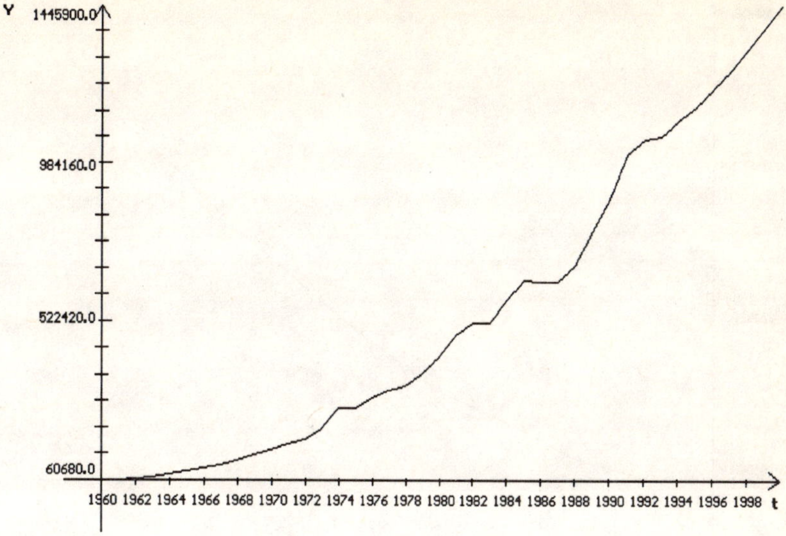

Figure 5 X Exports

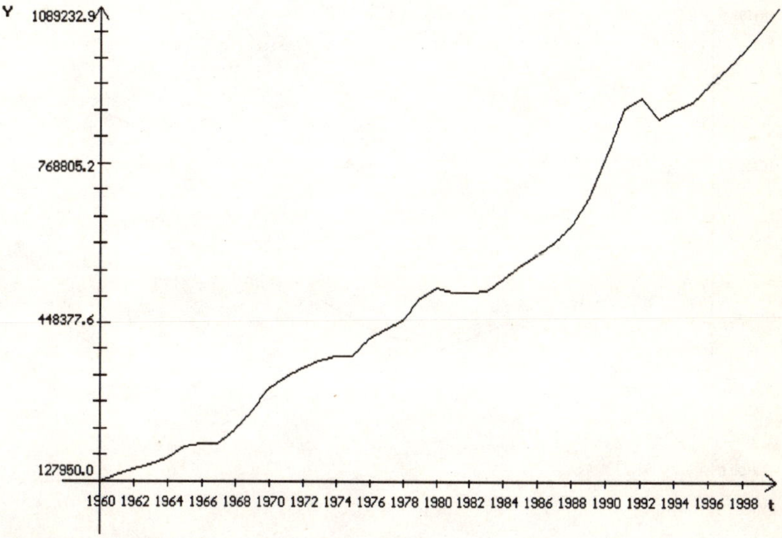

Figure 6 M85 Imports, in 1985 prices

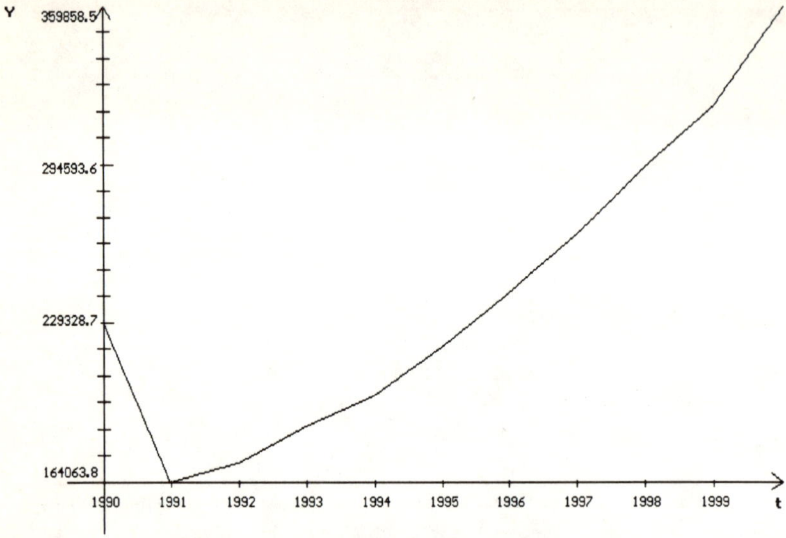

Figure 7 BSP85@ Gross national product in 1985 prices

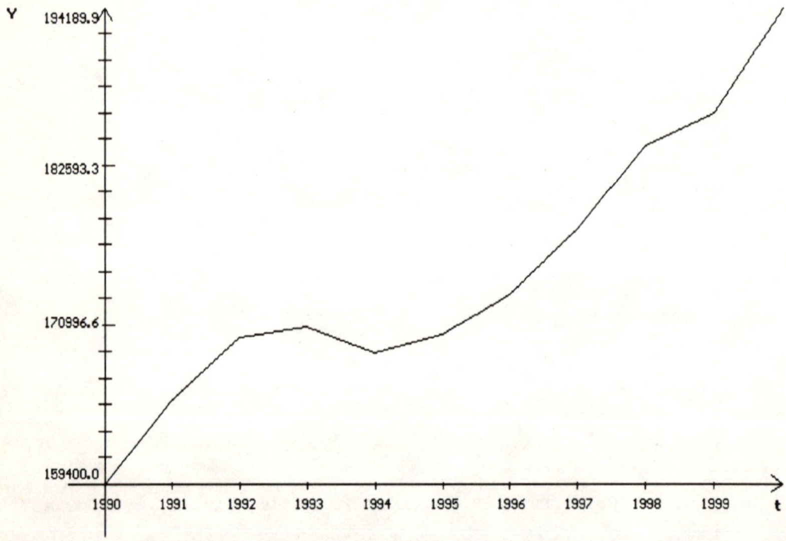

Figure 8 CPR85@ Private consumption in 1985 prices

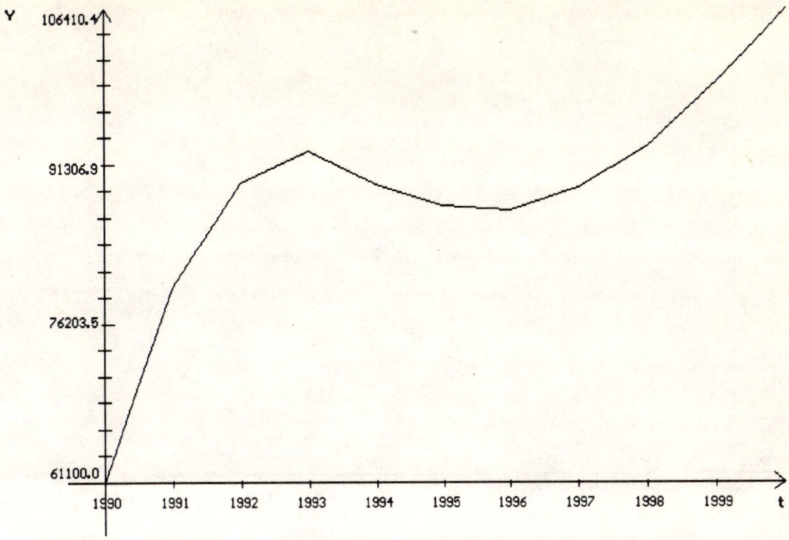

Figure 9 IAN85@ Gross fixed capital formation, in 1985 prices

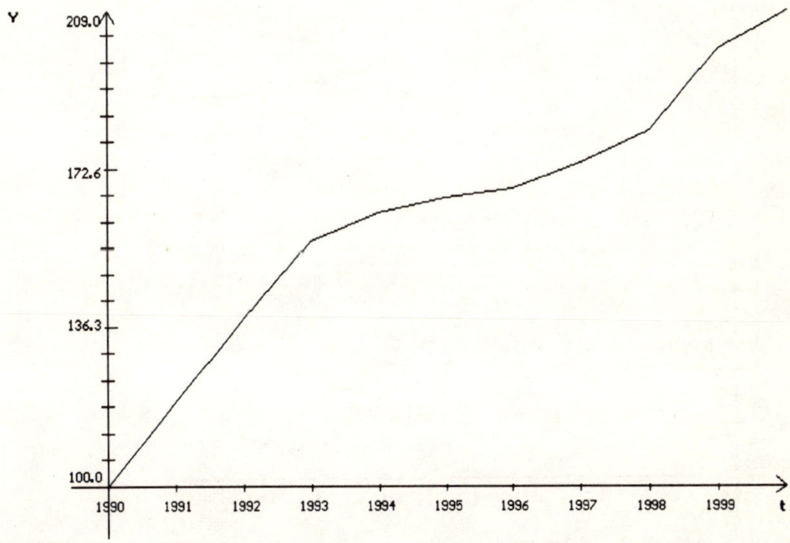

Figure 10 PBSP@ Price index, gross national product

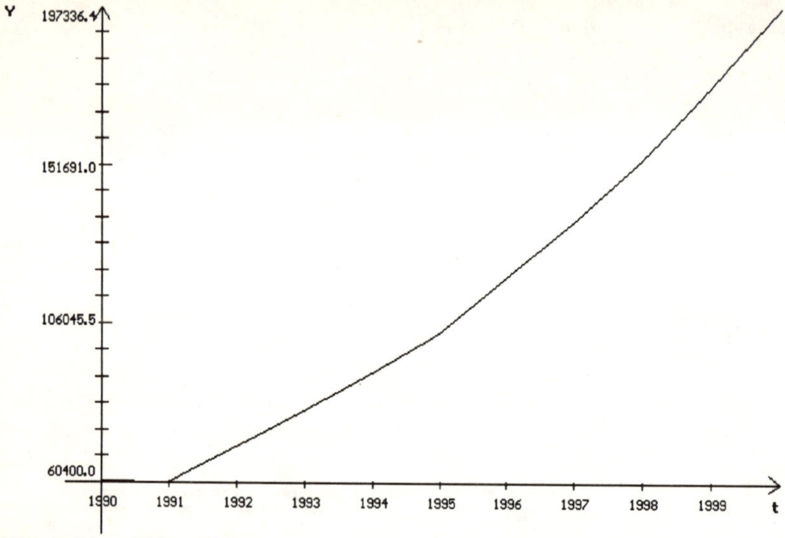

Figure 11 X@ Exports

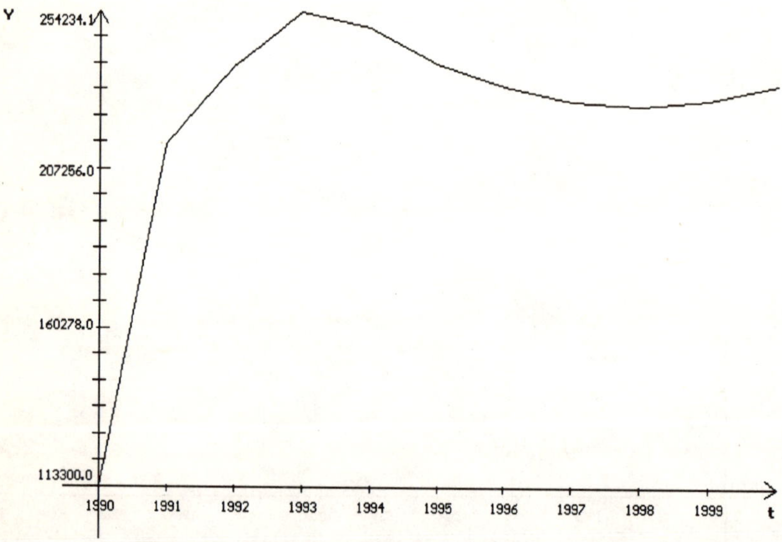

Figure 12 M85@ Imports, in 1985 prices

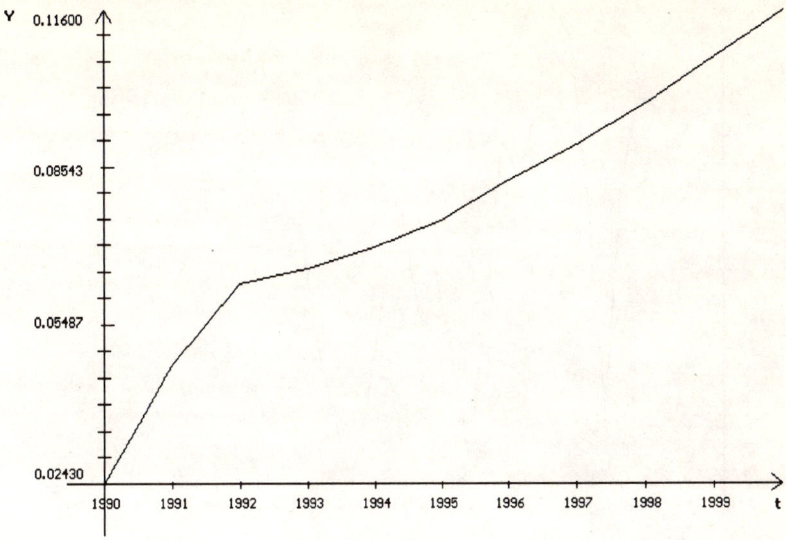

Figure 13 ALPHA Share of West German imports from East Germany to total imports

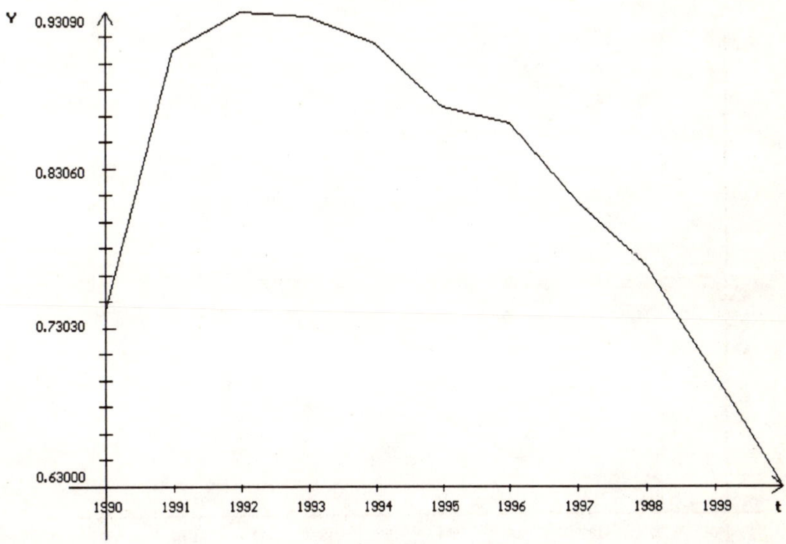

Figure 14 BETA Share of imports from West Germany to total East German imports

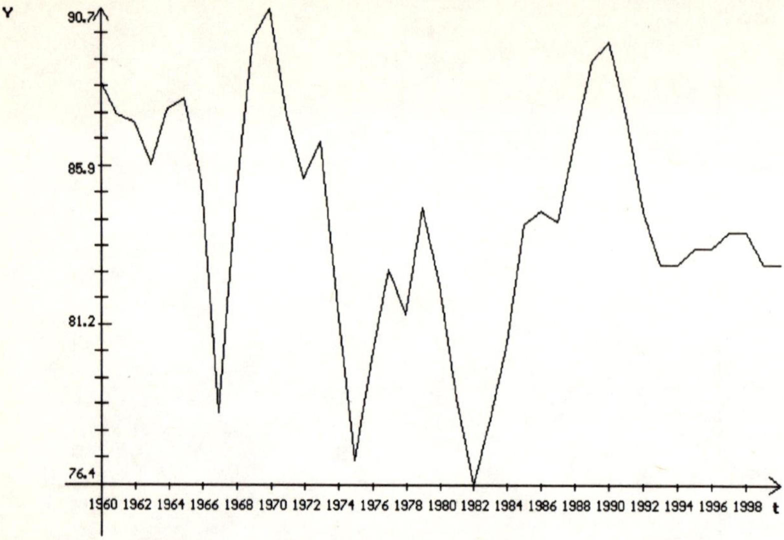

Figure 15 CAPIFO Degree of capacity utilization in the manufacturing sector

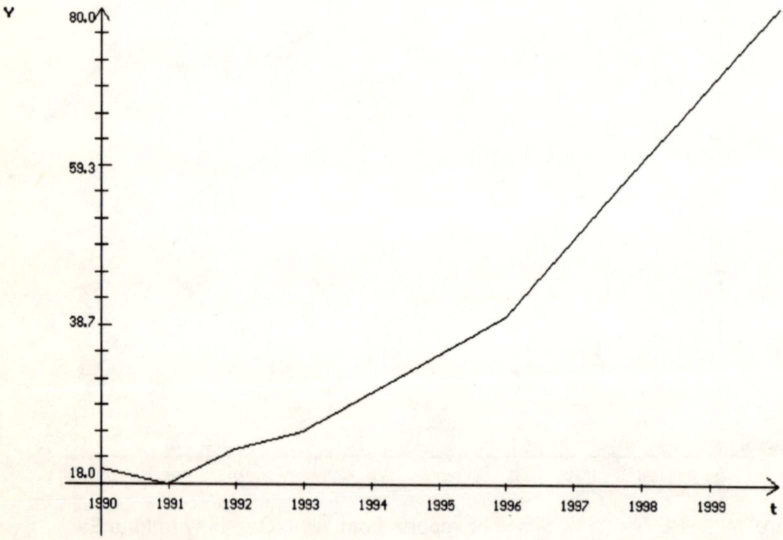

Figure 16 CAPIFO@ Degree of capacity utilization in the manufacturing sector

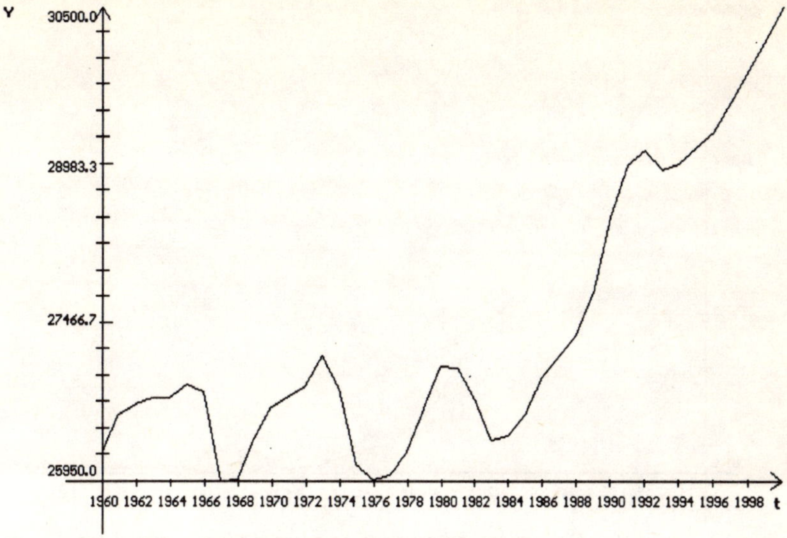

Figure 17 ET Workers (on the basis of resident status)

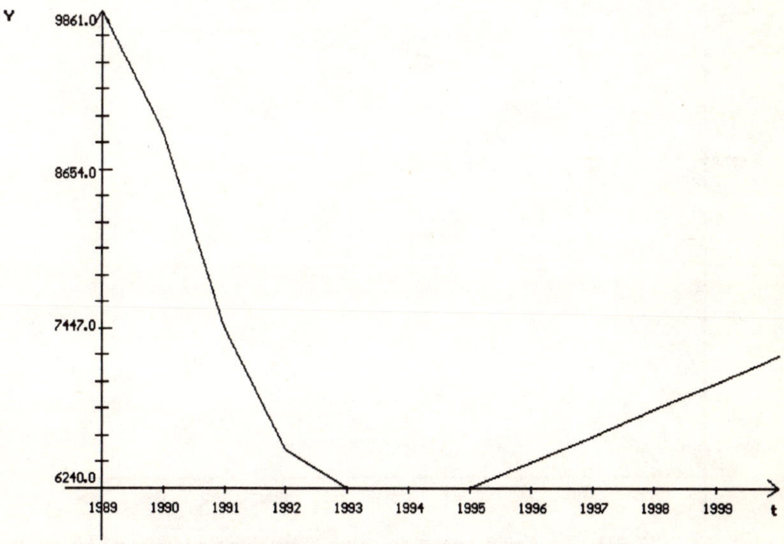

Figure 18 ET@ Workers (on the basis of resident status)

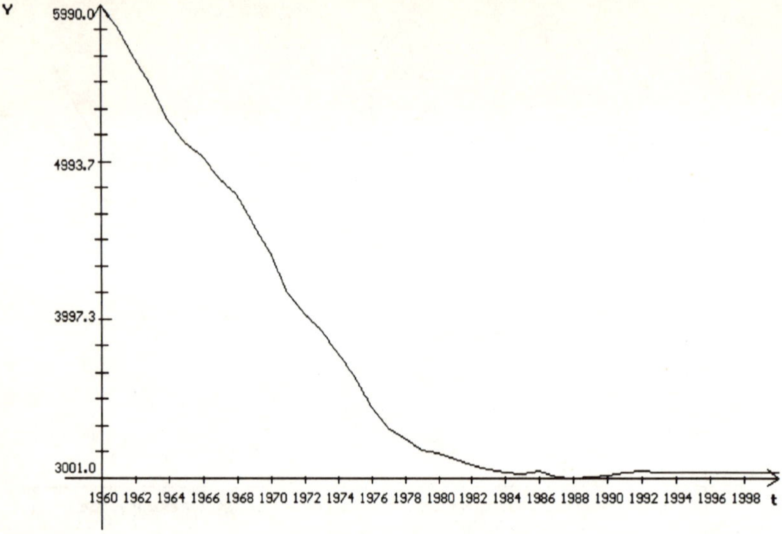

Figure 19 SELB Self employed persons and unpaid family members

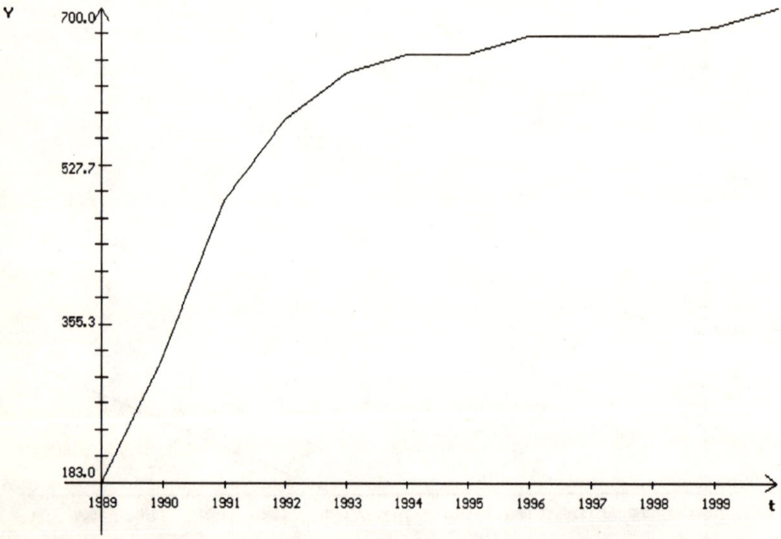

Figure 20 SELB@ Self employed persons and unpaid family members

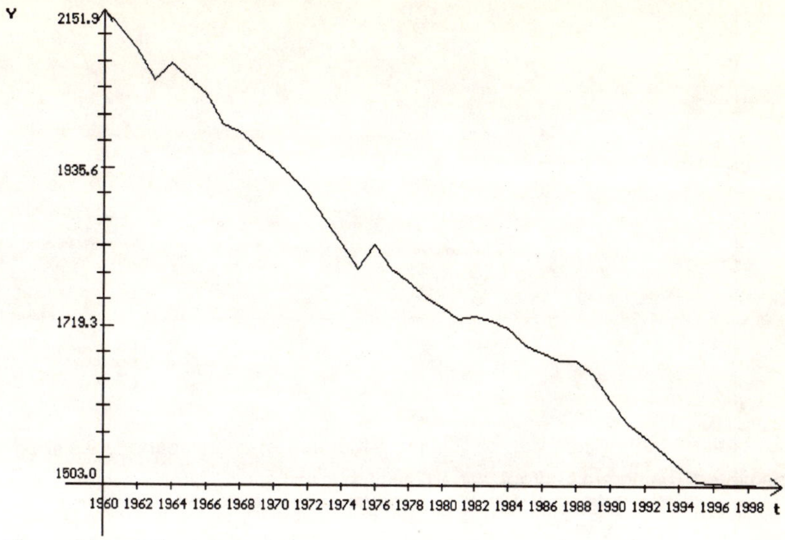

Figure 21 EH Annual average working hours

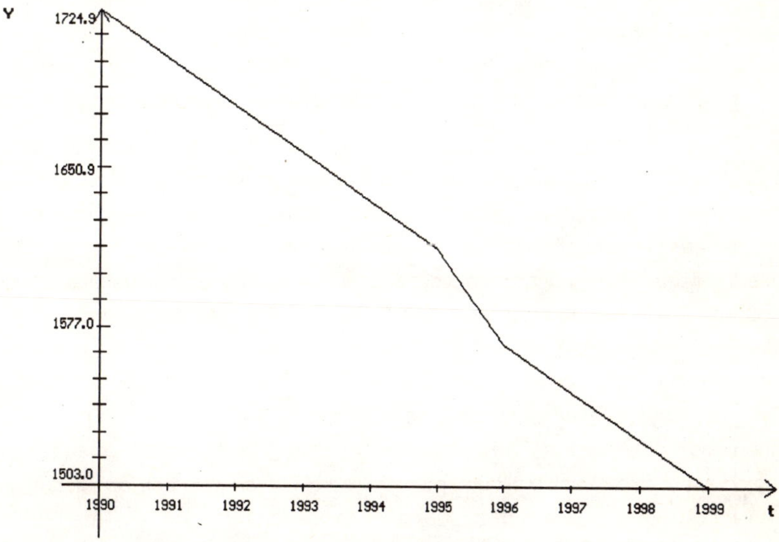

Figure 22 EH@ Annual average working hours

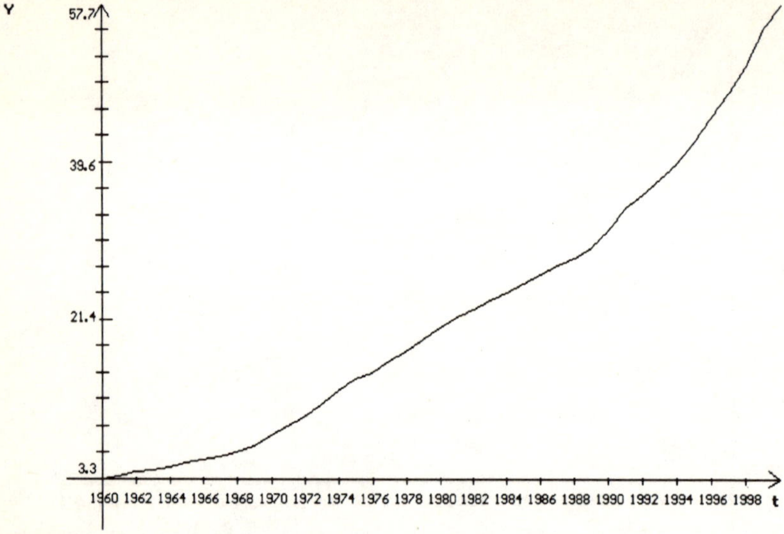

Figure 23 BUA_EH Total labour cost per hour

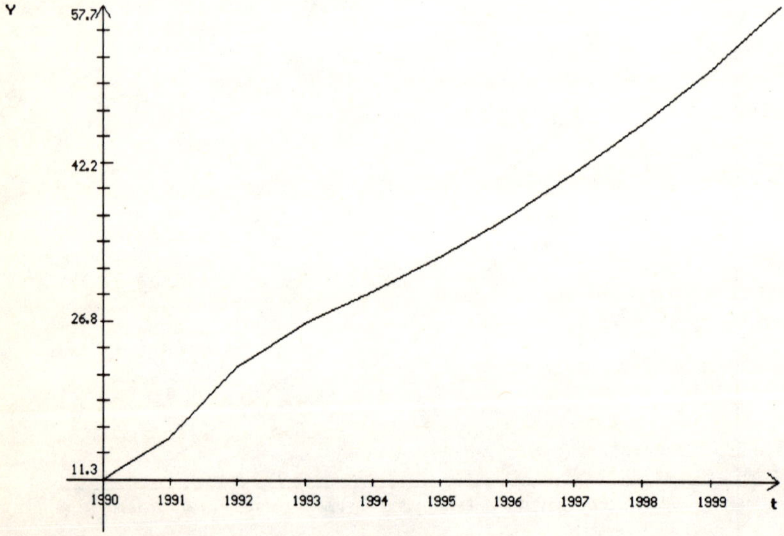

Figure 24 BUA_EH@ Total labour cost per hour

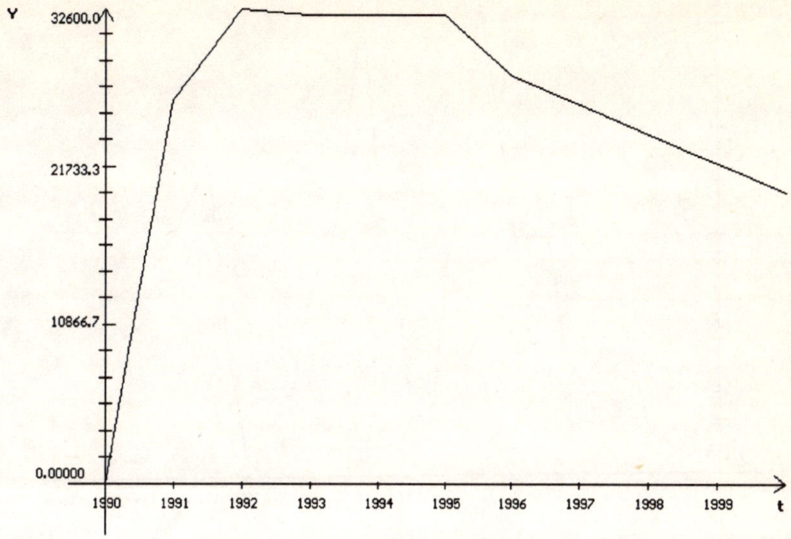

Figure 25 SL_HN_ST Social contributions of the West German government to East German households

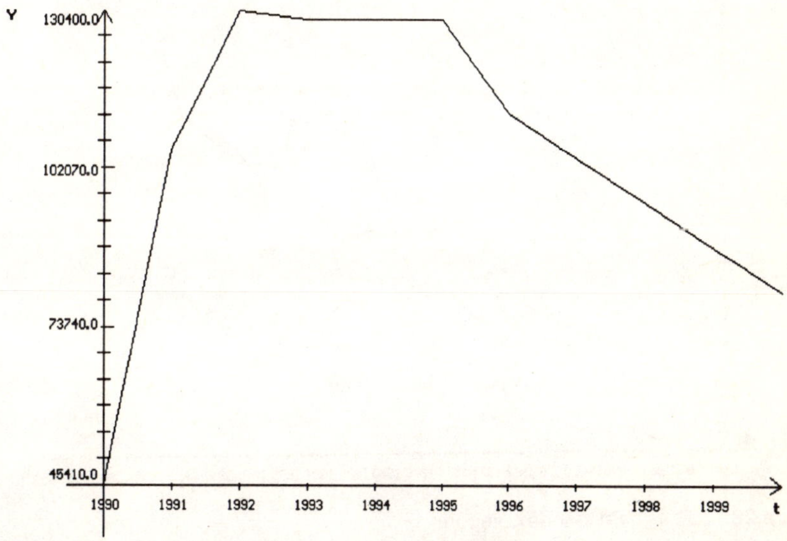

Figure 26 ZU_NL_ST Payments of the West German government to the East German government

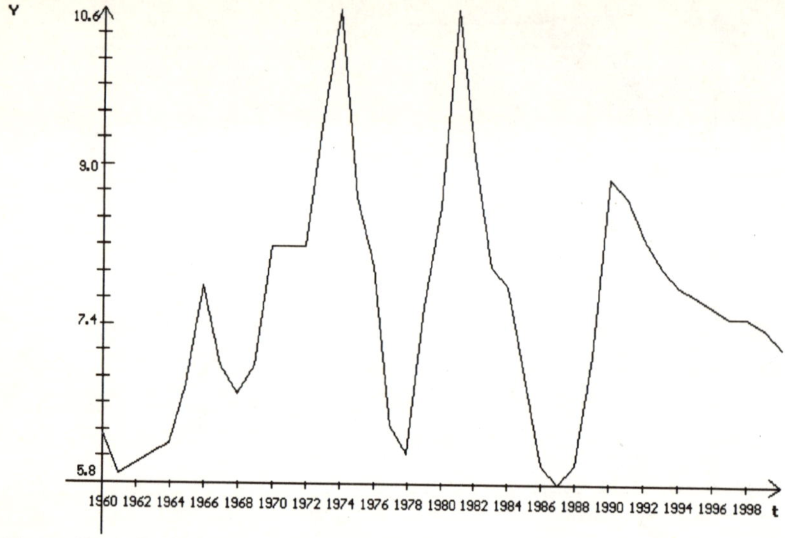

Figure 27 R_WPUM Average yield on circulating bearer bonds

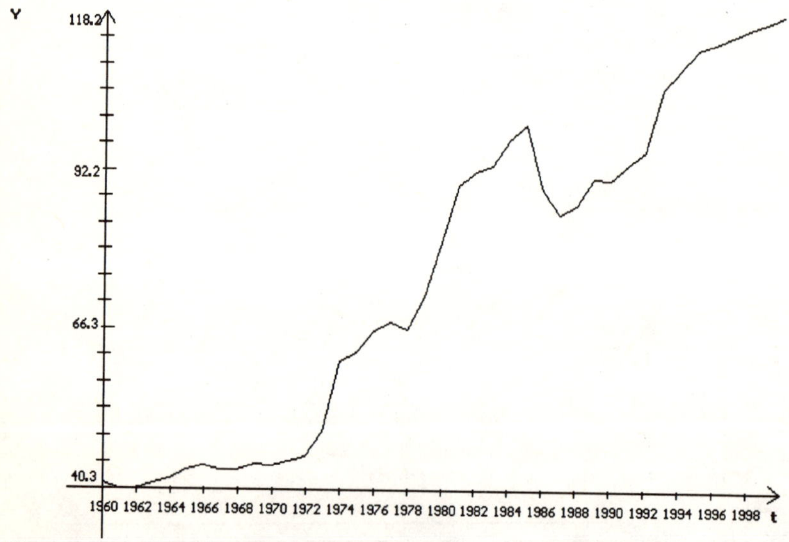

Figure 28 PM Price index, imports

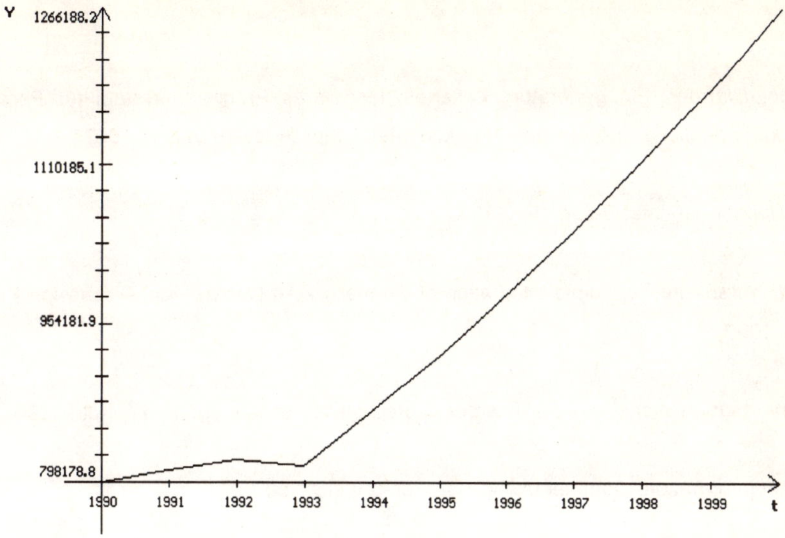

Figure 29 X_R Exports from West Germany to the rest of the world without without exports to East Germany

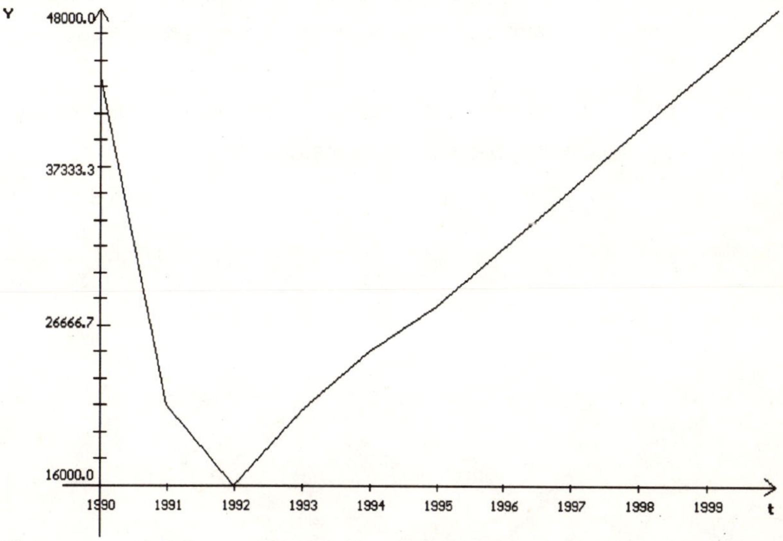

Figure 30 X_R@ Exports from East Germany to the rest of the world without exports to West Germany

References

[1] *Hubrich, Dietmar.* Ein generatororientiertes, modulares Programmsystem für Personalcomputer zur Erstellung und Anwendung ökonometrischer Modelle, Idstein 1992

[2] DIW Wochenberichte, Berlin 1990-1992

[3] *Siebert, Horst.* The Economic Integration of Germany - An Update. Kiel Discussion Papers 160a, Kiel 1990

[4] IWD. Informationsdienst des Instituts der deutschen Wirtschaft, Jg. 16-17, Köln 1990, 1991

[5] Brancheninformation, Commerzbank, Heft 10/90 v. 16.7.90

[6] Ifo-Schnelldienst, Ifo-Institut fuer Wirtschaftsforschung, München 1990-1992

[7] Ifo-Studien: *Gehrig, G. and Kuhlo, K. C.*, Ökonometrische Analyse des Produktionsprozesses, 7.Jg., 1961, H 1/2, Überprüfung der ökonometrischen Projektion von 1962, 18.Jg., 1972, H.2

[8] Volkswirtschaftliche Gesamtrechnungen, Fachserie 18, Reihe 1.3, Konten und Standardtabellen, 1991 Hauptbericht, Statistisches Bundesamt, 1992

APPENDIX 1.

ETAS, Conception and features of an econometric model generator

Dietmar Hubrich, Fachhochschule der Deutschen Bundesbank, Hachenburg,
Meinrad Rohner, Institute for Development, Environment and Quantitative Economic Research, Johann Wolfgang Goethe-University, Frankfurt/Main

1. Conception of the program system ETAS[4)]

Personal Computers are gaining increasing importance in supporting econometric model building. This has become especially true in recent years. At the beginning of the 6Os, regressions were difficult to compute at the very technical level, whereas at present such problems have become much better manageable due to the development in the field of high capacity computers as well as due to the progress in personal computer (PC) technology.
Today the potential user can avail himself of a great variety of statistical and econometric program systems. They frequently excel by their abundance of methods, but on the economic side of model building, they leave the user without any help. The program system ETAS, developed in intense research studies by the *Institute for Development, Environment and Quantitative Economic Research* in Frankfurt am Main, is trying to fill this gap with the realization of a PC-based model generator. This program system is well suited for micro- as well as for macroeconomic model building.

The implementation aims at automating the creation of econometric models as far as possible. Starting with a modelling idea for a given country in a limited period, a model is built by exploiting the electronically stored expert knowledge about hypotheses that are well founded by economic theory. Such a way of proceeding offers two decisive advantages:

(1) On principle, the builder of an econometric model is confronted with the problem of estimating a lot of regressions, one among them being destined to form part of the model finally. Testing different hypotheses and functional forms can demand quite some computing time. Furthermore the results have to be integrated into a definitional frame.

---

(4) Econometric Tools for Advanced Studies

Taking into consideration the unreliability of data and the time- and space variances of hypotheses it would be surprising if precise results could be obtained only from a small number of selected estimates. As a consequence the systematic examination of the statistical material is a scientific necessity. Thus hundreds, even thousands of individual regressions come into consideration and are subject to a procedure of selection and evaluation. The selection has to be made on the basis of statistical and economic criteria. The accomplishment of such a task is almost unsurmountable without computer assistance and automatization. Lacking the appropriate software the complete evaluation of the statistical material is often omitted, and estimates with dubious statistical properties are accepted for the model.

(2) Living models have to be updated on a regular basis. This can build up to a very demanding task. The program system ETAS allows to repeat the entire model generation in a reasonable time, because the automated process of evaluation and selection of viable hypotheses will use the updated statistical material, but rely at the same time on the databases containing the economic theory. No »fine tuning« is required, because this way of processing acknowledges that human behavior and technical details are subject to changes in the course of time: the entire model is organically updated. At the same time it is always possible and desirable to update the expert knowledge, too, and thus to reflect the progress in economic theory.

Generally it has been a fundamental aim of this software project to offer a program system that is as easy to use as possible. This has mainly been accomplished by developing a menu driven user interface. The researcher is not required to learn a programming language nor has he to learn cryptic commands. He should be free to ponder about the economic implications of his doing and not bother too much with controlling the program.

The model generator uses three media of information in the form of databases: a database containing time series, a database of definitional relationships between the economic aggregates and finally a database containing economic knowledge in the form of hypotheses about functional relationships between the aggregates. See Figure 1.

The *database of time series* plays a fundamental role within the entire program system. The user is asked to choose one of the available databases on initializing the system. All functions and processes will refer to this chosen database. It is easy to exchange a database later on without exiting the system. All time series can and should be extensively commented. A structure for

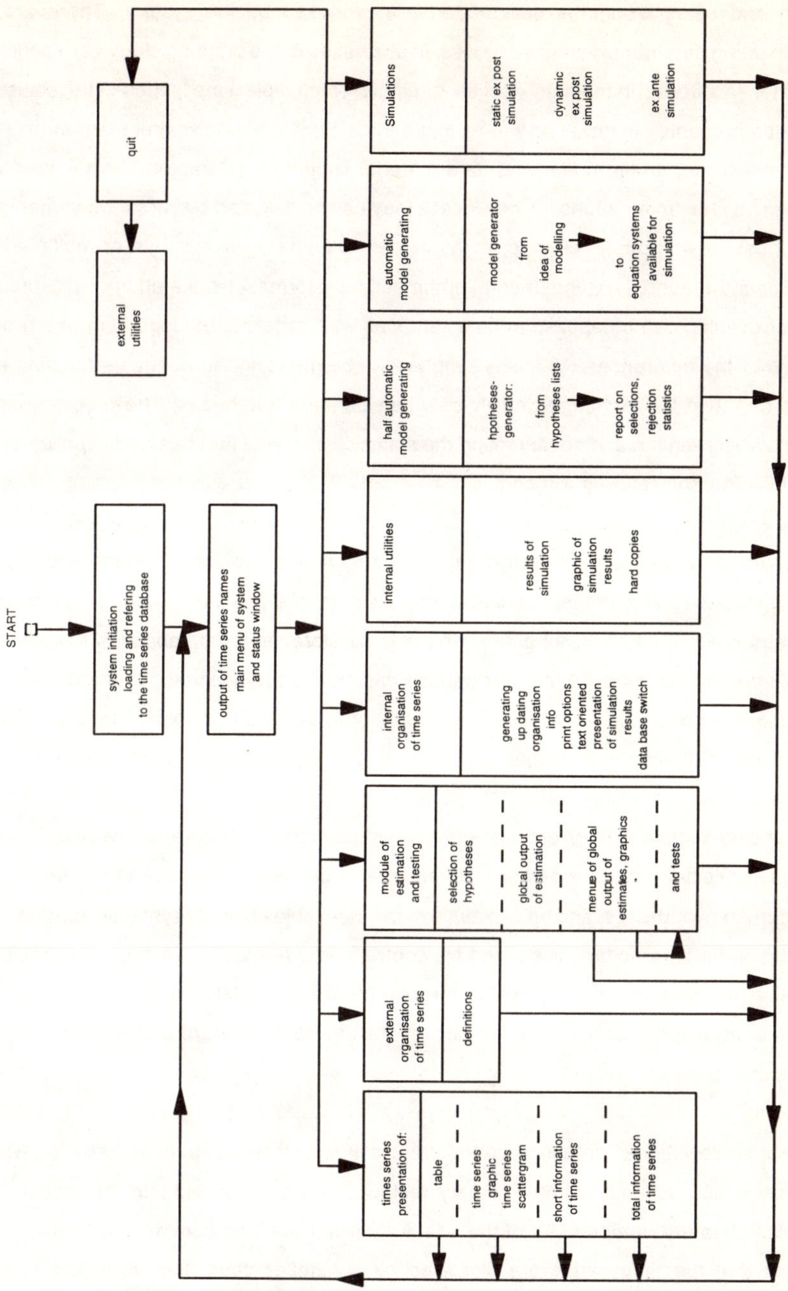

Fig. 1 The modularized concept of the programm system ETAS

commenting and categorizing the data material is proposed by the system. There are no restrictions in using mnemonic variables names. In all phases of the ongoing study or experiment the researcher is offered immediate access to single or multiple time series. The statistical material can be presented in tables as well as in graphical form (line and scatter diagrams). Thus complete transparency of the underlying data material should be guaranteed. Whenever time series have to be chosen for a function or process they can be selected by cursor movements.Of course it is possible to update, change, copy, delete, redefine or print single or multiple time series. Redefining means that fundamental arithmetic transformations like adding, subtracting, multiplying or dividing can be applied to time series as well as taking the logarithm, the growth rate, the lags or the differences. All this is simply done by pressing the adequate function key. Time series can also be exchanged easily between different databases. The program offers various forms of presenting and documenting the statistical material that has been applied in the process of building and revising a model.

The *databases of hypotheses and definitions* form part of the background information in the automatic construction of a model. Concepts and insights of the economic theory as well as knowledge about successful functional forms have to be stored in the database of hypotheses. Lead by a control file the model generator will use this knowledge according to the rules of the economic field in question, be it production, consumption, investment, labor or financial markets or any other object of economic studies.

The advantage of such a way of proceeding is obvious. Once a comprehensive database of hypotheses is collected, the researcher is freed to a large extent from the technical task to implement certain hypotheses, and he can avoid many inevitable errors of syntactic or referential nature. At the same time nothing is beyond his control and it remains always his responsibility to put together the final model. But due to the results of the model generator he has at his disposal many more statistically viable alternatives than there usually are available without this kind of computer support.

The *database of definitions* contains a collection of definitional linkages. In accordance with a particular accounting scheme, complementary restrictions are integrated into the model. The definitional linkages are independent of the user's particular naming conventions. This results from the fact that the time series are classified by a number code specific to the applied accounting scheme, e. g. the System of National Accounts (SNA).

The actual process of the model generation takes into consideration all preinformation available from the databases, the structuring ideas and particular definitional restrictions. The selection of certain equations is based on an evaluation procedure that can be specified flexibly and individually. Once a raw structure has been put together, it can be closed drawing on concepts from the database of definitions.

The system of equations thus created will automatically be tested regarding its identification, consistency, and complete data availability. In parallel a verification of the numeric consistency according to the definitional frame is carried out. In the end the researcher will dispose of a model that can immediately be run in the *simulation module*. Figure 1 shows that static or dynamic ex post and ex ante simulations are possible without modifying the equation system.

With these instruments in his hands the researcher can build several model variants and easily compare and test its conforming and deviating features.

At the same time the program supports more traditional ways to estimate single hypotheses by selecting the endogenous and exogenous variables merely with the cursor and the enter keys. All necessary handling information is given on screen. Thus input errors should practically not occur. This *manual estimation module* is especially useful in teaching economics but it proves helpful also in preliminary model studies and in the process of demonstrating certain concepts to a wider audience. The module of estimation is based on the Ordinary Least Squares (OLS) Method.

As soon as it is the aim to undertake more systematic studies the researcher can test his concepts with the *hypotheses generator*, a half-automatic module somewhere between the manual and the full-automatic operation mode. (See Figure 1 again.) In this context, the input requirement is no longer the specification of a definite hypothesis, but a prescription that contains competing hypotheses subject to economic and statistical constraints. The user can manually select equations that result from this process and add them to an equation system without running the model generator.

The entire complex of the program is rounded off by a collection of utilities, some of them accessible as internal menu options, some as stand-alone programs. These utilities serve mainly to import and export data and to document research results.

2. Summary of features of version 1.0

The following paragraph is meant to outline some features of the program system ETAS in it version 1.0[5]. First we look at the process of automatic model generation. This program module is called *model generator*. The process of model generating can be subdivided into three major steps: input, computing and presentation.

Automatic Operation Mode: Model Generator		
Input		
Create and edit modelling ideas with integrated editor.	Set statistical and economic restrictions.	Set statistical and economic priorities.
Keep database of hypotheses.	Keep database of definitional relationsships.	Keep track of and save the process of modelling.
Computing		
Automatic generation of hypotheses lists.	Automatic processing of the hypotheses lists and evaluation of results.	Automatic selection of "best" hypotheses according to priority criteria and restrictions.
Automatic generation of an equation system, available immediately for simulation.	Screen output during computation.	Set definitions in dialogue.
Test the equation system for identification and consistency.	Test numerically the consistency of the model.	Error comments during the runtime.
Presentation		
Save generator results and comments to file.	Display and edit results and model with integrated editor.	Present hypotheses lists and model variants.

Table 1 Survey of options during automatic model generation

A second principal option is the half-automatic model generation. This procedure is realized by means of a program module which is called *hypotheses generator*. Both generators use lists of hypotheses, i.e. permutative instructions to build series of stochastic equations. But, whereas the

(5) For a comprehensive description see Hubrich, Dietmar: Ein generatororientiertes, modulares Programmsystem für Personal Computer zur Entwicklung und Anwendung ökonometrischer Modelle. Idstein: Schulz-Kirchner Verlag, 1992

model generator can compose such a list automatically, in the case of the hypotheses generator the list must be put together manually. It can be advantageous, especially in the early phases of the modelling process, to test spontaneous ideas using the hypotheses generator instead of the more complex model generator. Again we can distinguish three major steps: input, computing and presentation.

Half-automatic Operation Mode: Hypotheses Generator		
Input		
Select hypotheses lists manually.	Create and edit hypotheses lists with integrated editor.	Use predefined hypotheses lists.
Set statistical limit values for falsifying the hypotheses.	Set economic restrictions for regression parameters.	Save new or modified hypotheses to file.
Computing		
Automatic handling of hypotheses lists according to combinatoric rules.	Error comments in great detail.	Automatic hypotheses selection according to statistical and economic restrictions.
Presentation		
Report of generator activities on file.	Diplay lists of selection files with integrated editor.	Statistical overview of reasons for rejection.
Save and print rejection statistics.	Menu-driven selection of equations for model.	Print hypotheses list in readable form.

Table 2 Survey of options during half-automatic model generation

Moreover, it is possible to estimate single equations. The program uses the time series stored in the data management module and offers additionally a wide variety of testing options. The non-automatic mode is subdivided into data management, estimation, testing and presentation of results.

Once a system of equations is found by use of one or more of the described procedures, the final application of the model will be the most important and intriguing part. To this purpose ETAS offers several modes of simulation which can be launched from within the same program environment. Equation systems can be solved in a static or dynamic ex post simulation, but of course in an ex ante simulation, too. The program relies on a solution algorithm of the Newton type. The structure of the program can again be best understood by looking at the three phases input, computing and presentation.

Non-automatic Operation Mode		
Management of Time Series		
Select time series menu driven.	Comment individual time series.	Integrate single equations into equation systems.
Fast access to individual time series due to index-sequential storage.	Effortless switch between different databases.	Import data from other sources.
Comment whole databases with integrated editor.	Create, change, copy or delete time series.	Complement database by redefining and transforming time series.
Estimation and Statistical Tests		
Form equations by selecting time series menu driven.	OLS-regression of up to 8 exogeneous variables, including 7 optional transformation.	Tests of parameter significance, autocorrelation, heteroscedasticy and residual distribution.
Presentation		
Line and scatter diagrams of time series.	Graphical evaluation of estimates (fit, partial and residues diagram).	View estimates with integrated editor.
Print tables and graphics or save into file.	Print individual time series or whole databases.	Export database as ASCII-file (limited or extended version).

Table 3 Survey of the non-automatic operation mode

At first sight the realization of such a project in a PC environment seems rather restrictive. PCs, however, offer a wide range of advantages in comparison with mainframe computers. Mainframes may dispose of higher computing capacities, but their control is often inconvenient and inflexible for the individual user.

As a rule mainframes of different manufacturers are incompatible. Consequently software development is closely constrained by specific technological environments. Hardware modifications almost inevitably require major software revisions.

On the other hand, the use of personal computers reduces these difficulties considerably. It is possible to offer cost conscious and problem oriented solutions at the same time, while questions of compatibility do not arise as long as software developer comply with the industry standard.

The use of PC's with 80386 or 80486 processors and the installment of a mathematical coprocessor can compensate to a large degree for the speed advantages of mainframe computers.

By far the most important argument in favor of personal computers is its mobility. This feature allows to tackle problems on the spot without taking the trouble of additional technical devices, provided software solutions are available. Once a software solution is implemented, it can be applied, unbound to specific places – not only in new fields of scientific research but also for commercial purposes.

Simulation		
Input		
Edit equation systems with integrated editor.	Simulation of linear and non-linear models.	Direct access to systems generated by the model generator.
Supplement systems manually.	Store and manage up to 99 variants of a model.	
Computing		
Static and dynamic ex post simulations.	Ex ante simulations.	Define values of exogeneous variables menu driven.
Simultaneous computation of up to 220 equations.	Interchange of forcasted data between different databases.	Save and display results during computation.
Presentation of Results		
Graphical evaluation of simulation results.	Compare model variants graphically and in tables.	Print or display computed values, ordered by variables or time.

Table 4 Survey of simulation options

3. Enhancements in version 1.1

ETAS is a box of econometric tools that can be used for teaching and researching as well. The way it supports the model builder is most probably unique in the field of statistical, econometric and simulation software. Within the project of preparing and building a financial model of the Federal Republic of Germany (FRG) it has already served well as it has been possible to put together a macroeconometric basis model in a surprisingly short time.

ETAS has originally been developed with yearly data in mind. Yet the task of modelling the financial sector requires without doubt time series with shorter periodicities: quarterly or even monthly data. Adapting the existing program system to this task is not quite easy. Nevertheless first steps have been taken to accomplish exactly this task.

We can announce by now the availability of an upgraded version of ETAS (numbered 1.1). The program has been enhanced in several respects most of which are particularly useful within the ongoing research project.

The most important enhancements at a glance:

(1) The database volume has been enlarged up to 600 time series.

(2) The database structure has been revised so as to simplify the import and export of data.

(3) First steps have been taken in order to handle quarterly data.

(4) Hardware requirements have been minimized. While a mathematical coprocessor is still supported (and recommended), it is not necessary anymore. The program can be used without effort on monochrome monitors.

(5) The setup of the program is more flexible now. The program can easily be installed on IBM-compatible PCs with different disk configurations.

(6) The user interface has been thoroughly improved so as to conform with widespread conventions.

These modifications and enhancements shall be described in more detail:

(1) One database can contain up to 600 time series. At the same time it is still possible to maintain as many parallel databases as disk capacity allows. It is easy to copy time series between different databases so that in reality the restriction of 600 variables per database should not be a problem.

(2) While importing hundreds of actualized and new time series from the Federal Statistical Office in Wiesbaden, it has proven useful to improve the available import and export routines. Without going into every detail here it should be much easier in the future to actualize data on a regular basis. There is no doubt that the same or slightly adapted procedures can be used to import data of statistical sources from other European countries.

The main format we now use as import medium is called *RDB-Format*. RDB-files are plain ASCII-files and can be edited with any ASCII-Editor. ETAS will convert existing RDB-file into its internal database format on request as it will export databases to the RDB-format from the internal format.

One side effect of these changes is that the required disk space for back-up copies has been reduced by approximately two thirds. Therefore it will be possible to interchange data between different research sites more easily, be it by using traditional or electronic mail.

(3) Quarterly data are automatically recognized in the import process and accordingly labelled and organized. The time indexation scheme has been revisioned to this same purpose. With the present version it is possible to estimate quarterly models that span over a period of twelve years. This should be enough for most purposes.

(4) Good software should run on minimal hardware, but it should use hardware extensions as available. Hardware and software requirements for version 1.1 of ETAS are:
– IBM-compatible PC with 530 KB free RAM
– Extended memory recommend, but not necessary
– DOS 3.2 or higher (MS-DOS 5.0 or OS/2 2.0 is recommended)
– High density disk drive (5¼" or 3½")
– Hard drive with about 5 MB of free disk space
– CGA-, EGA- or VGA-monitor
– Mathematical Coprocessor recommended, but not necessary anymore
– Color monitor recommended, but not required

(5) The installation procedure is more flexible now. The program can be installed from floppy drive A: or B: to any hard disk partition. The program is available on 4 high density diskettes.

(6) It is still unusual that econometric programs are menu-driven and therefore easy to use. ETAS never expected the user to learn a programming language and ease of use was a point of high priority from the very beginning of the development work. Even more effort has been taken now to make the user interface consistent and to adapt some international conventions established over the last years for MS-DOS software applications.

The main limits the program system ETAS is still suffering are due to limitations of the chosen operating system (MS-DOS) itself. The well known 640-KB-limit of MS-DOS (the addressable memory space) is not easily overcome. It has serious consequences for the length of time series that can be used in ETAS (maximum 50 periods at the moment) and the number of equations that can simultaneously be computed (maximum 220).

In the past it has been completely reasonable to use MS-DOS (or a virtual DOS machine in OS/2 2.0) as basis for econometric software development because it is by far the most wide spread operating system in the history of computing. Today there are attractive alternatives available, particularly OS/2 2.0. As a true 32-bit operating system OS/2 2.0 is capable of adressing a much larger adress space and it is therefore to be considered as the the ideal platform for future development efforts.

APPENDIX 2.

On portfolio models of the Federal Republic of Germany

Thomas Gehrig

Department of Economics, University of Basel, Basel

1. Introduction

In the recent two decades Western economies have witnessed an increasing mutual economic dependence. This largely followed the abolition of the Bretton Woods system of fixed exchange rates in 1972 and the widespread liberalization of financial markets in the 1980's. Increasingly, capital flows appear to dominate the short term determination of exchange rates and even more they effectively seem to constrain fiscal policy. For example the German Quellensteuer had to be abandoned in 1987 not only because of public resistance but also because of substantial amounts of capital flight.

This growing importance of financial markets is also reflected in the structure of numerous macro economic forecasting and simulation models covering (more) extensively financial markets. In this paper no attempt is made to survey this somewhat inaccessible literature. Rather emphasis is laid on evaluating three particular recent studies on (West-) Germany as a basis for potential further research. The models to be considered are: Diwischek (1989), Meyer, Ewerhart und Siebe (1990) and Tödter (1989). While the first study was undertaken as a research project at the University of Frankfurt, the second study was commissioned by the German Science Foundation and the third study is known as the Bundesbank model version 30/3/88.

All three studies attempt to provide forecasting and simulation tools for the national economy with exchange rates and foreign variables (such as interest rates) being given exogenously. Their common aim is to identify the structure of domestic financial markets and the mechanism of transmission of monetary policy on domestic real variables. In all three studies the financial sector is linked to a model of the real economy.

Not surprisingly economic theory gives little assistance in deriving asset demand systems. An important problem stems from the fact that financial markets act as information aggregators. Accordingly, behaviourial functions should incorporate the potential differences in information across different agents. For the case of symmetrically informed investors, however, a theory of portfolio behaviour is well established and this theory serves as the theoretical foundation of the three models.

We shall argue that in all three models the maintained specifications do not conform closely to the original portfolio approach. Rather the dynamic specification of some ad hoc adjustment process seems to dominate the empirical specification of asset demand functions. This points to various conclusions: First, classical portfolio theory might not be a good theory for financial markets at all. In particular, the implicit informational assumptions might be seriously in error. Second, classical portfolio theory might yield a good approximation of the real world, but expected returns and expected risk might vary over time. In this case we should have ways of tracing the time pattern of perceived risk and expected returns. Third, asset markets are not perfect in the sense that transactions costs or market power are not negligible and vary over time. Again, in this case we should have some idea about their dynamic evolution.

Naturally, the above list does not exhaust the list of possible explanations[6)], but all these arguments suggest that a proper structural approach for financial markets might prove exceedingly difficult. Therefore, as a first approximation one might feel tempted to estimate directly some reduced form parameters, even when it should be impossible to identify the true underlying (dynamic) structure. Accordingly, based on the surveyed empirical evidence vector-autoregression methods are suggested as useful tools for fruitful future research on asset markets.

This note is organized as follows. In section 2 a short account of portfolio theory is given, while section 3 presents the empirical studies covered. In section 4 these results are evaluated and section 5 suggests future research.

2. Aspects of portfolio theory

Before discussing the specific studies in detail it may seem worthwhile to provide a short account of the theory employed.

---

(6) Take the Roll (1982) critique for example as another explanation.

The theory of portfolio selection as introduced by Markowitz (1952) and Sharpe (1964) and Lintner (1965) characterizes market equilibrium in situations of uncertainty in which (risk averse) investors have to decide how to allocate some given wealth across various risky assets. One central assumption is that all investors agree on the (joint) distribution of the returns of all relevant assets. Accordingly, they maintain homogenous (not necessarily correct) expectations concerning the distribution of future returns of the various assets. On the basis of this assumption the theory provides decision rules for investors. In the presence of a risk free asset any optimal portfolio can be constructed as a linear combination of the risk free asset and the so-called market portfolio. The market portfolio is defined as the tangency portfolio on the efficient frontier relative to the risk free asset.

An immediate consequence of this result is that all investors should hold risky assets in identical proportions. Depending on their degree of risk aversion they should differ only in the relative position of the risky asset against the risk free asset.

A second consequence of the result is that the risk premia r_i-R of any risky asset i should be proportional to the risk premia of the market portfolio, i.e.

$$r_i - R = b_i\,(r_m - R) \quad \text{, for all assets i}$$

where:
r_i= rate of return on asset i
r_m= rate of return on the market portfolio
R = safe rate

Note, the determination of the market portfolio requires the full set of conceivable assets. Typically, this information is not available. Therefore, any empirical work may be doomed to fail. This is the Roll critique (1982) which extends to basically any empirical work on the capital asset pricing model.In principle both predictions of the basic portfolio model are testable. On a micro level such tests tend to reject the basic portfolio model. Numerous so-called stock market anomalies (Dimson, 1987) are ample proof of it. Given that private information may be of some value on stock markets the rejection of the basic theory is no surprise. Incorporating private information, however, will destroy the clear structure of predictions. For testing the generalized portfolio model some hypothesis on private information structures and possibly its dynamic evolution has to be maintained (Gehrig, 1991). The generalized portfolio selection model therefore remains likely to be unoperational.

For macro econometric modelling however, the original Markowitz model has never been applied. Rather following Brainard and Tobin (1968) the model typically is translated into an asset demand model (e.g. Müller U. (1989)). Obviously, portfolio theory then suggests a list of variables exogenous to investors' demand x_i for asset i. These are the rates of return for any conceivable asset as well as investor's net wealth W. Given n assets accordingly the investor's demand system can be formulated as:

$$x_1 = F_1(r_1,\dots,r_n, R, W)$$

$$\dots$$

$$x_n = F_n(r_1,\dots,r_n, R, W)$$

This system can be estimated, while care has to be taken to account properly for cross equation restrictions on the parameters imposed by the budget constraints.

It should be noted that this reformulation of the standard portfolio selection model does not permit a ready interpretation of the demand parameters in terms of expected returns and risks which lie at the heart of portfolio theory proper. According to the standard theory of portfolio selection the optimal choice will react sensitively especially with respect to expected returns and risks. While the asset demand equations typically control for expected returns the nature of risk is embodied in the parameters estimated. Drastic changes in the riskiness of particular assets typically would change these structural parameters. In the asset demand framework this type of analysis cannot readily be undertaken. Consequently, a discussion of alternative monetary policies implying different risk patterns for different types of assets might seriously suffer from this methodological defect of the asset demand framework.

All studies to be discussed below, however, do follow this approach. In addition linear homogeneity in investors' net wealth is imposed and accordingly demand systems for financial assets of the following form should ideally be estimated:

$$x_1 = f_1(r_1,\dots, r_n, R)\ W$$

$$\dots$$

$$x_n = f_n(r_1,\dots, r_n, R)\ W$$

In all studies considered an additional dynamic hypothesis is superimposed to the static demand system. It is assumed that "transactions costs" or adjustment costs will delay adjustment to the optimal portfolio. Such arguments may invalidate the theoretical justification for the empirical model. Obviously, if transaction costs exist, they have to be incorporated explicitly in the demand functions since apparently they affect expected asset returns and risks. A proper treatment of (differential) transaction costs should refer to some dynamic model of portfolio selection (Merton, 1973). Alternative approaches would seem rather ad hoc.

The prototype model, on which all the models to be discussed are based on is given by:

$$x_{1t} = f_{1t}(r_{1t}, \ldots, r_{nt}, R, x_{1,t-1}, \ldots x_{n,t-1})\,W$$

$$\ldots$$

$$x_{nt} = f_{nt}(r_{1t}, \ldots, r_{nt}, R, x_{1,t-1}, \ldots x_{n,t-1})\,W$$

In summary the return variables as well as the wealth variable are suggested by portfolio theory, while the dynamic specification is based on some type of ad hoc adjustment cost approach. The chosen specifications of asset demand functions explicitly imply the assumption of time invariant risk and return expectations of (identical) investors. In time series studies this assumption may not hold - at least it should be justified rigorously, possibly by way of testing. All studies considered fail this point.

3. Empirical portfolio models

In this section briefly three portfolio macro models of the financial markets in the Federal Republic of Germany are surveyed. While all three of them employ the same theoretical framework they differ significantly in the frequency of data, the disaggregation chosen, the mechanism which determines equilibrium prices and the econometric methodology.

Diwischek (1989):

Diwischek's study is based on annual data from 1960-1984.

The markets he considers are:

1. currency

2. sight deposits
3. demand deposits
4. savings accounts
5. "Geldkapital"
6. credit

The behaviour of the following agents is explained in the model:
1. private households and non-banks
2. banks

On the basis of the portfolio model outlined above demand equations are estimated for all agents for private households and non-banks (as one sector). Major modifications to the above asset demand system are the following:

i) Due to the multicollinearity of regressors and the limitation in degrees of freedom a typical demand function does contain the asset's own price and an alternative rate of return, which is the average rate of return of domestic bonds (denoted by RWPUM).

ii) Especially for short term assets such as currency and sight deposits an additional income or expenditure variable (such as disposable income or private consumption) are included. Obviously, the inclusion indicates evidence for motives to hold assets additional to portfolio considerations, namely transaction purposes.

The markets considered are markets, in which banks typically represent one side of the market. Further capital markets such as the stock market or the market for equity are not considered. Rather than estimating supply functions for banking services Diwischek assumes that banks simply quote prices and accept any market demand at such (equilibrium) price. Hence, only some form of reduced equation is estimated linking the interest rate in question to regulatory instruments controlled by the central bank and international rates. Accordingly, no hypothesis on (strategic) banking behaviour needs to be maintained.

Naturally, also the behaviour of the government, the central bank and the foreign sector are considered with exogenously given behaviour. In particular, components of foreign demand for domestic sight or time deposits are not modelled. Clearly, to do so one would need to model also the asset menu available to foreigners. On the other hand by not explaining the foreign sector important monetary developments might not be detected on the basis of the particular model.

The estimation was carried out by employing OLS for each demand and "supply" equation. Obviously, no attempt was made to employ some system estimator.

Meyer, Ewerhart, Siebe (1990):

The model employs annual data from 1971 to 1983.

The markets considered are:

1. currency
2. sight deposits
3. demand deposits
4. savings accounts
5. bonds
6. credit

The following agents are distinguished:

1. private households
2. private non-banks
3. banks
4. near banks (insurance)

For each type of agents and each market portfolio ("dynamic") demand functions are estimated. In particular for non-banks both asset demand and credit demand functions are estimated independently. So in contrast to Diwischek also the supply behaviour is endogenous and equilibrium rates of return are determined in market equilibrium by equating demand and supply. As in Diwischek single equation OLS-estimation is performed throughout. The restrictions imposed by budget identities were considered in the determination of equilibrium but not at the level of estimation. Again a system estimator might have produced more convincing results but no word is mentioned about such attempts in the study.

Tödter (1989):

The model is based on quarterly data from 71/1- 87/4.

As in Diwischek the markets are

1. currency
2. sight deposits
3. demand deposits
4. savings accounts
5. "Geldkapital"
6. credit

Also only the behaviour of two sectors is modelled

1. private households and non-banks
2. banks

Asset demand functions are modifications of the dynamic asset demand functions described above:

$$x_i = a_{oi} + a_{1i} r_i + a_{2i}\, z + a_{3i}\,(BSP/W) + a_{4i}\, x_i(-1)$$

where :

z = weighted (lagged holdings) average of returns

BSP = gross national product

The particular choice of demand function resembles Diwischek and provides a way of solving the multicollinearity problem. Also the inclusion of an activity variable (BSP) indicates the potential influence of transactions effects.

Banking behaviour remains unmodelled and as in Diwischek an implicit supply function is estimated relating the market rate of return to foreign rates and instruments controlled by the central bank. Also capital markets remain unmodelled.

The method of estimation is restricted least squares incorporating the restrictions derived from the wealth constraints.

4. Critical evaluation

a) Transactions motive versus savings (portfolio) motive:

The distinction between money and near monies held for transaction purposes and money held as a safe asset (with zero return but also zero risk) in a portfolio framework seems important. While the latter aspect may depend on risk return considerations, the former will largely depend on consumption behaviour and therefore is rather price insensitive. For policy issues a clear discrimination may be important.

The results of Diwischek suggest that especially assets with short maturities (currency, sight deposits, demand deposits) also perform the role of transactions media. None of the three studies however even attempts the difficult task of discriminating between these different motives.

b) Real capital and foreign sector:

In neither study investors are allowed to invest in real capital, i.e. in stocks or equity holdings. There may be practical reasons (data) for not incorporating stock markets in the empirical analysis. In this case however the portfolio justification for the empirical models estimated is particularly weak. Furthermore, none of the studies does allow for foreign investment of domestic investors. One obvious reason for cutting this link to international capital markets is an attempt to deal with only one of Hydra's heads. Its does however imply the serious drawback that cross equations restrictions derived from portfolio theory are meaningless in the domestic model since additional equations for foreign activities have to be included in the portfolio choice.

So basically what has been done in all studies essentially amounts to the estimation of some rather ad hoc asset demand system based on plausibility considerations. This is all the more problematic since the asset categories excluded probably are the most risky assets. Therefore they play an important role in any approch, which builds on a theory of risk diversification and risk reduction.

c) Assets versus liabilities:

Portfolio theory is a theory on asset allocation. Its application on negative assets, or say credits therefore, remains somewhat dubious. This criticism is especially directed towards the Meyer et.al. model. Although the disaggregation of the private sector into households and into non-banks in principle is to be welcomed, it runs into the problem of simultaneously formulating a demand equation for credits (short and long term) and a demand equation for assets such as demand deposits. Obviously, immediately further disaggregation is required into surplus firms and credit firms. Otherwise, no recourse to some sort of portfolio justification can be claimed. While ad hoc credit demand functions can be formulated they may closely follow asset demand equations. Nevertheless, economic theory provides little help in this respect and any specification needs to be ad hoc by necessity. In particular, there seems to be widespread agreement about imperfections in the credit market due to information problems (Gale, Hellwig, 1985).

d) Determination of equilibrium rates of returns

The formulation of asset supplies in Diwischek and Tödter implies that the banking sector determines prices and non-banks basically adjust their portfolios according to their demand functions. Hence savings behaviour does not really affect the determination of equilibrium prices but adjusts residually. While this approach may serve well descriptively it leaves the determination of the rates of return to a hypothesis on banking behaviour.

Banking behaviour on the other side is not motivated from a theoretical model but ad hoc specifications are given. Again an obvious reason is the lack of theoretical guidance in modelling banks. The point however to be made is that in both models the portfolio behaviour does not significantly help to determine interest rates.

In contrast Meyer et al. explicitly determine rates of return from equating estimated supply and demand. However, their methodology of estimation does not take account of the endogeneity of rates of returns. Rather single equation OLS-estimates are performed.

e) Dynamic specification

Finally in all three studies the explanatory power of asset demand functions seems to stem from the autoregressive element. Tödter is surprised about the high value of the adjustment parameters of about .85, which he interprets as evidence for substantial transaction costs. But also Diwischek's and Meyer's results are driven from the dynamic specification rather than the specific portfolio formulation. For example consider the estimated demand functions for time deposits:

Diwischek:

$$TE = .037\ BSP/W + .010\ ZTE - .015\ ZSP + .65\ TE_{-1}$$

BSP := gross national product

W := net wealth of non-banks

TE := time deposits demanded by private non-banks

ZTE:= interest on time deposits

ZSP:= interest on saving deposits

Meyer, Ewerhart, Siebe:

$$TEH = .077\ ZTE - .011\ ZSP + .32\ SH - .36\ TEH_{-1} + .30\ BH_{-1}$$

TEH := time deposits of private households

SH := change in net wealth of private households

BH := bond holdings of private households

Given the smooth behaviour of the time series in both cases a good deal of explanation might stem from the lagged terms rather than from rates of return. Furthermore, the explanatory power of rates of return is seriously hampered by the multicollinearity problem in relatively short data sets. Given that also the dynamic specification is rather ad hoc a theoretical justification for the estimated functions on the basis of portfolio theory does not seem very convincing.

5. Suggestions for further research

Based on the comments above still substantial work can and needs to be done. There are basically two strands along which progress can be hoped for: (i) improvement of the standard portfolio explanation or (ii) improvement of the dynamic specification.

(i) static specification:

The omission of the market for real capital is a serious impediment to a portfolio theoretic approach since probably the most risky assets are excluded from the analysis. On the other hand multicollinearity in rates of returns restricts severely specification of demand functions. Given that data for the financial model are available on a monthly basis it would seem worthwhile to repeat the exercises of Diwischek and Tödter on monthly data and explore how the estimation of asset demand functions is affected. With substantially more data at hand larger vectors of rates of return - those suggested by theory - can be handled and the multicollinearity problem should ease to some extent.

Furthermore, on the basis of the price predictions set out in section 2 the portfolio model could be tested. Risk premia of the various assets should be proportional to the risk premia of the market portfolio. Accordingly, risk premia of various assets should also be proportional. Of course, testing the model still is a first step towards estimating structural parameters.

Furthermore, with high frequency data it should be possible to get some ideas about the dynamic evolution of risk premia. So it should be a fruitful exercise to analyze the dynamic properties of the second moments of the financial variables of interest. This points to the need to employ conditional heteroscedasticity procedures such as developed by Engle (1982). Since in the next section I want to argue to take a less structural approach anyway at this point there is little need to pursue this line of thought and discuss the growing literature on ARCH (autoregressive conditional heteroscedasticity) and GARCH (generalized autoregressive conditional heteroscedasyticity) -methods.

One direction in which probably little progress can be expected is further disaggregation of private non-banks into households and non-banking firms. Portfolio behaviour of firms should by necessity incorporate the firms' investment options, which again might differ sector by sector. Also a disaggregation in the categories of financially constrained firms and surplus firms should be undertaken as argued in 3. Thus further disaggreagation entails the need to even more radical disaggregation. The smaller the aggregates, however, the more important are the demands on agents' information structures and the less likely is a satisfactory performance of a portfolio type model.

In principle, improvements could be expected by application of system estimators taking explicitly into account the endogeneity of rates of return. However, such an approach does have to rest on a solid theoretical foundation of asset supply, or in other words on a solid theory of banking behaviour. As such theories are not available (yet), the gains from system estimation may be small.

(ii) dynamic specifications:

The second strand for further work could follow the first intuitive attempts of Diwischek and Tödter in modelling supply. Given economic theory does provide little guidance in modelling behaviourial equations in asset markets any structural specification has to be chosen in a rather ad hoc way. Alternatively, one could follow the temptation to concentrate on the reduced form. In this case typically it is not possible to identify the underlying structural model, but for prediction or simulation purposes this may not be necessary. While neither Diwischek nor Tödter are able to comment on the explicit behaviour of banks they can simulate the portfolio behaviour of private non-banks.

Since the dynamic specification appears quite important this approach suggests to employ an explicitly dynamic approach. Following Sims (1980) we therefore propose to fit a (vector-) autoregressive process on the various rates of return and other monetary and real variables of interest. Based on monthly data such a programme should also be feasible. This approach might improve significantly forecasting and simulation properties of the integrated real and financial model. It may lack the rigorous support from economic theory, but in financial markets theory cannot impose strict structural restrictions anyway.

The attractive feature of vector-autoregressions is that no information is lost about structural relationships and that no a-priori information about cross equation restrictions is needed. Although it may be impossible to identify the exact underlying structural model for forecasting purposes this disadvantage may by compensated by the appealing feature that vector-autoregressions do enjoy the same forecasting properties as the true underlying structural model.

In vector-autoregressions there is no need to partition the variables of concern in endogenous and exogenous variables. Rather an autoregression fitted on all variables of interest would suggest automatically a reduced form relation between the variables considered. Exogeneity of variables would show up automatically in the parameters estimated. Also the dynamic specification suggests some pattern of dynamic "causation" [7].

To be more specific a system of order p to be estimated can be written as follows:

$$y_t=\sum_{\tau=1}^{p} A_\tau y_{t-\tau}+\varepsilon_t$$

where:

$$y_t \in \mathbf{R}^n, A_t \in \mathbf{R}^{nxn}$$

and ε_t is a random error and typically is assumed to be normally and intertemporally independantly distributed according to a multivariate Gaussian distribution $N(0, \Sigma_t)$. y_t is the vector of variables of interest, while A_t are coefficient matrices. The variables should be grouped into various subgroups:

a) prices
rate of inflation
private and public bond returns
stock returns
interest rates on time deposits and savings
accounts

b) wealth and income
gross national product
capital stock

---

(7) See Granger (1969) for example.

domestic production

private wealth

c) fiscal variables

tax rates

government debt

d) monetary variables

money supply (various measures)

discount rate

reserve requirements

e) foreign variables

real exchange rate (or specific exchange rates)

return on foreign bonds

return on froeign stocks

exports and imports

Clearly, given the limited time horizon of 30 years of monthly data for monetary variables work with large vectors and long lags will be impossible. So preliminary work should start with fairly low-dimensional vectors and a low dimensional lag-structure. One problem arises, when real production or wealth and income data enter the analysis, since these are observed only quarterly. Estimation methods have to be developed to deal with such cases.

Furthermore estimation of the coefficient matrices may be complicated by the likely phenomenon that many of the variables of concern would seem to be cointegrated. Special techniques to deal with non- stationarity have been developed by Sims, Stock and Watson (1990) for the class of models considered here[8)]. In case of stationary variables it is well known that OLS-estimation of the coefficients yields consistent estimates.

One comment on the special case p=1 is in order. A block diagonal structure of the Matrix A_1 then can be interpreted as seperating variables in exogenous and endogenous variables, in the sense that these exogenous variables (Granger-) cause the endogenous ones. The interesting

(8) See also Johansen (1991).

feature is that this division arises endogenously from the data. In this sense a priori information is not required for the application of this technique.

An interesting exercise could be to test the forecasting properties of some version of the suggested vector-autoregression relative to the structural models surveyed earlier. In principle a sufficiently rich vector autoregression should yield results of at least the same quality asymptotically.

Furthermore, the approach suggested for financial markets can be combined with real models of lower frequency. In principle, monthly interventions can be evaluated with respect to some quarterly or annual model of the real sector. If investment is found to depend on some end of year cost of capital this variable could be targeted with monthly interventions given the parameters of the autoregressive process.

By way of summarizing it seems useful to estimate a structural portfolio model and/or a reduced form vector autoregression on the rates of returns with monthly data. In the case of structural estimation problems related to the multicollinearity problem will be reduced. Such estimates should be contrasted to the lower frequency studies of Diwischek and Tödter. Also the vector autoregression should give valuable insights concerning Granger causation and possibly the role of adjustment costs. Finally, forecasting and simulation properties of both variants should be contrasted against each other.

6. Literature

Engle, R. (1982): "Autoregressive Conditional Heteroscedasticity with Estimates of the Variance of UK-Inflation", Econometrica, 50, pp.987-1007

Dimson, E. ed. (1987): "Stock Market Anomalies", Cambridge University Press, 1987

Diwischek,W.(1989): "Der Geld- und Kreditmarkt im Rahmen eines makroökonometrischen Modells für die Bundesrepublik Deutschland", Schulz-Kirchner, Idstein, 1989

Gale, Hellwig (1985): "Incentive Compatible Debt Contracts: The One-Period Problem", Review of Economic Studies, 1985

Gehrig, Th. (1991): "Ein internationales Kapitalmarktmodell mit unterschiedlich informierten Anlegern", forthcoming in: Schweizerische Zeitschrift für Volkswirtschaft und Statistik

Granger, C. (1969): "Investigating Causal Relationships by Econometric Models and Cross-Spectral Methods", Econometrica, 55, pp.251-276

Johansen,S. (1991): "Estimation and Hypothesis Testing of Cointegration Vectors in Gaussian Vector Autoregressive Models", Econometrica, forthcoming

Markowitz, H.M. (1952): "Portfolio Selection", Journal of Finance, Vol.7 pp.77-91

Merton, R.C. (1973): "An Intertemporal Capital Asset Pricing Model", Econometrica, pp.867-887

Meyer, Ewerhart, Siebe (1990): "Dollarkurs und Beschäftigung", Duncker und Humblot, Berlin

Müller,U (1989): "Die Passivseite der Bankbilanz: ein Portfolio-Ansatz", Schweizerische Zeitschrift für Volkswirtschaft und Statistik, pp.55-66

Lintner, J. (1965): "Valuation of Risk Assets and the Selection of Risky Investment in Stock Portfolios and Capital Budgets", Review of Economics and Statistics, Vol.47, pp.13-37

Roll, R. (1977): "A Critique of the Asset Pricing Theory's Tests; Part 1: On Past and Potential Testability of the Theory", Journal of Financial Economics, pp.129-176

Sharpe, W. (1964): "A Theory of Market Equilibrium under Condition of Risk", Journal of Finance, Vol.19, pp.429-442

Sims, C. (1980): "Macroeconomics and Reality", Econometrica, Vol.48.1, pp.1-48

Sims,C. Stock,J. Watson,M.(1989): "Inference in Linear Time Series Models with unit Roots", Econometrica, 58, pp.113-144

Tödter, K.H. (1989): "Das Ökonometrische Model der Deutschen Bundesbank: Entwicklung, Struktur und Perspektiven", mimeo, Feb.1989

PART 2

POLAND

CHAPTER 4

QUARTERLY MODEL WK-91 OF THE POLISH ECONOMY IN TRANSITION[1]

Grażyna Juszczak, Maria Magdalena Kaźmierska,
Nina Łapinska-Sobczak, Władysław Welfe

Institute of Econometrics and Statistics
University of Łódź

4.1. Introduction

The transition from a centrally planned, command economy to a developed market economy is a long lasting process. The '80s in Poland were characterised by a series of attempts to implement economic reforms. Although they did not reach their general targets - they brought the departure from the command type planning and central allocation of resources on behalf of direct links between producers and users, broadening the sphere of the freely negotiated prices and wages and, at last, growing significance of financial instruments of economic policy.

However, it was the stabilisation plan introduced in 1990 that brought full freedom of prices formation which, together with deflationary fiscal policy (control over wages, high taxes) and tight monetary policy (high rate of interests), resulted not only in depressing the hyper inflation, but also fruited with regaining economic equilibrium, first of all the market equilibrium. The adjustment market mechanisms started to work. However, it remained unclear to what extent the state enterprises would show their readiness to follow the market signals[2]. The basic tools of the economic policy became the instruments of fiscal policy (taxes, subsidies) and monetary policy (rate of interests on credits and deposits).

Moreover, one should stress that the economic adjustments, especially in financial flows, became more and more intensive in time. One can risk a hypothesis that the deep recession in the industry - due to underestimation of the impact of anti-inflationary policy package introduced by January 1st, 1990 - continued to exist because of inflexible financial policy, i.e.

---

[1] The concept of the model was presented for discussion at the ACE Workshop in Mittelberg (June 1991) and EEA Congress in Cambridge (August-September 1991). The empirical results were shown at the ACE Seminar in Paris (October 1991) and at Macromodels' 91 in Jachranka-Poland (December 1991) as well as at the ESEM '92 in Brussels (August 1992) and EEA Congress in Dublin (August 1992). See Juszczak et al. [1991a, 1991b, 1992a, 1992b].

[2] The reaction to the drop in demand in 1990 was immediate- it took the form of a fall in the output, along with the lack of explicit willingness or ability to adjust, either in the form of price reduction or diminution of costs. Hence, it was uncertain whether, taking into account the high degree of monopolization of industry, an increase in expenditures will bring about an increase in output or, to what extent, an increase in prices (despite the low rate of utilization of production capacities). A likely increase of production was in the '90s additionally constrained because of the negative impact of the special anti inflationary tax, punishing state own firms when the rate of increase in their wage bill exceeded certain portion of the rate of inflation.

lack of prompt reaction to the changes taking place from month to month and from quarter to quarter.

This analysis let us draw the following conclusions. First, it was indispensable to broaden the scope of analyses based upon the simulation models - into the widely understood financial flows, with including observations of price movements into them. Second, forecasts and results of these analyses must be available in a monthly or at least quarterly periods, if one wants to provide information on the short term adjustments combined with the analysis of possible economic policy options.

Short term analyses of fluctuations in macro variables, financial flows, etc., have been regularly performed in all developed market economies for many years. To mention some of them: the USA - McCarthy [1972]), France - (Malgrange [1983], Courbis [1986]), Finland - (Tarkka [1990], Bank... [1979]), Italy - (D'Adda [1976]), the Netherlands - (Fase [1984]), Spain - (Uriel [1981]), Germany - (Macro econometric [1988], Hansen [1975]).

It all proved the need to construct a forecasting-simulation econometric macro model for Poland, covering the financial flows, and also the movements of prices. We mean here a quarterly model, which is supported not only by the above arguments, but also by the fact that it is the only way to escape the necessity to introduce changes in the structural parameters or calibrating them as in the case of annual models. The monthly or quarterly time series describing the above variables have been available only for a couple of years and they become outdated very fast. Furthermore, due to practical reasons, a possibly fast and frequent updating of quarterly forecasts (for example, every month) and simulation analyses are needed.

This chapter includes, first of all, the discussion of the assumptions on the quarterly macro econometric model of the Polish economy. The initial assumptions supported by the emerging theory of the transition period (Portes [1991]) were modified, taking into account restricted accessibility to data and the results of numerous discussions, which led to the construction of the model. We begin the general characteristics of the model's structure with including the problems of unobservable macro aggregates. Then major economic mechanisms described by the model are outlined. Specification of equations within particular blocks in the light of first empirical findings is discussed next. The paper also reports the results of the parameters estimation of particular equations (see Appendix 2) as well as the first results of the solution of the model. The model in its current version will be labelled WK-91.

4.2. Data base, extraneous information and estimation techniques

The data base was compiled using two main sources: Monthly Bulletins of the GUS (Central Statistical Office) and Bulletin of the NBP (Polish National Bank). In principle, it covers the period starting from 1989 (for several variables from 1988). First estimation exercises were performed using data up to the 2nd quarter of 1991. Hence, the sample was small, which explains, why the time series were not seasonally adjusted; it will probably change in the next years. The framework is based on definitions used in statistical publications of 1991. The constant prices of 1990 were applied. The data cover an increasing number of variables (approaching 100 time series). However, they did not include macro-aggregates still unavailable in the official statistics. Hence, we made our own estimate described below in Section 4.3.1.

The use of time series on real flows (expressed in 1990 prices) was constrained mainly to equations relating macro- aggregates. As the majority of variables represent financial flows and are expressed in current prices and strong similarity of price movements was observed - the regression equations mostly relate current values of these variables. As the sample is very short (10-14 observations), we made reference to composite explanatory variables, looking for extraneous information mainly from the I-O tables (for instance in defining the participation of industry in the demand of particular final users). The equations of the model are systematically updated and revised. The first 1991 version was completed in June 1991 (Juszczak et al. [1991a]) and the most recent revised in September 1991 (Juszczak et al. [1991b]).

In quarterly models the lags in behaviour play important role. Small size of the sample prevented from the use of standard techniques of estimation of the lag distributions. Hence, we used the search procedures. The last 1991 version of the model introduces lags in equations explaining not only employment but also households' expenditures, government budget incomes and expenditures, and price formation. The introduction of expectations will be the next step in model development.

The 1991 version of the model consists of 83 equations of which 16 are identities. Some of the 67 stochastic equations are, however, bridge equations, being in fact approximations of identities. There are 4 explicit exogenous variables and 14 dummies (the majority of them was introduced to account for seasonality; others to represent the policy changes). The initial versions of the model are linear and only OLS was applied. In the next phase non-linearity will be introduced and consistent estimation procedures tried, to allow for the simultaneity bias.

4.3. General structure of the model

4.3.1. Macro aggregates in the quarterly model - general framework

A consistent image of the quarterly macro model of the national economy can be created by starting with the framework of a national accounts system (either in the SNA or MPS system) and of financial flows by analysing particular components of the subsystem of flow of funds accounts (financial balances). The latter describes, in a more or less coherent way, the processes of distribution of the national product and national income, distinguishing the basic economic agents participating in this process. These are producers (business) and public institutions (non-profit organisations), households, the government - represented by the budget, banking system and foreign sector.

The block of the macro model's equations explaining economic macro categories should cover the following groups of macro variables[3]:

in SNA system:		in MPS system:
Gross domestic product (XNA) and its industrial components:		Net material product (national income produced) (X) and its industrial components:
XXQNA	- manufacturing and mining industry	**XQ**
XXBNA	- building industry	**XB**
XXRNA	- agriculture	**XR**
XPONA	- other branches	**XPO**
Gross domestic product to be distributed, i.e. domestic absorption (XGNA) and its components:		National income distributed (XG) and its components:
CNA	- personal consumption	**C**
GNA	- government consumption	**G**
JNA	- investment outlays	**JA**
DRNA	- increase of inventories	**DR**

Carrying such a program into effect we had to overcome the problem of data scarcity[4]. For quarterly periods, the available time series include only related variables or some of the components of the macro aggregates describing production and distribution of the national income (for example, value added in industry could be represented by the sales of production which is available for firms with 6 or more employees only)[5].

However, in this situation, we did not consider it appropriate to give up the estimation and forecasts of unobservable macro aggregates. There exists a variety of procedures suitable for distributing and interpolating time series of macro aggregates using the information on dynamics in related series of selected indicators. More specifically, the values of particular macro aggregates for quarterly periods can be calculated from the relations, which, on the basis of annual data, are established between the macro aggregates and relevant indicators, the values of which are also observable in quarterly periods. It is being assumed here that the parameters of the bridge equations representing the above relationships remain valid for

[3]The meaning of particular symbols is explained in the list of variables (see Appendix 1).
[4]Macro models based on annual data tyipically used MPS macro aggregates. The model builders had to allow for a switch to SNA system, which posed some problems as the annual time series were available for the '80s only, as in the Polish case.
[5]Situation in this area is completely different from that which has been taking place in the developed market economies for at least twenty years, where the data on macro aggregates are available every quarter. In majority of countries, however, they are generated by using the methodology described below however, but not from direct calculations based on data reporting.

quarterly periods. Indicators can be selected from major components of the macro aggregates or other related variables. The relevant procedures and the techniques used in deriving the quarterly values of the macro aggregates are described in details in Chapter 6, Section 6.2.

Let us only mention that, in general, two approaches can be distinguished in defining the indicators for bridge equations: first, relating a particular macro aggregate to its approximate measure, for instance GDP originating in building industry was related to basic output of building enterprises; second, using the behavioural type of relationship between the macro aggregate and explanatory variables, the values of which were also reported on quarterly base. Here we have for instance personal consumption as a function of a proxy for real personal income. Unless the quarterly data are not seasonally adjusted, this approach may lead to biased estimates of seasonal patterns. The personal consumption may show somewhat different pattern than incomes (it will be certainly biased downwards in the 4th quarter). Moreover, this approach predetermines specification of the structural equation for a particular macro aggregate.

Following the above methodology, the quarterly characteristics of all the above mentioned macro aggregates for the years 1989-1991 were obtained. The quarterly data on macro variables linking the GDP produced and distributed, i.e. on exports (E) and imports (M), were available, however not without problems related to the coverage of the private sector activities (especially that of imports). The information on the production factors was far from complete. It is constrained to the employment in 6 major industries (both public and private) - except for private agriculture sector. There is no data on hours worked nor on fixed capital.

Hence, the model can explain the above macro variables mostly from the demand side, which is in line with the maintained hypothesis (see below) that the Polish economy, is in principle, demand constrained (driven). There are few chances to determine the fixed capital and production capacities in the future as well as the degree of their utilisation, first of all in the industry and to analyse the supply side. The relationships between macro categories are shown in figure 4.1.

The model's building strategy assumes that it is the demand for particular components of the Gross Domestic Product (GDP) which is explained first. Value added in industry, construction, agriculture and other activities are, in fact, derived from equations similar to the bridge equations mentioned above (see Chapter 6). For example, GDP originating in mining and manufacturing industries (XXQNA) depends on the demand for product (sales) from this sector (SQQ). The latter variable, as it is shown in the next sections, depends on the proxies of demand of the final and intermediate users.

The components of Net Material Product (NMP) are derived by means of bridge equations linking these variables to the respective components of GDP.

Hence, the totals are obtained by adding up particular components for GDP:

$$\mathbf{XNA = XXQNA + XXBNA + XXRNA + XPONA} \qquad (4.1)$$

for NMP:

$$X = XQ + XB + XR + XPO \tag{4.2}$$

Allowing for the changes in foreign trade we can define domestic final demand i.e. the GDP to be distributed (domestically absorbed) (XGNA):

$$XGNA = XNA + M - E \tag{4.3}$$

and, respectively, national income distributed (XG):

$$XG = X + M - E \tag{4.4}$$

The components of domestic final demand except for inventory changes, are explained using behavioural equations either directly or indirectly via bridge equations as it is shown in the next sections. Following the general strategy, the final demand components of the SNA system were explained first and the variables representing the components of the MPS system were respectively linked, using bridge equations (except for personal consumption and investment outlays). The inventory changes were generated as residuals by subtracting from GDP (or national income) to be distributed - the remaining components of final domestic demand.

Figure 4.1. Relationships between macro categories in WK-91 model

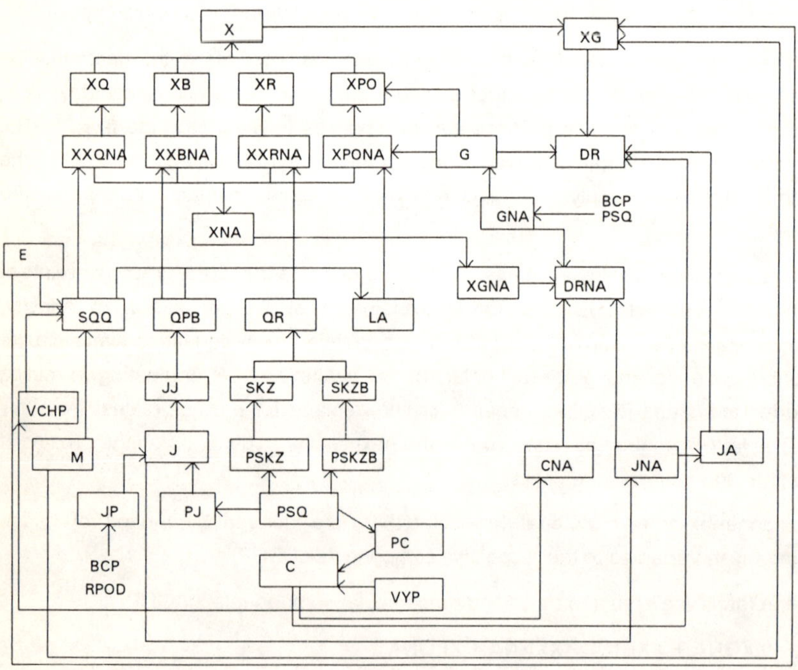

4.3.2. General assumptions on functioning of the economy in transition

The structure of the model and the relations between its variables should approximate the very mechanisms of functioning of the national economy. Models for the centrally planned economy were, generally, supply determined [6]. In a developed market economy we deal, most often, with demand-oriented models with somewhat elaborated supply side.

For the transition period from the centrally planned to the market economy no simple mixture of these two approaches can be advocated, as the transition of economic mechanisms is neither unique nor similarly phased in time (compare Portes [1991]). The dominating, in particular periods, economic mechanisms depend on the degree of departure from a command type management and central allocation of resources towards the market forces determined behaviour of the producers. This is a long-lasting process and it turns out that full abandoning of central, command type planning does not transform the state-owned firms into profit maximisers as long as they are not commercialised. Being wage-bill maximisers, they show lower efficiency, lower ability to respond to market signals, behave asymmetrically in their response to demand changes (if it declines they cut off their supplies and output first of all, but not the prices; if it increases they tend to increase prices instead of increasing capacity utilisation rates).

On the other hand, much depends on the characteristics of the growing impact of fiscal and monetary policies. Will they allow for maintenance of shortage economies (of various intensity) or will they promote regaining of market equilibrium (as it happened in Poland in 1990) and continue stabilisation policies? A shock therapy may reverse the economic regimes within a short period of time - hence the shift from a supply determined to a demand oriented economy can be represented by a shift of economic regimes in the model. Otherwise, mixed regimes must be assumed.

Happily enough, when starting the construction of a quarterly model for the Polish economy generally from 1990, we could safely assume that the Polish economy was demand determined. However, we had to keep in mind that behaviour of the dominating (in industry) state-owned firms is somewhat specific. Taking into account the rigidities in response to market signals, including price changes, we could assume that the macro economic mechanisms tend to be similar to those, which are attributed to the economic regime known as Keynesian unemployment rather than classical unemployment [7].

Below we shall show major relationships between the macro variables and blocks of equations describing the behaviour of particular groups of economic units. In the next sections the structure of particular blocks will be discussed in some more details. It will cover the blocks explaining final demand and its links to the production sector, activities of enterprises

---

[6] The latest annual models for Czechoslovakia and Poland contained, however, well elaborated demand side, allowing for shortages, using disequilibrium approach. See Welfe W. [1991].

[7] Hence, there is not much argument left in favour of empirical general equilibrium models, which assume perfect immediate market adjustments (of prices and of activities of economic agents).

(producers), the activities of the households, foreign agents, then of the government (its budget) and banking system and the system of prices.

The structure of particular model's blocks will be shown in Figure 4.2. reflecting major relations between the model's variables (except for details related to generation of macro-variables to be found in Figure 4.1).

Figure 4.2. Interrelations between variables of the WK-91 model

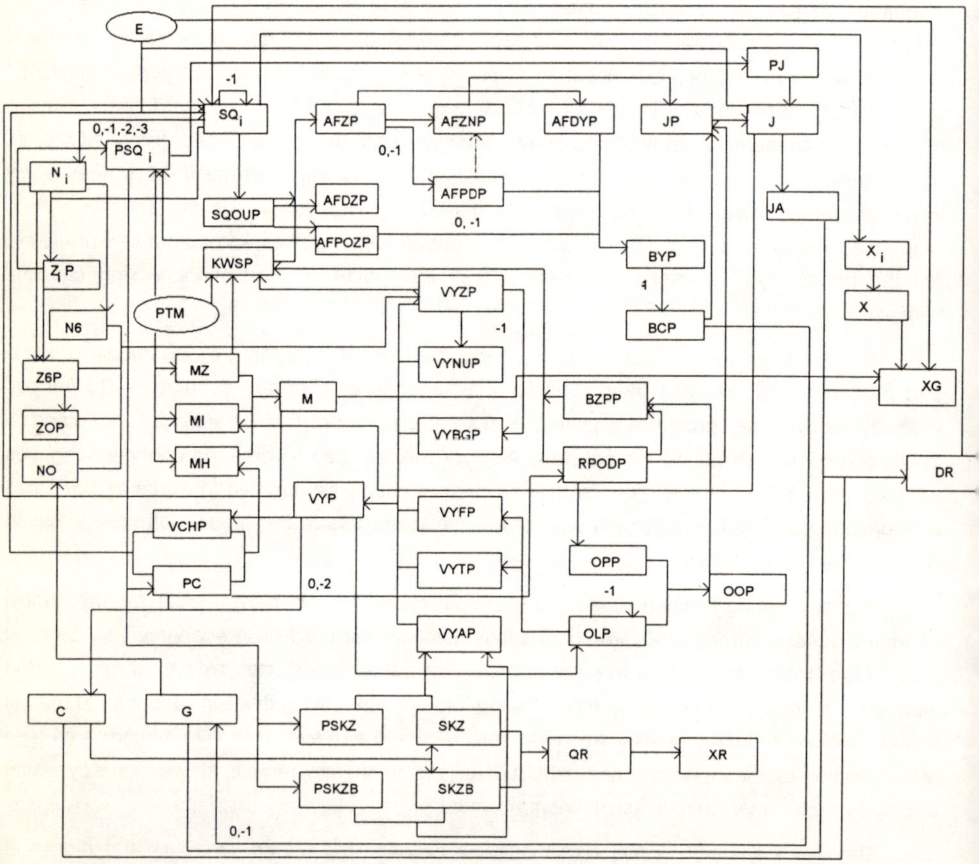

4.3.3. Major macro-relations

The most characteristic of a demand determined system is the feedback known as (Keynesian) multiplier. It plays an important role in explaining recession in the Polish economy between 1990-1992 (its impact was ignored for a long period by the leading monetarists). This feedback can be identified in the model in the following way: the real expenditures of the households (VCHP/PX) codetermine the demand for industrial products. This is being split into demand for domestic industrial products (SQQ) and imports (MH). The relative prices of imports to domestic prices (the imports prices are exogenous - in fact they depend on exchange rate and customs duty being implicit policy instruments) affect the changes in demand allocation. The industrial production affects transportation (LA) and, allowing for lags

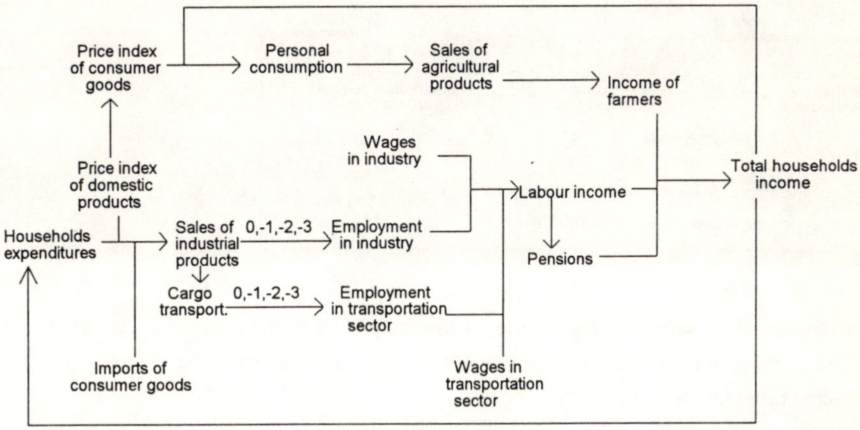

not exceeding 4 quarters, employment in these sectors. Given average wages total labour income (VYZP) is obtained, which affects the social benefits (VYBGP). Allowing for income from agriculture (VYAP) which depends on the agricultural output and this on consumers' demand (C) - total income of households VYP is obtained. It determines their total expenditures (VCHP) and given prices - the real expenditures, which closes the loop traversing through industry and transportation and, on the other hand, it determines the personal consumption which closes the feedback involving agriculture activities.

The above feedback is strengthened due to the endogenization of government budget expenditures (BCP). Its impact is, however, limited as the public demand does not affect in the model the demand for industrial commodities. An increment in the budget expenditures, through an increase of material expenditures (G) brings about an increase in the wage bill of employees paid from the budget (NO*ZOP), a portion of which returns to the budget via personal income tax. The additions to personal income allow an increase in the consumer's demand, thus in industrial activities (total sales SQOUP) and (except for wage bill discussed above - dotted lines in the arrow scheme) in firms' profits (AFZP).

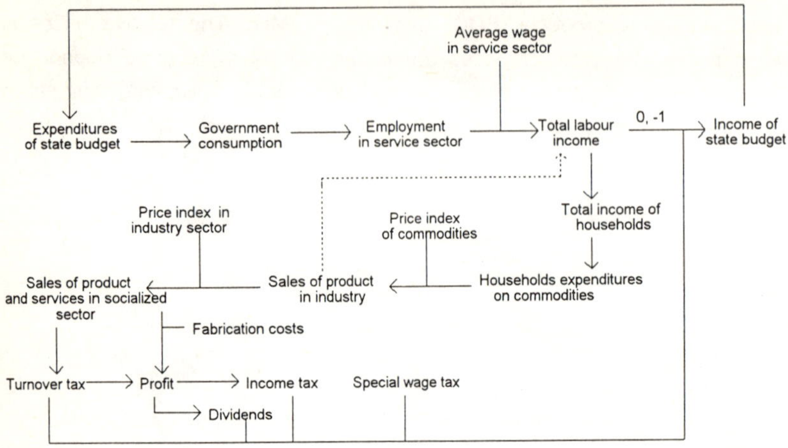

Hence, an increase in payments from turnover tax, corporate income tax, etc. follows which flow into the budget. As the budget receipts (BYP) determine its expenditures, we have an additional simultaneous feedback in the model.

What may seem unusual is that the budget deficit is residual in the model. However, it can be easily exogenized in the simulation exercises by means of respective adjustments of the parameters explaining budget expenditures (BCP). The same applies to other forms of likely government interventions. The wage rates of employees paid from the budget (ZOP) may be extraordinary raised by adjusting either constant or regression coefficients in the wage function, the tax rates can be adjusted in the same manner in respective equations explaining tax flows (AFPOZP, etc.).

The interrelationships typical of the growth mechanisms are not fully represented in the model (this is mainly due to the data constraints mentioned in the previous sections). The accelerator type feedback includes the following relationships. The total investment (J) codetermines demand for industrial products (the imports are being subtracted) and determines the output of construction industry. Given the prices, fabrication costs and tax payments - the net profits in the production sector are then determined (AFZNP). They influence directly the investment outlays (JP). On the other hand, total sales affect budget incomes from turnover tax, profits - incomes from the corporate income tax (and other taxes). Budget receipts determine budget expenditures (BCP) - being the second source of financing investment outlays. Another source of investment financing are bank loans, which are represented in the investment outlays equations by interest rate on the long term credits. Deflating the investment funds by prices of investment goods (PJ) we obtain the total investment (J).

Notice, that the government interventions can be carried out only indirectly - by changing the rates of taxation, allocation of the government expenditures and changes in the interest rates - all by means of parameter changes in respective equations.

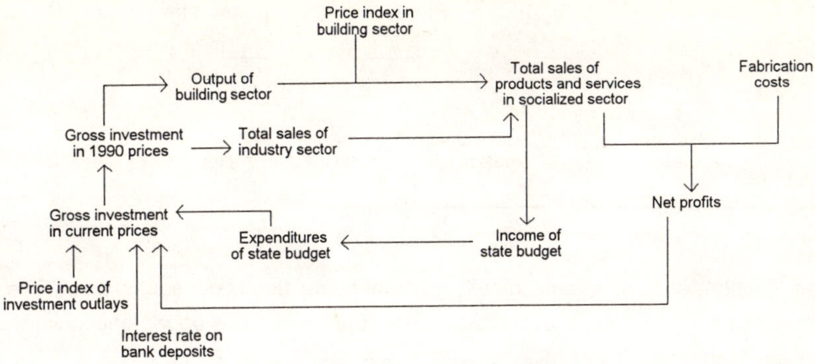

The likely shortcomings are due to the simplifying assumption that financial constraints are the major determinants of investment outlays. Hence, for the time being, the expectations of future demand were neglected as well as the degree of utilisation of existing fixed capital. Also, there is no link to the building up of productive capacities.

Following our remarks in the previous section, one should expect asymmetric behaviour of producers, their response - in terms of supply adjustments - to the demand decrease should be more sensitive than to the increase in demand (crowding out effects). As we were not able to test this hypothesis because of data scarcity, the simulation exercises using the estimated (average) response parameters may sometimes lead to inconclusive results.

The transition period is typically characterised by relaxing the control over prices to adjust the relative prices to free market prices, to constrain the subsidies and to regain market equilibrium, which leads to high rates of inflation. The stabilisation policies are then introduced, aimed at repressing the inflation with deflationary fiscal and monetary measures. Hence, the analysis of the inflation mechanisms and its adequate description by introducing the inflationary loop becomes a fundamentally part of the model. Studying properties of this feedback as well as the impact of external factors affecting inflation is one of the most important objectives in the model's construction. In this model, mainly the short-term adjustments are of interest. Let us assume at the point of departure, a certain level of the consumer's goods prices (PC). Each movement towards their increase results in the pressure on increasing the wages and salaries. The negotiations are led at firms levels and, for large public owned enterprises being wage-bill maximises, there is a natural tendency to retain, if not increase, the real value of wages by means of relevant nominal wage increases. This tendency is being hampered by superimposing special, highly progressive tax on wage increases exceeding the tax free rate of growth, calculated as an admissible fraction of the actual rate of inflation. In principle, the average wage increase may be compensated by an increase in labour productivity. The latter factor does not play any significant role - as we observe only slight changes in its level (-2%, +2%) compared to 40%-50% increase in nominal wages (at annual rates). Increased wage costs, being an important component of the production costs, are immediately transferred

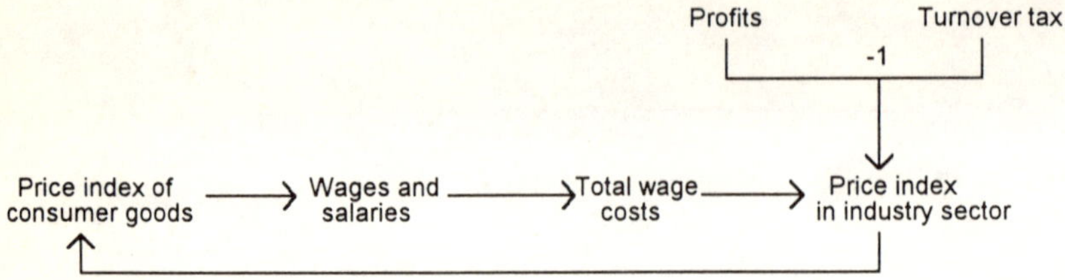

on prices, provided that there is not a demand ceiling or that production is not subsidised[8]. The domestic goods' prices at the producers level (PSQ) affect the consumer's goods prices which closes the inflationary loop.

The impact of demand pressures on prices is only indirectly reflected through the changes in profits (AFZP) being residual. They, allowing for one quarter lag transmit these impulses on the producers prices. The lack of capacity utilisation measure prevented us from the use of this typical proxy as the measure of disequilibrium intensity.

As the producer's prices depend also on taxes, especially the turnover tax (AFPOZP), which can also affect consumer's prices - the tax policy may use this channel additionally - to control the inflation.

The analysis of inflationary spiral can be combined with the previously discussed economic mechanisms, where prices and wages were assumed as predetermined. The wage increase, keeping the employment unchanged, will be followed by an increase in labour income and total nominal income. However, an increase in real incomes, and thus in consumer's demand, will follow only if the price increase induced by this wage increase will not compensate for the growth of nominal incomes.

Again, if an increase in producer's prices induced by an increase in labour costs is higher (lower) than the total costs increase, the profits will rise (decline). It will affect the investment activities as the real value of profits increases (declines). On the other hand, an increase in profits (also due to other factors) as well as in turnover tax affect positively the producer's prices with a quarter lag .

The description of relationships characteristic of money and capital flows and their links to real flows is only fragmentary because of the underdevelopment of the money and capital markets. The nominal personal incomes determine the additions to savings deposits of households, the interest rate being an important additional factor. These deposits (OLP) and the bank deposits of enterprises (OPP) which depend on total industrial sales add up to total deposits (OOP).

They form the basis for lending activities - the net loans (measured by increase in firms' debt BZPP) depend on net increase in total deposits and in interest rates (RPOD). The total

[8] The present policy tends towards systematic reduction in subsidies and one can deduce by observing the statistical data, that the level of subsidies has been considerably reduced in the last two years. Their share in the total expenditures of the state budget dropped from 40% to ca 10%.

debt of firms determines their expenditures on interest-payments. Following the increase in data availability we intend to split the information on banking activities, separating the short-term from the medium- and long-term loans. It will enable to analyse the sources of financing investment activities more directly - except for firms profits and government expenditures - the loans provided by the banking system and the sales of shares in the capital market will play the decisive role. At the moment, we have substituted the two latter items in the investment function by an estimate of the impact of average interest rate.

The interest rate is related to the discount rate, being the major instrument of monetary policy of the central bank. It can, by changing the discount rate, create more advantageous conditions of financing investment outlays from the bank credit, since, if the discount rate decreases, commercial banks can decrease the interest rate on the credits for their clients. However, due to high rates of inflation, the interests rates still depend, via the interests on saving deposits, on the changes in the index of consumer prices. Thus, the real interest rates continue to be positive.

However, such situation seems temporary. Due to the deep recession in industry, enterprises suffer from the lack of liquidity and development funds. Taking advantage of credits, which are very expensive (interest rates may reach 70% - 100% annually) causes that the locally manufactured products, bearing high credits costs in their prices can hardly compete with the cheap imported goods (not only from the Far East). So, with the inflation rate still being high, it seems likely that the rates of interest both on the savings and credits will decrease. Then savings, particularly those of individuals, will be invested instead of being banked. This will call for a re specification of the equation explaining exchange rate. (See also Èapinska-Sobczak [1991]).

4.4. Specification and empirical results for major blocks of variables

In this section the foundations of specification of the structural equations and the major results of estimation of these equations parameters will be reported. The complete simulation version of the quarterly model including the detailed results of estimation and all the identities is shown in Appendix 2. Absolute values of t-Student statistics are given in brackets below the parameter estimates.

4.4.1. Final demand components

The personal consumption of commodities and services (C) financed from the real disposable income can be explained referring to the standard concept of consumer demand function. Simple specification was suggested relating the consumer demand to a proxy for real disposable income being equal to deflated money receipts of the households (VYP/PC). As its dynamization occurred unsuccessful, a simple static demand function was used for estimation. The examination of the latest data has shown, however, that the inertia of households behaviour during the recession period are very strong (the decline in real incomes is hardly followed by relevant decline of expenditures - real savings decline and this especially applies to expenditures on housing and energy). Hence, lagged consumption (preferably for the quarter, when it reached maximum) will be tried again after the sample is extended.

$$\mathbf{C} = -329.27 + 0.77310^{*}\mathbf{(VYP/PC)} \qquad (4.5)$$
$$\quad (1.0) \qquad (178.0)$$

$R^2 = 0.999 \qquad DW = 2.51$

The marginal propensity to consume equals 0.773. It is rather low and it results from the use of the concept of total receipts of the households (including gross-profits of private sector) instead of personal, disposable income, which is not available.

The total personal consumption (CNA) includes, except all elements of C, also the individual consumption of non-material services (educational, health protection etc.) financed from public budget, being reported in MPS system (after subtracting labour costs) as a fraction of G. Hence, total requirements of the households can be explained using a quasi-bridge equation, which relates the requirements to personal consumption from real personal incomes (C) and, additionally, to other (social) consumption (G) in the same way as the data was generated:

$$\mathbf{CNA} = 1.1009^{*}C + 0.6339^{*}\mathbf{G} \qquad (4.6)$$
$$\quad (41.8) \qquad (4.9)$$

$R^2 = 1.000 \qquad DW = 0.90$

The other gross (social) consumption (GNA) was related to the deflated total government budget expenditures (BCP/PC). The marginal share is as low as 12%, which is due to the fact, that the wage bill and transfers, but not the expenditures on commodities, form the major part of the budget. The fit is poor, however the introduction of lags reduces serial correlation. The weights for the current and lagged variables were found using search procedure:

$$\mathbf{GNA} = 4632.9 + 0.1229^{*}\mathbf{\{0.4^{*}(BCP/PC)+0.6^{*}[BCP(1)/PC(1)]\}} \qquad (4.7)$$
$$\quad (2.4) \qquad (2.5)$$

$R^2 = 0.479 \qquad DW = 1.73$

The quality of fit of both equations shown above is completely different. This fact is connected with the way of generating quarterly time series for both endogenous variables. The values of CNA were obtained on the basis of the same relation as in regression equation above, estimated for annual data. For that reason, the R^2 statistics is equal 1 in this case. On the other hand, the values of quarterly data for variable GNA were obtained relating this variable to total consumption (CNA) - see Chapter 6. The fit for the annual data of the '80s was high, but it occurred that the above relationship ceased to remain stable for the years 1990-1991. Social consumption did not follow the decline in personal consumption, especially in 1990. Hence, the fit was poor for the quarterly data and we are looking for an improved form of bridge equation to generate the values of GNA.

Net investment outlays (JNA) depend on total investment outlays (J). It was implicitly assumed that depreciation forms a constant share of total investment outlays; this approximation seems acceptable for a short-term analysis. The level of investment activities in general depends on the producers expectations with respect to the future capacity increase and the opportunity costs. We had, however, to take into account that in Poland, the expectations were highly uncertain (which explains the low propensities to invest also from foreign firms). The major constraining factors affecting the investment decisions were, in fact, the available autonomous investment funds (foreign capital had to be ignored for the past) and the interest rate charged by banks offering credit lines. This made it possible to specify the investment function in current prices (JP). Hence, the investment outlays are explained by taking into account the main sources of financing investment i.e. net profits of enterprises (AFZNP) and government budget expenditures (BCP) as well as the changes in interest rates (RPOD):

$$\mathbf{JP} = \underset{(0.9)}{2172.7} + \underset{(1.5)}{0.1823}{*}\mathbf{AFZNP} + \underset{(11.8)}{0.5390}{*}\mathbf{BCP} - \underset{(1.6)}{28.765}{*}\mathbf{RPOD} \tag{4.8}$$

$R^2 = 0.967$ DW = 2.90

The highest statistical significance was obtained for variable BCP, but the value of parameter (0.54) is certainly overestimated. We expect to get better results for this equation after updating the sample.

The inventory changes were obtained as residuals from the balance equations:

$$\mathbf{DRNA = XGNA - CNA - GNA - JNA} \tag{4.9}$$

and respectively

$$\mathbf{DR = XG - C - G - JA} \tag{4.10}$$

The above equations close the system at the macro level. We intend to split the inventory formation into:

a) depending on the expected changes in activity levels,

b) being the result of demand-supply adjustments (changes in buffer stocks being residuals in balance equations).

The remaining blocks of the model will include the available (in the monthly-quarterly aspect) characteristics of real and financial flows of particular groups of economic agents and then prices.

4.4.2. Wages, incomes and money expenditures of households

The basic information concerning wages includes wages in 6 major sectors (industry, building, transportation, telecommunication, trade, communal services). The wages are in general negotiated at the firms level the rate of inflation being the crucial factor under high levels of inflation (70% in 1991). The impact of growing living costs was represented, however, in a linear form being an approximation of non-linear indexation scheme; the elasticity of wages with respect to the living costs were close to the upper levels of indexation coefficient (typically 0.6 in 1991), defining wage increase free of special prohibitive tax on wages. The long-term impact of productivity changes was also introduced. On the other hand, we were unable to follow the Philips curve specification as unemployment is a new phenomenon and its impact not necessarily follows classical schemes [9]. Hence, wages in particular industries were related to the general rate of inflation and the productivity of labour in each industry. For example, the results for manufacturing and mining industry are as follows:

$$\mathbf{ZQP} = \underset{(2.2)}{-798.70} + \underset{(14.2)}{947.57}*\mathbf{PC} + \underset{(2.4)}{23.908}*\mathbf{(SQQ/NQ)} \qquad (4.11)$$

$R^2 = 0.989$ DW = 1.62

where PC - index of consumers prices, SQQ/NQ - proxy for labour productivity (ratio of sales to employment).

A similar specification was applied to explain wages in building industry, transportation and trade. Wages in services sector follow (according to the present legal regulations) the wages in major industries. The rate of unemployment will be introduced as an explanatory variable in the near future after thorough testing of its impact.

Total labour incomes of households (VYZP) depend on wages in 6 major industries (Z6P) multiplied by employment in these industries (N6) and wages in services (ZOP) multiplied by employment in this sector (NO):

$$\mathbf{VYZP} = \underset{(0.1)}{32.781} + \underset{(68.9)}{0.9115}*[0.001*3*\mathbf{(Z6P*N6+ZOP*NO)]} \qquad (4.12)$$

$R^2 = 0.998$ DW = 1.59

---

[9] For more discussion see Welfe A. [1991].

It is the most important source of income as its share in the total incomes has reached ca 40% in the last years. This percentage, however, is systematically decreasing on behalf of the income (profits) from the private sector.

Incomes from social benefits also form a large percentage share (ca 18%) of the total incomes. They follow lagged labour income, as the pensions are indexed on the average wages (with quarterly lags):

$$\mathbf{VYBGP} = \underset{(0.6)}{913.84} + \underset{(13.0)}{0.6169}{*}\mathbf{VYZP(1)} \qquad (4.13)$$

$R^2 = 0.966 \qquad DW = 1.69$

Other incomes, especially in the private agriculture and business sector, should be linked with the available financial characteristics of their activities. For incomes from agriculture (VYAP) there are: the value of purchase of cattle for slaughter (SKZ*PSKZ) and the value of procurement of cereals (SKZB*PSKZB):

$$\mathbf{VYAP} = \underset{(0.9)}{-1121.0} + \underset{(5.1)}{0.0028}{*}\mathbf{(SKZ{*}PSKZ)} + \underset{(1.7)}{0.0087}{*}\mathbf{(SKZB{*}PSKZB)} \qquad (4.14)$$

$R^2 = 0.813 \qquad DW = 2.44$

The R2 statistics is not high for this equation as the two available indicators of agriculture activities cover only a part of total activities of this sector. For the growing incomes (profits) of the private business (except agriculture) (VYNUP) no reliable proxy for its activity could be found. Hence, they were related to the total labour income (VYZP).

The latter components are incomes from interest rates and dividends on stock and bonds as well as received loans. They depend on savings deposits and interest rates.

The consumer demand for commodities is explained in a similar way as the total consumers demand. Its specification followed, however, that assumed for this block - relating the variables in current prices. Hence, households expenditures on commodities are the function of nominal value of the purchasing fund (VYP):

$$\mathbf{VCHP} = \underset{(1.4)}{2801.8} + \underset{(22.3)}{0.5034}{*}\mathbf{VYP} \qquad (4.15)$$

$R^2 = 0.984 \qquad DW = 1.10$

Disaggregation of expenditures is unlikely. Its substitute would be distinguishing the retail sales and their major components like foodstuffs and alcoholic beverages, completed with estimates of sales in the private sector. Characteristics of inventory changes in trade channels would supplement this information. At present, this information is mainly available only for annual time intervals.

The model distinguishes also financial expenditures of the households both on taxes and fiscal charges and on credit repayment, which establishes links between the household sector, the state budget and the banking system. Households expenditures on taxes and charges take into account the fact that taxes are paid with some delay to the period of obtaining the incomes:

$$\mathbf{VCVP} = \underset{(1.3)}{-648.88} + \underset{(13.3)}{0.0804}\mathbf{*[0.5*VYP+0.5*VYP(1)]} \qquad (4.16)$$

$R^2 = 0.962 \qquad DW = 2.00$

Households expenditures on credit repayment are the function of incomes instead of accumulated credits granted (because of too small number of observations). Testing of specifications which assumed lagged incomes or weighted sum of current and lagged incomes was not successful, however.

$$\mathbf{VCFP} = \underset{(9.3)}{-133.74} + \underset{(9.3)}{0.6753}\mathbf{*VYFP} \qquad (4.17)$$

$R^2 = 0.916 \qquad DW = 1.55$

Equations explaining households saving are discussed below (Section 4.4.5).

4.4.3. Activities and financial position of enterprises in production and services sector

Activities of the business sector composed of public (socialised) and private enterprises are represented by the value of their output and/or sales. In the manufacturing and mining industry, the volume of the production sales (SQQ) will be mostly interpreted as the realisation of the composite demand of the final users (households (VCHP/PC), investors (J), and exporters (E) - the allocation coefficients being derived from the I-0 tables) and inventory demand (DR). The demand of intermediate users is represented by the lagged production sales. In order to introduce foreign competition, the total demand for industrial products is adjusted by subtracting imports of final goods (MH+MI). It is, of course, assumed that the producers supply follows the composite demand.

$$\mathbf{SQQ + MH + MI} = \underset{(2.4)}{28035.3} + \underset{(9.7)}{1.7101}\mathbf{*[0.582*(VCHP/PCX)+0.172*J+0.826*E]}$$

$$+ \underset{(2.0)}{0.1726}\mathbf{*SQQ(1)} + \underset{(4.0)}{0.8868}\mathbf{*DR} \qquad (4.18)$$

$R^2 = 0.974 \qquad DW = 0.72$

This specification needs certain improvements, as it ignores the mechanisms of formation of the producers demand expectations - not necessarily equal to effective demand. Its modification will become possible after we succeed in splitting the inventory increase into related to the increase of demand for it and fluctuations due to changes in the ratio of supplies (following demand expectations) and effective demand for domestic products.

More serious objection can be raised by claiming that the producers' behaviour in the transition period seriously differs from that which is standard for developed market economies. As it was mentioned earlier, an asymmetric behaviour was observed: a decline in demand was followed by a decline in the output without typical market adjustments aimed at decreasing sales prices and or fabrication costs. On the other hand, the increase in demand may bring crowding out effects (an increase in prices) instead of a relevant increase of output and supplies. However, it can be claimed that if in this case - the price increase takes place, it will negatively affect the initial final and intermediate demand. The price increase will attract competitive imports and this will have an additional negative impact on the demand for domestic product. At the very end it will be the effective demand which will determine the supplies and output. The problem will be thus shifted to the specification of producer's prices and imports. The former should show the real impact of changes in demand - supply ratio. The imports equations must be sensitive enough to relative price changes. These comments apply, to some extent, also to the equations explaining output or sales of other industries, shown below.

The basic output of construction industry depends on investment outlays on buildings and constructions:

$$\mathbf{QPB} = \underset{(47.5)}{0.6192}{*}\mathbf{JJ} + \underset{(16.2)}{3720.0}{*}\mathbf{(Z1+Z2)} + \underset{(6.1)}{2149.2}{*}\mathbf{Z3} - \underset{(8.7)}{3573.0}{*}\mathbf{U894}$$

$$- \underset{(7.8)}{1978.8}{*}\mathbf{U8912} + \underset{(7.2)}{2963.2}{*}\mathbf{U903} \qquad (4.19)$$

$R^2 = 0.983$ DW = 2.45

This sphere is characterised by many fluctuations. Some of them are seasonal ones (variable Z1, Z2 and Z3 express the influence of this kind of fluctuations) and others are accidental (dummy variables u894, u8912, u903). We expect some better results for this relation in the future.

As regards agriculture there will be employed these quantitative characteristics (and partly concerning values of sales) which are available in quarterly periods and refer to purchases of agricultural products by trade organisations rather (cattle for slaughter - SKZ, procurement of cereals - SKZB) than the output itself.

$$\mathbf{QR} = 0.00014 + 36.509^{*}\mathbf{SKZ} + 5.4177^{*}\mathbf{SKZB} \qquad (4.20)$$
$$(0.1) \qquad (59^{*}10^{5}) \qquad (2^{*}10^{7})$$

$R^2 = 1.000$ DW = 0.72

High goodness of fit is connected with the way of generating the quarterly time series for QR.

The transportation of cargo depends on the activities of manufacturing and mining industry and building industry being a weighted sum with the weights taken from the I-O table.

$$\mathbf{LA} = -109.29 + 0.0536^{*}\mathbf{(0.037^{*}SQQ+0.011^{*}QPB)} \qquad (4.21)$$
$$(4.2) \qquad (11.4)$$

$R^2 = 0.942$ DW = 1.93

The financial position of enterprises will, first of all, refer to the receipts from the sales of output in the industry (SQQ), building (QPBP) and transportation (LA) (particularly in the socialised one), generated on the basis of information on the "production sold" (in fixed prices by industries) outlined above and the level of producers (wholesale) prices (PSQ and PQB):

$$\mathbf{SQOUP} = 3559.4 + 1.2566^{*}\mathbf{(SQQ^{*}PSQ+QPB^{*}PQB+LA^{*}PSQ^{*}}19.85\mathbf{)} \qquad (4.22)$$
$$(1.1) \qquad (49.9)$$

$R^2 = 0.997$ DW = 1.45

Special attention had to be paid to the characteristics of transportation activities as variable LA is a quantitative one. Because of this, the coefficient 19.85 was taken into account to calculate the value of transportation output [10].

On the other hand, the subject of the analyses are the fabrication costs (KWSP) and financial accumulation of enterprises and its components: turnover tax (AFPOZP), subsidies (AFDZP) and gross profits (AFZP). In a market economy the gross profits are typically obtained as a residual from the following identity:

$$\mathbf{AFZP = SQOUP - KWSP - AFPOZP + AFDZP} \qquad (4.23)$$

The net profits of enterprises are obtained from gross profits after deduction of numerous taxes: income tax, "dividend" paid on fixed assets and tax on wage increase

---

[10] Coefficient 19.85 is the value of cargo transportation of 1 thousand ton in m. zloties (in 1990 constant prices) obtained for 1989.

exceeding the assumed portion of the rate of inflation (the latter paid by the state-owned firms only). The equation explaining fabrication costs adds up their major observable components - wage bill (VYZP), imports of intermediate goods (MZ*PTM) and payments of interest rate (BZPP*RPOD):

$$\mathbf{KWSP} = \underset{(0.1)}{-684.40} + \underset{(10.1)}{3.4213}^{*}\mathbf{VYZP} + \underset{(1.8)}{2.3282}^{*}\mathbf{(MZ^{*}PTM)} + \underset{(2.2)}{0.2296}^{*}\mathbf{(BZPP^{*}RPOD/100)}$$

$R^2 = 0.992$ DW = 1.31 (4.24)

As the costs of domestic material inputs were omitted on the right hand side, the coefficients standing with labour costs and imports are higher than one .

The equations explaining taxes allow, first of all, for the fluctuations in the tax base (sales, profits, wage bill, etc.). The turnover tax (AFPOZP) is more recently becoming the basic source of the state budget incomes. In the near future, it is to be replaced by the value added tax. As the tax rates differ among commodities, the relationship between its value and the value of sales was made stochastic. The turnover tax, as an indirect tax, is the basic instrument of fiscal macro-policy. By introducing low rates of the tax, central authorities can support particular spheres of activities, or, by imposing high tax, may constrain the areas which are not preferred (for instance imports of manufactured products).

The significance of subsidies (AFDZP) is heavily decreasing, as a result of the economic reforms. Their value in the last months has been fixed at the level of ca. 10% of the total expenditures of the state budget.

Gross profit was, through the income tax (AFPDP), one of the basic sources of the state budget incomes. Nowadays the tax's rate is fixed - 40%, but due to various exempts from the tax, its equation in the model cannot be deterministic, either. This tax, when compared to the turnover tax, is a much less effective tool of the financial policy, because of numerous and effective ways of hiding incomes by the tax-payers (especially in private sector) and declining profitability (especially of public firms). Then dividends (AFDYP) are also paid out from the profit of public firms, the tax base being the assets transferred by the state to these firms.

The changes in tax rates, being the fiscal policy instruments, can be introduced in the form of parameter changes of particular equations.

In this block, the characteristics of resources and their changes will be to some degree, taken into account, i.e. changes in assets and investment activities in real and nominal terms.

4.4.4. Foreign trade

The foreign trade will be represented in the model to a much greater extent than at the moment - both in real and nominal terms (values will be expressed in current domestic and transaction Zl, and in US dollars). At the initial stage, however, only real commodity flows will be explained. Imports decomposed according to their designation (consumption - MH, investments - MI, intermediate - MZ) will be explained from the demand side. They depend not only on the level of respective activities (output - SQOUP for intermediate, households expenditures - VCHP for consumption and investment outlays on machinery and equipment - JV for investment commodities). They also depend on relative prices (imports prices - PTM versus respective domestic prices - PSQ, PC or PJ) to reflect the competitiveness of imports. The estimation results are as follows:

Imports of intermediate commodities:

$$\mathbf{MZ} = \underset{(1.1)}{2548.7} + \underset{(1.9)}{0.0171}*\mathbf{(SQOUP/PSQ)} - \underset{(0.2)}{516.66}*\mathbf{(PTM/PSQ)} + \underset{(5.9)}{6372.1}*\mathbf{Z4}$$

R^2=0.907 DW=1.73 (4.25)

Imports of consumer goods :

$$\mathbf{MH} = \underset{(2.6)}{17787.4} + \underset{(0.4)}{0.0366}*\mathbf{(VCHP/PC)} - \underset{(1.8)}{11376.7}*\mathbf{(PTM/PC)} - \underset{(1.2)}{3530.9}*\mathbf{Z3}$$

R^2 = 0.603 DW = 1.84 (4.26)

Imports of investment goods:

$$\mathbf{MI} = \underset{(1.4)}{3867.1} + \underset{(3.9)}{0.4717}*\mathbf{JV} - \underset{(0.8)}{1878.9}*\mathbf{(PTM/PJ)} + \underset{(4.8)}{7239.3}*\mathbf{U912}$$

R^2 = 0.888 DW = 2.39 (4.27)

The impact of relative prices is not statistically significant in the three equations shown above but as the signs of the appropriate parameters are correct, we prefer to retain this specification for imports equations, hoping that its accuracy will improve after sample extensions and employing the information on movements of imports prices decomposed in a similar way as domestic prices.

Exports are exogenous. They will be endogenized in the near future and considered mainly from the demand side, although the supply approach will be simultaneously analysed in order to solve the adjustment problems (including the export price formation).

4.4.5. The banking system activities

The above blocks of equations were associated with selected characteristics of the banking system activities. On the one hand, the information about the level of banking deposits (savings) and cash as well as foreign currency deposits of households and enterprises and their increase, money supply, comes into play.

The equations explaining households' money savings increase relate it to their incomes and the interest rate on deposits:

$$\mathbf{OLP - OLP(1)} = \underset{(0.8)}{3767.9} + \underset{(2.9)}{0.1103}*\mathbf{VYP} + \underset{(0.9)}{25.355}*\mathbf{RPOD} + \underset{(4.6)}{27826.0}*\mathbf{U894}$$

$$R^2 = 0.850 \qquad DW = 2.30 \qquad (4.28)$$

The approximate propensity to save (11%) is high compared to historical standards, which may partly reflect the fact that in 1989 forced savings were included in the data. The untypical increase in households savings was observed in the fourth quarter of 1989. For this reason dummy variable u894 was introduced. The interest rate variable has proved statistically insignificant. As this variable plays an increasing role in generating households savings we decided not to give RPOD up as explanatory variable.

The firms deposits are naturally linked to the level of their activities. The impact of interest rate changes occurred negligible:

$$\mathbf{OPP} = \underset{(1.0)}{3590.9} + \underset{(10.1)}{0.2319}*\mathbf{SQOUP} \qquad (4.29)$$

$$R^2 = 0.927 \qquad DW = 2.47$$

On the other hand, the information about the crediting activities is only scarcely available. The major components of commercial and investment loans were only recently published. The available data with respect to production sector provided information about the level of debt only. Hence, we abandoned the idea of explaining "flows" and decided to explain "stocks". It was assumed, that the debt level depends mainly on available deposits as well as on the interest rate:

$$\mathbf{BZPP} = \underset{(0.3)}{4056.9} + \underset{(8.9)}{2.0293}*\mathbf{OPP} - \underset{(1.4)}{103.30}*\mathbf{RPOD} \qquad (4.30)$$

$$R^2 = 0.927 \qquad DW = 1.46$$

For the interest rate - a system of interest rates should be defined. At the initial stage, an interest rate on long term deposits was selected as their representative (up to now all of them show similar rates of change). It was endogenized by relating it to the lagged rate of inflation following the postulate broadly advocated in the past that the real interest rates should be positive in tendency:

$$\mathbf{RPOD1} = -0.0130 + 0.4207^{*}\mathbf{[PC/PC(2)]} \qquad (4.31)$$
$$\quad (0.1) \qquad (8.1)$$

$R^2 = 0.917 \qquad DW = 1.64$

Its partial exogenization is made possible through constant adjustments to allow for NBP autonomous decisions in changing the refinancing interest rate. We shall further develop the equations describing the money and capital markets following their development.

4.4.6. State budget

The block of equations depicting the total revenues and expenditures of the state budget explains these categories in nominal terms only, which results from the constraints in the information included in the available statistics on appropriate deflators. Along with expanding the information referring to the incomes and expenditures in quarterly periods, an appropriate decomposition of these items is predicted. The total incomes (BYP) will result from the generalisation of incomes from taxes as well as from the sale out of the state owned assets:

$$\mathbf{BYP} = -1702.9 + 1.2651^{*}\mathbf{\{[0.8^{*}(AFPDP+AFPOZP+AFDYP+AFPZP+0.13^{*}VYZP) +}$$
$$\quad (0.5) \qquad (11.9)$$

$$\mathbf{+\ 0.2^{*}[AFPDP(1)+AFPOZP(1)+AFDYP(1)+AFPZP(1)+0.13^{*}VYZP(1)]\}}$$

$R^2 = 0.952 \qquad DW = 2.34 \qquad (4.32)$

The weighted sum of current and previous period taxes was used for explaining the fact that not all the taxes are immediately paid by enterprises to the budget.

The expenditures will be linked to the subsidies and autonomous government expenditures, the role of which is systematically growing. At the moment they are related to the available total income (current and previous quarter):

$$\mathbf{BCP} = 369.67 + 1.0567^{*}\mathbf{[0.8^{*}BYP+0.2^{*}BYP(1)]} \qquad (4.33)$$
$$\quad (0.1) \qquad (15.0)$$

$R^2 = 0.970 \qquad DW = 2.13$

The budget deficit is residual. It can be partly exogenized however, by adjusting the expenditures respectively for an autonomous adjustment process (see Welfe A. [1990]).

4.4.7. Prices

The block of prices is rather complex. First of all, it includes the deflators of the production sold in manufacturing and mining and also building industry. The changes in the producers prices (deflators of the production sales) are linked to the changes in the labour costs and imports prices of materials, as well as to the lagged profits and taxes to reflect the market and fiscal inflationary pressures:

$$\mathbf{PSQ} = \underset{(0.7)}{-0.0192} + \underset{(3.2)}{0.2412}*\mathbf{PTM} + \underset{(13.6)}{4.9143}*\mathbf{[(3*ZQP*NQ/100)/SQQ]} + \underset{(47.5)}{0.5321}*\mathbf{\{[AFZP(1)+AFPOZP(1)]/SQQ(1)\}} \qquad (4.34)$$

$R^2 = 0.996 \qquad DW = 3.01$

As it was mentioned earlier the specification should allow more directly for the expected demand pressures. Hence, in the future, changes in the degree of utilisation of the production potential or inventory changes will be the likely candidates to be introduced as explanatory variables instead of lagged profits. Other elements of the price system are the prices of agricultural products, of investment goods, of consumer goods (retail prices), and in the future: exports prices and foreign currency exchange rates. Basically, they are associated with the producer's prices. First attempts to dynamize these equations have been recently made. The imports prices, and the potential market tensions will be taken into account in our further research after the sample extension. It must be added that the imports transaction prices (in Zl) will be decomposed into imports prices (in US $ or other foreign currencies), respective exchange rates and custom duties and turnover tax margins, being financial policy instruments.

4.4.8. Employment

A completion of the discussed system will be the block explaining changes in the employment (particularly, in the private sector) and the unemployment rates. The demand for employees depends on the output. It is characterised by significant lags to express the strong labour hoarding effects. For example, for manufacturing and mining industry the parameter estimates of demand function for employees are as follows:

$$\mathbf{NQ} = \underset{(11.0)}{3231.1} + \underset{(4.7)}{0.0096}*\mathbf{[0.1*SQQ+0.3*SQQ(1)+0.3*SQQ(2)+0.3*SQQ(3)]}$$

$R^2 = 0.818 \qquad DW = 2.00 \qquad (4.35)$

The lag structure was established after testing alternative lag distributions.

The equation explaining labour supply and unemployment rate will be introduced in the next phase of research.

4.5. The model as a system. First conclusions

The structure of the model equations is such, that it restricts the number of the exogenous variables. They are composed of variables which are:

a) really external against the national economy, i.e. the characteristics of international trade (exports and imports prices at the moment) and possibly the weather conditions

b) express the instruments of fiscal and monetary policy. The latter include either specific variables (for example tax on wage increase exceeding assumed ceilings or in the future - foreign currency exchange rates) or more frequently changes in the equations parameters (for example, in the rates of interest on deposits and credits, in the level of deficit-surplus of the state budget via its expenditures, in the rates of indexation, tax rates).

The quarterly model WK-91 in its last simulation version of December 1991 contains 67 stochastic equations (including 9 bridge equations) and 16 identities. It is a simultaneous and dynamic simulation system. All its equations are shown in Appendix 2, as it was mentioned above.

Let us remind, that the consumption multiplier is characterised by lags not exceeding 4 quarters (mainly due to the lags in employment adjustments). The consumers', demand codetermines the industrial output, which affects the employment and labour income being the main determinant of real incomes and of consumers demand. The accelerator has a specific form - the investment demand codetermines the industrial output and it affects the profits being one of the sources of investment outlays. The inflationary spiral (loop) is also included - the increase in retail prices is followed by the wage increase and the latter affects the producers prices (via labour cost increase); the producers prices determine the retail prices.

The model was initially solved using the G-package on PC - microcomputers. It has been recently placed in the STS estimation system and SIMUL-package is being used for simulation exercises. Around 20 iterations were needed to obtain the first control solution. The initial model testing has shown, that the major macro-variables are well represented in the ex-post dynamic simulations. However, several variables and some blocks, especially prices showing biased estimates and instability, need further refinements. In the first line the model dynamization has been broadened - as far as it is only possible - with 10-14 quarterly observations at our disposal. After introducing particular lags and lag distributions the fits improved, serial correlation declined and stability increased. The first attempt to introduce the expectations into the behavioural equations was made and is described in Chapter 5. It also contains the first results of multiplier analysis.

The next steps in the model's development will be: the introduction of nonlinearities and the use of consistent estimation procedures.

Our intention is to update the model systematically by regular reestimation of its parameters quarter by quarter and testing for the stability of estimates and ex-post forecasts. We hope to make the model operational in the near future.

REFERENCES

Bank of Finland Quarterly Model, Version 1 MB LINK [1979], Research Department, Bank of Finland, Helsinki

Corrado C. [1988] - Reducing Uncertainty in Current Analysis and Projections: the Estimation of Monthly GNP, Special Studies Paper - Division of Research and Statistics, Federal Reserve Board, Washington

Courbis R., P. Salmon [1986] - Le Modele PROTEE, un modele trimestriele de l'economie francaise, Presentation generale et utilisation. II-eme Seminaire Franco-Polonais sur la Modelisation, Nanterre 29-30 mai (Papier GAMA, no 544)

D'Adda C., E.De Antoni, G.Gambetta, P.Onofri, A.Stagni [1976] - Un Modello per l'economia italiana, il Mulino

Fase M.M.G. [1984] - The Monetary Sector of the Netherlands in 50 Equations; a Quarterly Model for the Netherlands 1970-1979, in: J.P. Ancot ed. Analysing the Structure of Econometric Models, Advanced Studies in Theoretical and Applied Econometrics vol 2., Martinus Nijhoff, The Hague, Boston, p. 195-228

Hansen G., U.Westfal [1975] - A Quarterly Econometric Model for the Federal Republic of Germany. Special Features and Forecasting Results, paper on Congress of Econometric Society, Toronto

Juszczak G., M.M.Kaźmierska, N.Łapinska-Sobczak, W.Welfe [1991a]- Short-Term Models of Financial Flows for the Polish Economy in Transition, paper presented at the A.C.E. Seminar, Simulations and Financial Models, Mittelberg 1991, and at the European Economic Association Congress, Cambridge August 31-September 2, 1991, Materiały IEiS no 2/91. Discussion Papers, Łódź

Juszczak G, M.M.Kaźmierska, N.Łapinska-Sobczak, W.Welfe [1991b]- Short Term Macro econometric Model of the Polish Economy in Transition, paper presented for the A.C.E. Seminar: The Concept of a System of ` Models and Forecasts, Paris, October 23-25, 1991, Materiały IEiS no 37/91, Łódź,

Juszczak G, M.M.Kaźmierska, N.Łapinska-Sobczak, W.Welfe [1992a]- Quarterly Model of the Polish Economy in Transition (with Special Emphasis on Financial Flows, paper presented at the European Meeting of the Econometric Society August, 24-27, 1992, Brussels, Materiały IEiS no 17/92, Discussion Papers, Łódź,

Juszczak G, M.M.Kaźmierska, N.Łapinska-Sobczak, W.Welfe [1992b]- Real and Financial Flows in the Polish Economy in Transition Period. (A Quarterly Model) paper presented at the Annual Congress of the EEA, Dublin, August 29-31, 1992, Materiały IEiS, UŁ, no 14/92 Discussion Papers, Łódź,

Kaźmierska M.M., S.Narel [1992] - Unobservable Macro aggregates in the Quarterly Econometric Model of the Polish Economy, paper to be presented at the Annual Congress of the EEA, Dublin, August 29-31, 1992, Materiały IEiS no 18/92, Discussion Papers, Łódź

Łapinska-Sobczak N. [1991] - The Structure of the Quarterly Model of the Polish Economy in the Transition Period to the Market Economy, paper presented at the Workshop - A.C.E. Seminar, Simulations and Financial Models, Mittelberg 1991, Materiały IEiS no 25/91, Łódź

Mc Carthy M.D. [1972] - The Wharton Quarterly Econometric Forecasting Model MARK III, Studies in Quantitative Economics no 6., University of Pennsylvania

Macro econometric Model of the Deutsche Bundesbank. Model Version 30/03/88 [1988], Deutsche Bundesbank

Malgrange P. [1983] - Steady Growth Paths in a Short Run Dynamic Model: The Case of the French Quarterly Model "Metric", paper CEPREMAP, no 8321, Octobre

Portes R. [1991] - Introduction, of: European Economy, The Path of Reform in Central and Eastern Europe, Special Edition, no 2, Commission of the European Communities, Brussels-Luxemburg

Tarkka J., H.L.Maennistoe, A.Willman [1990] - The BOF4 Quarterly Model of the Finnish Economy, Bank of Finland

Uriel E., J.Akaide, J.B.Pena, J.B.Raymond, A.Rodriquez [1981] - The PREFICO Model: A Quarterly Model of the Spanish Economy, paper for Project LINK Meeting, New York

Welfe A. [1990] - State Budget and Inflation Processes. Estimates for Poland, Journal of Public Economics, 43, p. 61-180.

Welfe A. [1991] - Modelling Wages in Centrally Planned Economies: the Case of Poland, Economics of Planning, 24, p.47-58,

Welfe W. [1991] - Multisectoral Econometric Models of the Centrally Planned Economies and the Disequilibria, Economics of Planning, vol. 24.

CHAPTER 5

DYNAMIC EXPECTATIONS IN THE QUARTERLY MODEL OF THE POLISH ECONOMY

Maria Magdalena Kaźmierska, Wojciech Zatoń

Institute of Econometrics and Statistics, University of Łódź

5.1. Introduction

This chapter provides a short description of our efforts to introduce expectations in the most strategic equations of the quarterly model of the Polish economy (WK-91RE version), some notes on the rational expectations (RE) algorithm for solving the RE models and presents the results of most important policy simulations.

The WK-91RE version of the model includes dynamic expectations reflecting the increased flexibility of market reactions to the changes in economic policy in Poland. The transition from a centrally planned to a market economy is in progress and requires from the economic agents more caution and considering information not only from the past and the present but also taking into account by them the expected development in order to adjust their present behaviour to the rapidly changing economic situation.

The simulation experiments are carried out in three ways: a) by assuming that changes in economic policy are known in advance; b) changes are not known in advance - agents are "surprised"; c) the above two versions are compared with the results based on the primary version of the model omitting dynamic expectations.

5.2. Expectations in the model

WK-91RE model differs from its primary, "static" version, WK-91, in 5 equations where expectations are introduced. We have limited the time horizon for expectations to 1 quarter, because of the short sample available for quarterly data. Below, we give a description of these equations. The specification present in WK-91 model is listed first, and then the corresponding version including expectations - name of dependent variable in this equation is underlined. The equations were estimated using the OLS method. The numbers in parentheses below parameter estimates are t-ratios, R2 the coefficient of determination, R2C is the coefficient of determination adjusted for the degrees of freedom, D-W is the Durbin-Watson statistics, V the coefficient of variation, MAPE is the mean absolute percentage error, and SAMPLE is the estimation period for a given equation.

Credits taken out by enterprises (their total debt) (BK) depend on the money supply represented by total bank deposits of enterprises and households (OOP), and the interest rate (RPOD).

Credits taken out by enterprises

$$\mathbf{BK} = -40658.3 + 0.84443 * \mathbf{OOP} - 27.0142 * \mathbf{RPOD} \qquad (5.1)$$

(7.09) (32.0) (1.66)

R2=0.998 R2C=0.997 D-W=2.33 V=2.55 MAPE=2.33 SAMPLE 1989.4 - 1991.2

$$\underline{\mathbf{BK}} = -37118.9 + 0.83198 * \mathbf{OOP} - 43.0276 * \mathbf{[0.6*RPOD + 0.4*RPOD(+1)]} \qquad (5.2)$$

(7.11) (36.3) (2.53)

R2=0.999 R2C=0.998 D-W=2.66 V=2.06 MAPE=1.16 SAMPLE 1989.4 - 1991.2

Prevailing part of credits are loans required by producers. They, in their decisions, take into account not only the current interest rate, but also its level expected one period ahead. This factor is important in Poland where interest rate is high (109% on the average in 1990), but is systematically declining, following the decreasing rate of inflation, and cases of failures to pay off the credit are still frequent enough. The absolute value of estimated coefficient increased and it became statistically significant. The weights were established using search procedure.

Investment outlays, nominal

$$\mathbf{JP} = -1464.66 + 0.89541 * \mathbf{[0.3*BK + 0.1*BCP + 0.1*AFZP(1)]} - 17472.2 * \mathbf{(U911 + U912)} \qquad (5.3)$$

(0.32) (6.26) (3.82)

R2=0.909 R2C=0.863 D-W=2.89 V=14.88 MAPE=9.28 SAMPLE 1989.4 - 1991.2

$$\underline{\mathbf{JP}} = -15118.5 + 0.61220 * \mathbf{[0.3*BK + 0.1*BCP + 0.1*AFZP(1)]} +$$

(-1.19) (4.51)

$$0.44339 * \mathbf{AFZP(+1)} + 16952.7 * \mathbf{U904} \qquad (5.4)$$

(1.99) (5.03)

R2=0.960 R2C=0.920 D-W=2.47 V=11.4 MAPE=7.73 SAMPLE 1989.4 - 1991.2

This equation explains the value of investment outlays, taking into account the availability of investment funds. Main sources of investment financing are: credits (BK) - their level absorbed by the enterprises is regulated by the changes in the interest rate (see equation above), state budget expenditures (BCP), and gross profits of enterprises (AFZP) gained one period before. Two points, both resulting from the infirmity of the statistical sources on the quarterly data for Polish economy, need explaining. First, share coefficients of outlays on investment from different sources of financing are the averages on the 1990 quarterly data (these statistics were not reported for the quarters in the years prior to 1990). Keeping these coefficients as fixed for the whole estimation period, it was necessary to introduce dummy variables (U911, U912 and U904. equal 1 in periods indicated in labels and 0 in the others). Second, due to the only partial (not for all quarters) availability of the data for the net profits of enterprises we had to apply gross profits instead. Profits expected one quarter ahead are the factor strongly stimulating investment activities which was later confirmed by the simulation experiments. The goodness of fit increased and average cross declined.

Bank deposits of households

$$\mathbf{OLP - OLP(1)} = \underset{(0.77)}{2572.19} + \underset{(5.06)}{0.14031} * \mathbf{VYP} + \underset{(1.98)}{25.7966} * \mathbf{RPOD} + \underset{(6.92)}{27901.3} * \mathbf{U894} + \underset{(2.66)}{- 10869.8} * \mathbf{U911} \qquad (5.5)$$

R2=0.946 R2C=0.892 D-W=2.40 V=19.16 MAPE=18.64 SAMPLE 1989.2 - 1991.2

$$\underline{\mathbf{OLP - OLP(1)}} = \underset{(1.89)}{-12858.4} + \underset{(4.15)}{0.22112} * \mathbf{VYP} + \underset{(4.15)}{134.964} * \mathbf{[RPOD(+1) - RPOD]} + \underset{(4.23)}{160.729} * \mathbf{RPOD} - \underset{(2.40)}{13407.7} * \mathbf{(U904 + U911)} \qquad (5.6)$$

R2=0.867 R2C=0.734 D-W=1.97 V=30.0 MAPE=22.9 SAMPLE 1989.2 - 1991.2

Increase in households money savings depends on their incomes (VYP) and the interest rate level (RPOD). Additional factor influencing the increment of savings is the expected movement in the interest rate. The introduction of this variable made the impact of interest rates statistically significant. Dummy variables which are present in the equations (U894, U904 and U911 equal 1 in periods indicated in labels and 0 in others) express two effects : a) increase in savings just before starting the stabilisation program in Poland (since 1.01.1990) announcing high inflation rate but, at the same time, advantageous interest rate on bank deposits; b) decrease in savings (since 1990.4/1991.1) and spending them on the current consumption, because of the continued rigorous restrictions imposed on increase in wages being again an element of the stabilisation program.

State budget expenditures, total

$$\mathbf{BCP} = \underset{(0.36)}{1134.02} + \underset{(13.2)}{1.05056} * \mathbf{[0.7*BYP + 0.3*BYP(1)]} \qquad (5.7)$$

R2=0.961 R2C=0.956 D-W=2.71 V=12.93 MAPE=10.46 SAMPLE 1989.2 - 1991.2

BCP = -967.558 + 1.07926 * **[0.7*BYP + 0.2*BYP(1) + 0.1*BYP(+1)]** (5.8)
(-0.29) (12.9)

R2=0.960 R2C=0.954 D-W=2.29 V=13.19 MAPE=10.65 SAMPLE 1989.2 - 1991.2

State budget expenditures are the function of a weighted sum of its receipts coming from the current and previous quarters. Taking into account the receipts expected one period ahead as an explanatory variable shows the way of constructing the budget with anticipating future incomes when planning current expenditures. The weights were obtained using search procedures.

Agriculture output

QR + MH = 7519.95 + 0.38218 * **(C + 0.06*E)** + 14408.3 * **Z3** (5.9)
(0.98) (2.99) (4.73)

R2=0.857 R2C=0.816 D-W=2.57 V=12.13 MAPE=8.47 SAMPLE 1989.1 - 1991.2

QR + MH = 3652.53 + 0.43777 * **(C + 0.06*E)** + 0.23691 *
(0.56) (4.04) (2.09)

{ { [PSKZ(+1) + PSKZB(+1)]/2 }/ PC(+1) - [(PSKZ + PSKZB)/2] / PC } / { [RPOD(+1) - RPOD] / 100 } + 15183.3 * **Z3** (5.10)
(6.0)

2=0.917 R2C=0.876 D-W=1.92 V=9.8 MAPE=6.33 SAMPLE 1989.1 - 1991.2

Total demand for agricultural products (QR, domestic agriculture output + MH, imports of consumer goods) is determined by the private consumption (C) and exports (E). It seemed justifiable to include also the impact of factors determining domestic supplies of agricultural products. From the supply side, the decisive factor is the production profitability measured by the relation of a change in real incomes from agriculture (represented by the relation of procurement prices, PSKZ - prices of cattle and pigs for slaughter, PSKZB - prices of cereals to retail prices of consumer goods and services PC) to a change in indirect production costs (including, above all, repayment of the short-term credits, and showed in the equation through the fluctuations in interest rate). Dummy variable Z3 (equal 1 in a corresponding quarter of every year) cumulates seasonal effects.

5.3. Rational expectations algorithm

This section gives a short description of the basic algorithm for solving rational expectations models, following Fair, Taylor [1983]. This algorithm was used to solve WK-91DE model.

Consider the dynamic rational expectations model given by :

$$f_i(\mathbf{y}_{t-p},\ldots,\mathbf{y}_{t-1},\mathbf{y}_t,E\mathbf{y}_{t+1},\ldots,E\mathbf{y}_{t+h},\mathbf{x}) = u_{it}\ ,\ i=1,\ldots,n \qquad (5.11)$$

where **y** is an n-dimensional vector of endogenous variables at time t,, **x** is a vector of exogenous variables (it may contain variables with lags and leads), E is the expectations operator and u is a random disturbance with mean zero. In the basic algorithm we consider the model without serial correlation and assume that $Eu_{it}u_{is}=0$ for $t \neq s$. In the notation of (5.11), p is a maximum lag and h is a maximum lead on endogenous variables. Because of the presence of expected endogenous variables in (5.11) we cannot, in general, define the termination date for solution of (5.11). We assume an integer k as a number of periods beyond the horizon h for which the model should be solved. Thus, the time structure for the solution of (5.11) can be illustrated as in the figure 5.1.

Figure 5.1. Time Structure in RE Models.

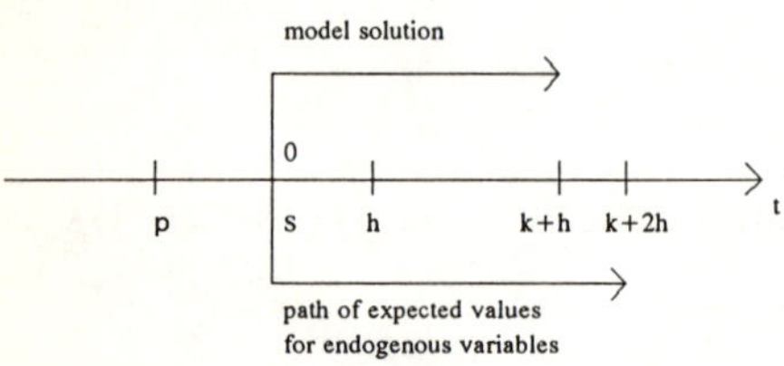

From figure 5.1 it follows that we must solve the model for k+h periods, having expected values for endogenous variables for k+2h periods. The solution algorithm is presented on figure 5.2.

We start in period s that refers to the zero point on the time axis. An initial number k is denoted by K, and $e_r(i,k)$ (where i=0 and k=K) is an initial path of expected values for endogenous variables, r=0,1,...,k+2h. First, we solve the model for r periods, r=0,1,...,k+h, allowing maximum MAXIT1 iterations for every period and checking convergence for endogenous variables assuming ε as a convergence criterion. This procedure is just a dynamic solution of the model using Gauss-Seidel or Newton's method and, in the RE algorithm, iterations in this procedure are called Type I iterations.

Having convergent solution of the model for k+h periods, we get a new path of expected values for endogenous variables $e_r(i,k)$ and examine convergence for corresponding elements of the $e_r(i,k)$ and $e_r(i-1,k)$ vectors. If the computed absolute difference for any of the elements is greater than the convergence criterion τ, we replace an old path $e_r(i-1,k)$ with a new one $e_r(i,k)$ and solve the model again for k+h periods. Every pass of the solution algorithm through all periods is called a Type II iteration and we assume MAXIT2 to be a maximum number of Type II iterations allowed for the solution process.

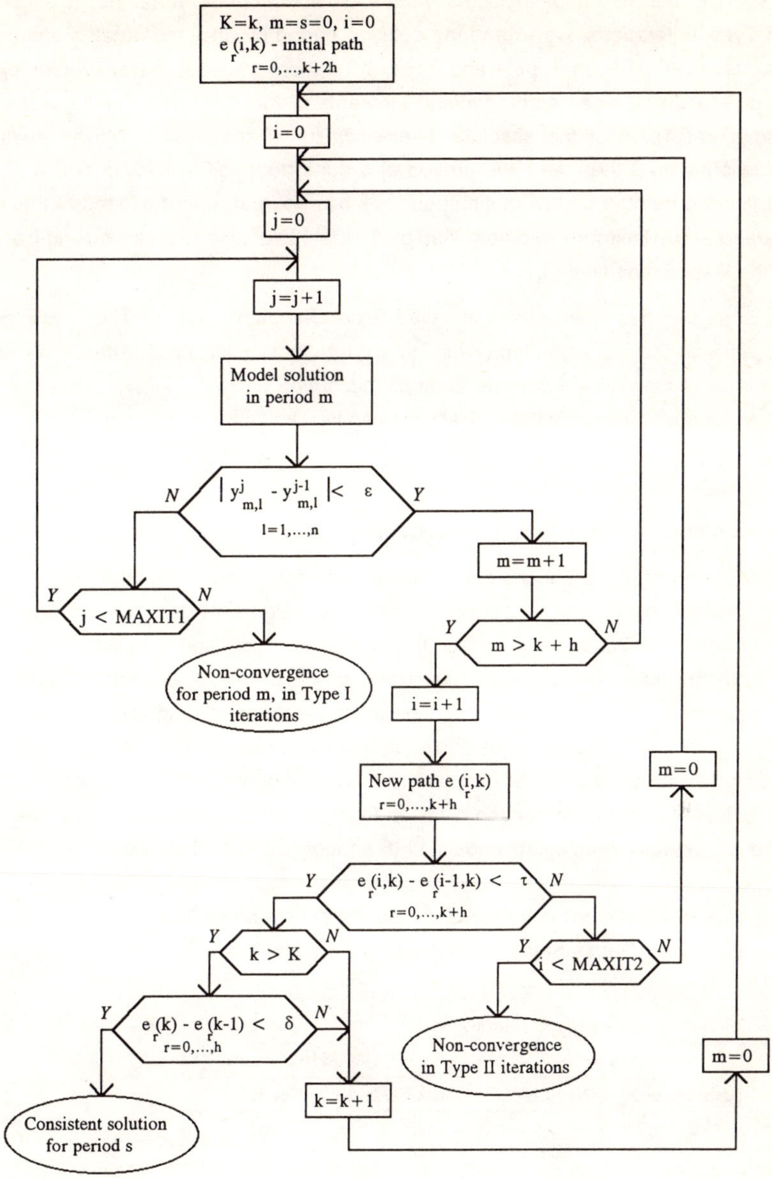

Figure 5.2. Rational expectations algorithm.

As $e_r(k)$ is the vector of expected values for endogenous variables in a convergent solution in Type II iterations, we extend the solution period by one, repeat all steps and, after passing successfully through Type I and Type II iterations, we get a new vector $e_r(k)$. We check the difference between corresponding elements of the $e_r(k)$ and $e_r(k-1)$ vectors within the horizon h, r=0,1,...,h. If the absolute differences for all these elements are less than a convergence criterion δ then we have arrived at a consistent solution for period s, if not, we increase again the number of the solution periods k by one, and repeat all steps - this is called Type III iteration. The limit for k is determined by the data available (we can extend the solution period on the last data available).

The algorithm described above is called "extended path" method. The tolerance levels for convergence in the RE algorithm (ε for Type I iterations, τ for Type II iterations and δ for Type III iterations) may differ from one another (according to Fair, Taylor (1983) the relation between them should be: $\varepsilon<\tau<\delta$) but in practice, we often apply the same check for iterations of all types.

5.4. Estimation and base solution of the model

The 59 stochastic equations of the model were estimated using OLS. For the simulation purpose, the equations were reordered using algorithm described in Don, Gallo [1987]. The simultaneous block of the model is large and consists of 72 equations from the total number of 84 (there are only 1 pre recursive and 11 post recursive equations). Having a set of 5 feedback variables distinguished in the simultaneous block, we could apply Newton's method for the solution of the model. As a tool for simulation we used the SIMPC program (see Manual SIMPC 3.0 [1990] for details). In WK-91RE model, a horizon h for endogenous expectations is 1, and the number of endogenous expectations equals 42 (6 endogenous variables with one lead

Table 5.1. Number of iterations in the base solution of WK-91 and WK-91RE models for the Gauss-Seidel and Newton solution methods.

Type II Iterations	Type I iterations (*)			
	WK-91		WK-91RE	
	Gauss-Seidel	Newton	Gauss-Seidel	Newton
1	150	74	135	68
2	-	-	105	64
3	-	-	26	44
4	-	-	7	7
Total	150	74	273	183

(*) For each Type II iteration, total number of passes through the simultaneous block of the model for 7 periods is reported. For Newton scheme it includes iterations for (re)evaluation of the Jacobian.

each, times 7 periods, 1990.1-1991.3), however expectations for 1991.3 (beyond the solution period) never get changed. Thus, we need 36 endogenous variables with expectations to converge in Type II iterations. We applied the same convergence criterion (0.0001) for iterations of all types, and tested Gauss-Seidel and Newton algorithms for the solution of the model. Table 5.1 reports the number of Type I and Type II iterations required to obtain the base solution of the model. To arrive at a consistent solution within a horizon h, one Type III iteration was needed.

It results from Table 5.1 that the Newton method considerably outperforms the Gauss-Seidel scheme. Table 5.2 is a compilation of the mean absolute percentage errors (MAPE) obtained in estimation and base solution, and is a kind of model validation (for each interval, number of equations with a corresponding MAPE value is given).

Table 5.2. Distribution of MAPE values for estimation and base solution in period 1989.4-1991.2

MAPE	Estimation	Base solution	
		WK-91	WK-91RE
0 - 5	20	8	8
5.1 - 10	12	9	14
10.1 - 20	15	47	51
> 20	12	20	11
Total	59	84	84

5.5. Results of policy simulations

We prepared four simulation experiments, each of them in three variants. The experiments, performed on the base solution, consisted in introducing, in the third quarter of 1990, the following policy changes :

- 10% increase in exports,
- 10% increase in import prices,
- 10% increase in interest rate on long term deposits
- 10% increase in wages for 4 main sectors

The variants for all the experiments were as follows:

a) the simulation was performed on the original version of the WK-91 model excluding dynamic expectations - call this variant "static",

b) using the WK-91RE version of the model, we started simulation in the fourth quarter of 1989 assuming in this way that a policy change is known three periods in advance - this variant is called "dynamic",

c) as in b) we used the WK-91RE version of the model but started simulation in the third quarter of 1990 assuming that a policy change is not known in advance - call this variant "surprise".

The results are described below and presented (for selected variables) on graphs as percentage deviations from the base solution.

The strongest effects of a policy change in each of the four experiments are observed in variant "dynamic" and we concentrate on them while describing the results.

Increase in exports

Expecting the change in exports in 1990.3 we observe the increased economic activity already 2-3 periods before. NMP increases in first periods (4.6% in 1990.3) improving financial abilities of enterprises and the state budget thus giving an impulse to the investment process (10.2% of increase in profits, 10.2% of increase in investment). At the same time, growing demand can be realised through the small variations in production factors, because of the low degree of their utilisation. Fluctuations in employment follow the changes in production with a delay of 2-3 quarters. In the first periods (1990.1-1990.3) net output increases at a faster rate than production costs (mainly wages) bringing about the fall in domestic prices (2% in 1990.3), keeping import prices exogenous. In 1990.3 total imports increase by 1.9% because of an increase in imports of investment goods (6.4%) while the imports of consumer goods decrease by 3.2%. In the next periods growing production costs stimulate inflation (4.4% increase in prices in 1991.2). Similar reactions appear in other variants but are weaker.

Increase in import prices

In this experiment one can easily see the considerable influence of expected profits on the level of investment outlays and, consequently, on the production. 10% increase in import prices in 1990.3 brings about 7% increase in production costs and 8.8% increase in sale revenues. It results from raising production prices, more than justified, by the increase in imports prices. In this way producers gain additional profits on sales. Expecting a 15% increase in profits in 1990.3 producers decided to augment investment outlays by 3.8% already in 1990.1 and 15% in 1990.2. Finally, NMP rises by 0.5% and 2.7% respectively. In "static" variant, the reactions are different because expected profits are not considered for taking investment decisions. High inflation rate (6.3% in 1990.3) causes the decline in real investment outlays by 3% and NMP drops by 0.2%. Increase by 10% in import prices gives 6.3% increase in overall price index resulting in 7% increase in wages. In the next quarters the changes in prices and wages show the same dynamics due to the producers efforts to keep profits at the maximum level reached in 1990.3.

Figure 5.3. Effect of an Increase in Exports.
(percentage differences between variant and base solution)

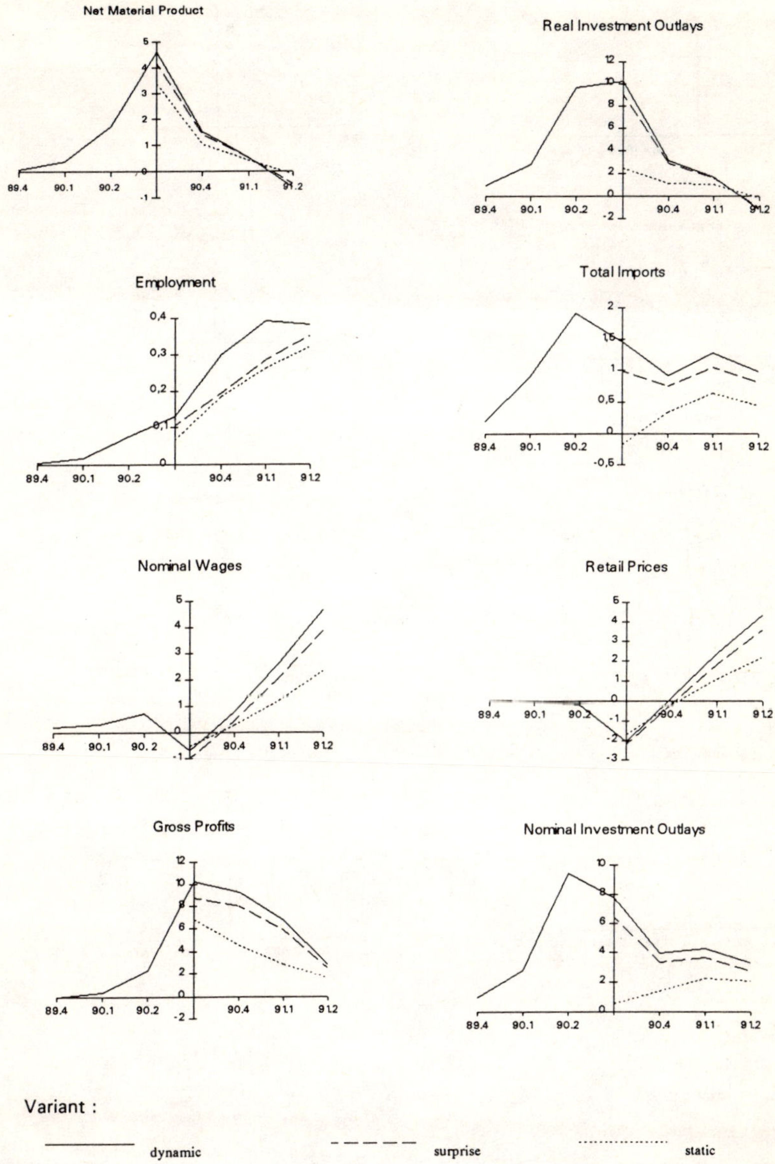

Figure 5.4. Effect of an Increase in Imports Prices.
(percentage differences between variant and base solution)

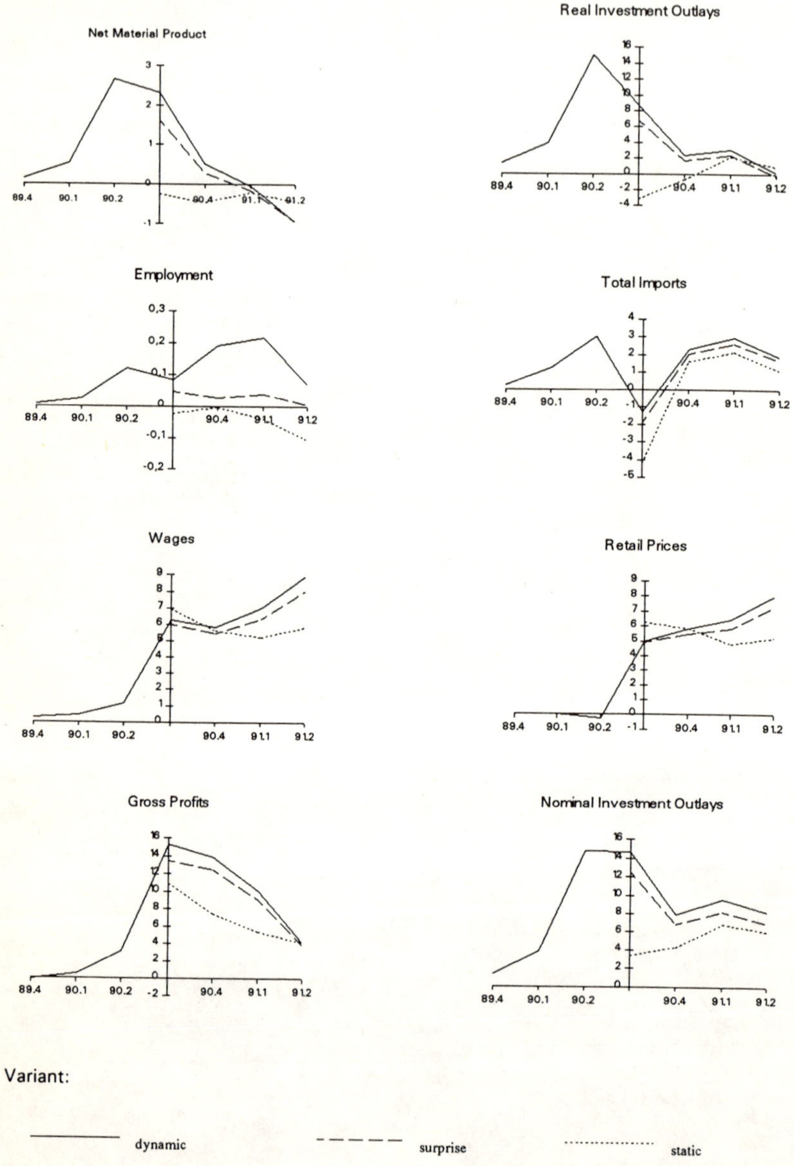

Figure 5.5. Effect of an Increase in Interest Rate.
(percentage differences between variant and base solution)

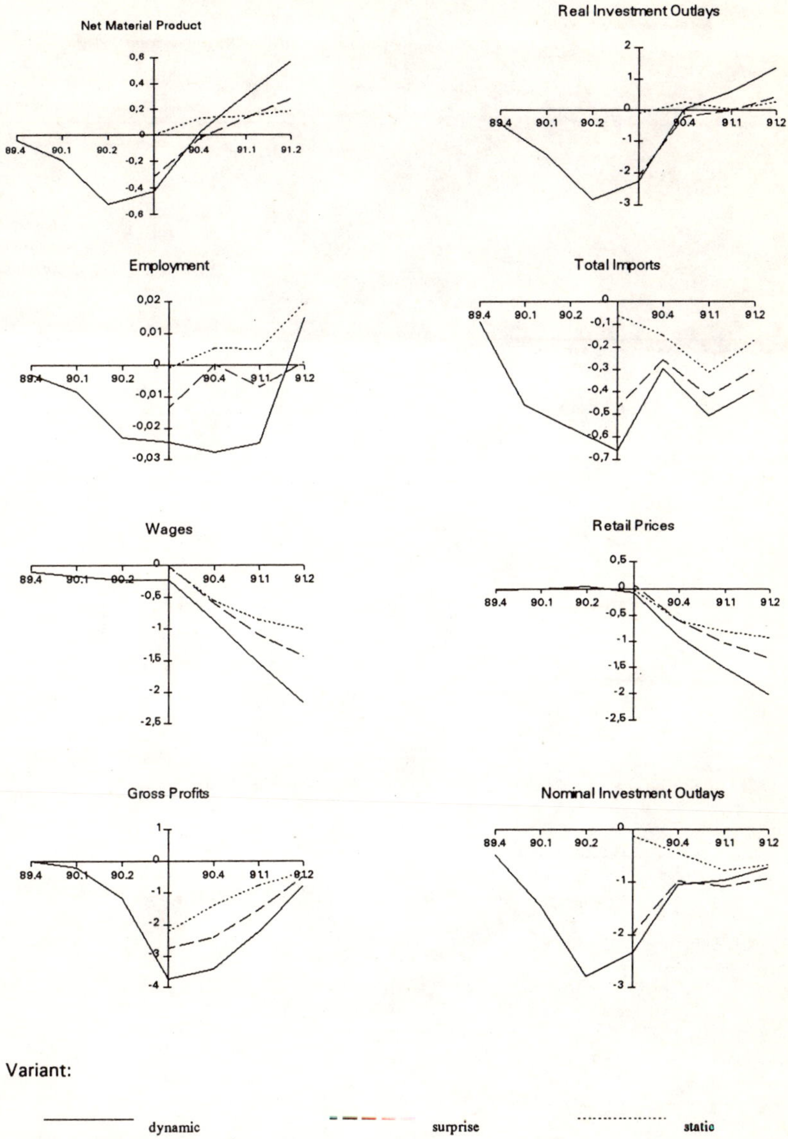

Figure 5.6. Effect of an Increase in Wages.
(percentage differences between variant and base solution)

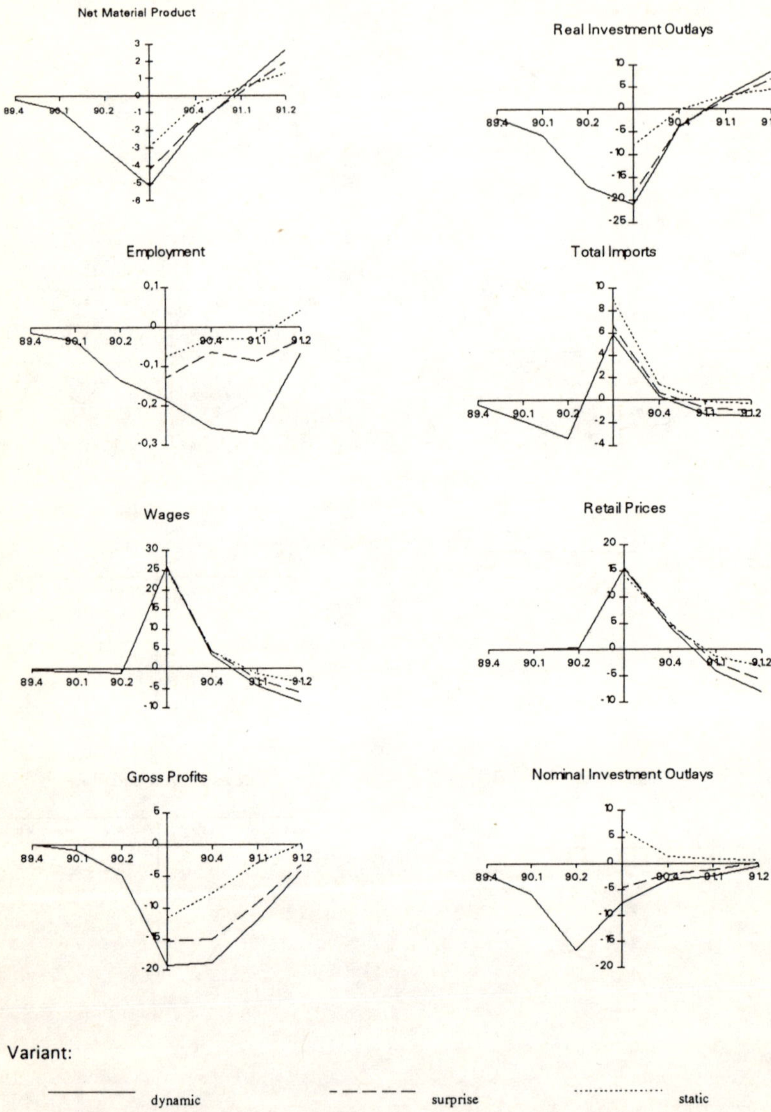

Increase in interest rate

Increase by 10% in interest rate in 1990.3 gives 0.5% increase in production costs and a decrease in profits resulting from paying off the higher interest on credits. Anticipating this, producers cut down investment outlays already in 1990.1 by 1.4%, by 2.8% in 1990.2 and 2.3% in 1990.3 which resulted in a decline in output by 0.2%, 0.5% and 0.4% respectively. Total decrease in profits determined by the increase in production costs and reduction of sale revenues reaches 3.7%. The increase in interest rate is not reflected in forming producer prices which are sensitive only to changes in labour and material costs. Difficulties related to sales tell producers to lower prices in the next quarter so as to assure the level of profits previously obtained. It has been starting the deflation mechanism since 1990.4.

Increase in wages

Original impulse raising wages by 10% in 1990.3 gives, through the inflation mechanism, the final augmentation in wages by 25% and 15.6% increase in prices. Resulting from that, the 24.6% increase in production costs decreases profits by 19.2%, although incomes from sale go up by 15.5%. Producers response to the expected deterioration of financial conditions is analogous to that described in section above: reduction of investment outlays already in 1990.1 by 5.8% and by 17% in 1990.2 followed by the decrease in NMP by 0.8% and 3% respectively. The decline in investment demand is not fully compensated by the increase in consumer demand. The result is that imports of investment goods decline by 4.8% in 1990.1 and 11.3% in 1990.2 (by 8.4% in 1990.3, but substantial increase in imports of consumer goods in this quarter by 23.5% gives an increase of total imports). Rising imports cut additionally demand for the domestic output. Since 1990.4, without further inflation stimulus, prices and wages decrease mainly due to a fall in the unit production costs.

5.6. Conclusions

The WK-91RE model is a first attempt to construct a quarterly model of the Polish economy including expectations. Our problem was that the sample was short and due to some missing quarterly data we could not verify hypotheses concerning rational expectations. The question of the availability of the complete statistics for the quarterly data for the Polish economy is quite serious and in the future may still cause problems. Undoubtedly, the model needs improvements and a new version is being prepared. The aim of this analysis was to see to what extent the mechanisms typical of the market economy are already present in the Polish economy and whether the expectations are involved in the decision making process. The results obtained with the WK-91RE model and presented above show that the market reactions to the expected changes in the economic policy are important. Through the simulation experiments we could examine the functioning of the model and its dynamic properties. The two main feedbacks in the model turned out to be: the dependence investment - production and the inflation mechanism, the strength of which seems to be a little overestimated. Still the important question remains whether the expectations introduced in the model are rational or not, and this will be a subject of our next study.

REFERENCES

Don, F. J. H., and Gallo, G. M. (1987), Solving Large Sparse Systems of Equations in Econometric Models, Journal of Forecasting 6: 167-180.

Fair, R.C., and Taylor, J.B. [1983], Solution and Maximum Likelihood Estimation of Dynamic Non-linear Rational Expectations Models, Econometrica 51: 1169-1185.

Manual SIMPC 3.0 - standard/student version [September 1990], Don Econometrics, The Hague.

CHAPTER 6

DATA BASE FOR THE QUARTERLY MODEL WK-91 OF THE POLISH ECONOMY

Grażyna Juszczak, Maria M. Kaźmierska, Sławomir Narel

Institute of Econometrics and Statistics, University of Łódź

6.1 General remarks

Main sources of the short-term data base for the quarterly model of the Polish economy are the GUS (Central Statistical Office) publications "Informacja Statystyczna" (Statistical Information), issued every month, starting from April 1989 till February 1991, and "Biuletyn Statystyczny" (Statistical Bulletin) also released monthly from March 1991 as well as the NBP (National Polish Bank) publication: "Miesięczny Biuletyn Informacyjny" (Monthly Statistical Bulletin) published since January 1990. Information included in the above mentioned periodicals concerns monthly observations starting from January 1988 (only for selected categories) or from January 1989 (for a majority of categories). Some of the time series appeared as late as from 1990 (interest rates, households money incomes and expenditures) or from 1991(the structure of government budget incomes and expenditures) others were deleted (the structure of retail sales). The definitions of several variables were changed over time (financial results of enterprises), which causes additional difficulties. The variables are expressed in the Bulletins in different ways - some are shown in absolute terms, others as indices of different base (no seasonal adjustments were available at all). To meet these differences we introduced the following classification of forms of the variables which were used in publications. In order to ensure immediate identification of the way of expressing each variable in the data bank, their symbols were constructed according to the scheme shown below.

Let X denotes any economic category. This symbol possesses setups of letters at the end, denoting respectively:

$XM_{i,t}$ - absolute value of variable X in month "i" and year "t",

$XNM_{i,t}$ - absolute value of variable X since the beginning of year "t" until month "i" (cumulative values), i.e.

$$XNM_{i,t} = \sum_{k=1}^{i} XM_{k,t} \qquad i=1,...,12; \qquad (6.1.1)$$

$X1M_{i,t}$ - index of variable X denoting the relation of its value in month "i" with respect to the value from the previous month (previous month = 100), i.e.

$$X1M_{i,t} = (XM_{i,t} / XM_{i-1,t})*100 \qquad i=1,...,12; \qquad (6.1.2)$$

where index $0,t \equiv 12,t-1$

$XYM_{i,t}$ - index of variable X denoting the relation of its value in month "i" in year "t" with respect to the value carried out in month "i" in the previous year (the previous year =100), i.e.

$$XYM_{i,t} = (XM_{i,t} / XM_{i,t-1})*100 \qquad i=1,...,12 ; \qquad (6.1.3)$$

$XNYM_{i,t}$ - index of variable X expressing the relation of its accumulated value from the beginning of the year till month "i" with respect to the value from analogous period of the previous year (analogous period of the previous year=100), i.e.

$$XNYM_{i,t} = (\sum_{k=1}^{i} XM_{k,t} / \sum_{k=1}^{i} XM_{k,t-1})*100 \qquad i=1,...,12 . \qquad (6.1.4)$$

Information is written in the system SYMPHONY on micro computer IBM/PC. They were transferred from the Bulletins in the same form they are published. However, this original set of data can not be directly used when constructing an econometric model because the statistical series included in the model are not comparable without suitable transformations (some of them are expressed as chain indices, others compare cumulative values, etc.). Hence, it was decided to construct an "Operational Bank". It should include all the information defined as absolute quantities ($XM_{i,t}$); it is possible then to take advantage of these series as well as generate their various needed transformations along the presented above definitions.

First of all, the transformations had to be defined which allowed to obtain absolute values (XM) from previously defined transformed variables.

For series defined according to formula (1), obtaining information of the XM type needs simple transformation:

$$XM_{i,t} = XNM_{i,t} - XNM_{i-1,t} . \qquad (6.1.5)$$

Far more difficult is to transform series being indices (formulas (2)-(4)), if we do not have at disposal additional information. This especially applies to deflators of the final demand components (consumption, investment outlays, exports) and imports. They had to be defined as indices of the present level of prices with respect to their average level in 1990. The choice of such a base was convenient for the following reasons: first, because of the feasibility of conversion of the categories expressed in the current prices into constant (1990) prices, second, it enables to relate to the categories observed in the yearly and quarterly horizons (for the sake of combining the monthly, quarterly and the yearly models). Let us mention, that only deflators of the output sold in 9 branches of the industry could be immediately defined in this way, using the information of the output value expressed both in the constant (1990 year) and current prices.

The deflators of final demand components (consumption and exports in zloties), as well as imports in zloties, were calculated using the published information of their chain monthly indices and the assumption that the deflator for 1990 should equal one. Let us start with indices of a single commodity X for individual months. Assuming the average price level in 1990 as the base, they can be written as:

$$PXM_{1,90} = PXM_{1,90}$$

$$PXM_{2,90} = PXM_{1,90} * IPXM_{2,90}$$

$$PXM_{3,90} = PXM_{2,90} * IPXM_{3,90} = PXM_{1,90} * \prod_{i=2}^{3} IPXM_{i,90} \tag{6.1.6}$$

...

...

...

$$PXM_{12,90} = PXM_{11,90} * IPXM_{12,90} = PXM_{1,90} * \prod_{i=2}^{12} IPXM_{i,90} \quad ,$$

where:

$PXM_{i,90}$ - X variable deflator in i-th month of 1990,

$IPXM_{i,90}$ - chain index of X variable prices dynamics defined as:

$$IPXM_{i,90} = PXM_{i,90} / PXM_{i-1,90} = PX1M_{i,90}/100 \tag{6.1.7}$$

On the other hand, the deflator for the total year 1990 will have the form:

$$PX_{90} = \frac{\sum_{k=1}^{12} XPM_{k,90}}{\sum_{k=1}^{12} (XPM_{k,90} / PXM_{k,90})} = 1 \tag{6.1.8}$$

Substituting $PXM_{k,t}$ from (6) and solving for $PXM_{1,90}$ we have:

$$PXM_{1,90} = \frac{\sum_{k=1}^{12} XPM_{k,90} / \prod_{i=2}^{k} IPXM_{i,90}}{\sum_{k=1}^{12} XPM_{k,90}} \tag{6.1.9}$$

Thus, using the calculated value of deflator of January 1990 ($PXM_{1,90}$) and indices of prices, there were determined then values of deflators for all months (as the inversion of formula (2)).

To calculate the deflators of exports and imports in terms of foreign currencies, there were used the following simple transformations, with the known deflators expressed in zloties and exchange rates:

- deflators of exports:

-to the 1st currency area (prices in transfer rubles)

$$PDERM = PTERM * \frac{WZLR_0}{WZLR} \quad (6.1.10)$$

where:

WZLRM - average zloty/ruble exchange rate

$$WZLR_0 = \frac{\sum_{1,90}^{12,90} WZLRM}{12}$$; average ruble exchange rate in 1990

PTERM - deflator of exports to the 1st currency area (transaction prices in Zl)

-to the 2nd currency area (prices in US dollars):

$$PDE\$M = PTE\$M * \frac{WZLD_0}{WZLDM} \quad (6.1.11)$$

where:

WZLDM - average zloty/dollar exchange ratio

$$WZLD_0 = \frac{\sum_{1,90}^{12,90} WZLDM}{12}$$; average dollar exchange ratio in 1990

PTE$M - deflator of exports to the 2nd currency area

-deflators of imports:

-from 1st currency area (prices in transfer rubles)

$$PDMRM = PTMRM * \frac{WZLR_0}{WZLRM} \quad (6.1.12)$$

where:

PTMRM - deflator of imports to the 1st currency area (transaction prices in Zl)

-from the 2nd currency area (prices in US dollars)

$$PDM\$M = PTM\$M * \frac{WZLD_0}{WZLDM} \qquad (6.1.13)$$

Total deflators of exports and imports were determined from the identities:

$$PTEM = EPM / EM \qquad (6.1.14)$$

where:

EPM - total exports in current prices, being the sum of exports to the 1st (ERPM) and 2nd (E$PM) currency area

EM - total exports in constant prices (the sum as above: ERM and E$M) and analogously:

$$PTMM = MPM / MM \qquad (6.1.15)$$

where:

MPM - total imports in current prices (the sum of MRPM and M$PM),

MM - total imports in constant prices (the sum of MRM and M$M).

For investment outlays there are distinguished two groups of outlays: on buildings and constructions (JJM, JJPM) and on machinery and equipment (JVM, JVPM). The values in current prices (JJPM and JVPM) were available only for 1990 and 1991, whereas in constant (1990) prices were available for 1989 and 1990. Hence, these time series were completed according to the following relations:

-deflators PJJM and PJVM for 1990 were obtained from the relations:

PJJM = JJPM / JJM

PJVM = JVPM / JVM

-PJJM and PJVM were extended for 1989 and 1991 on the basis of price dynamic indices of the construction-assembling works

-values of JJM and JVM in 1991 were extended according to the formula:

JJM = JJPM / PJJM

JVM = JVPM / PJVM

-values of JJPM and JVPM in 1989 were completed according to the formula:

JJPM = JJM * PJJM

JVPM = JVM * PJVM

The total investment outlays deflator was defined as identity:

$$PJM = JPM / JM \qquad (6.1.16)$$

where:

JPM - investment outlays in current prices,

JM - investment outlays in constant prices.

The primary obstacle, when constructing the short-term data base for the Polish economy, was missing monthly or the quarterly information concerning "macrocategories", i.e., gross domestic product or national income produced (with particular sectors distinguished) and GDP or national income distributed (defining its components). The procedure used to solve this problem is described in the next paragraph.

Along the above rules the first monthly data base was compiled as early as April 1991 and contained 247 time series. However, changes taking place in the Polish economy in the recent period affected the official statistics again. Statistical data published by the GUS for 1991 considerably differ from the data published for the previous years. The changes tend in three directions:

-giving up the reports writing in some fields,

-publishing new series,

-changes in the range or definition of particular variables.

Thus, simple extension of the time series already existing in the data base was not always possible. In the first of the mentioned cases, we were forced to give up using these variables. They included, among others, retail sales of commodities by groups of products. The abandoning of publishing of these variables is associated with the privatisation of majority of trading units and creating - instead of the old one - branch shops - multiprofile units. In such a case, registration of commodities sales by selected groups is impeded. Additional change in the reporting was associated with the fact that sales of agricultural products have not been registered since 1991. Lack of precise information resulted in the impossibility both to extend the sales series according to the old definition as well as to complete the newly defined category for the passed periods. The change resulted also in giving up completion of the consumer's expenditures deflators series by groups of products.

For the new data which have been published from January 1991, there occurred the problem of their backward extension for the earlier periods. Some of them, e.g. composition of the state budget revenues and expenditures are very important, having in mind the potential applications of the model. However, shortness of the time series causes that they were not included into the 1991 data base. It is likely that we shall decide to estimate the lacking information backwards at the next stage, making use of annual data and of the procedures aimed at distribution of this data, assuming, for example, a fixed monthly structure for a whole year.

Fundamental changes in the data base concern these categories which have changed their coverage in the recent period or need a change in how they are generated due to changes in the published characteristics. First, previous reports (and the publications) covered mainly the state-owned firms. Since the beginning of the year 1991 all types of economic subjects, independently of the form of ownership, are covered by the reporting system, however. Second, for small economic units (alternatively defined for banks and financial status) - instead of regular reports, there was introduced an inquiry based on representative samples. For previous years, much information is not available in terms of the new approach. In such situations we tried to bridge the old and new time series. Having the published information for January 1991 expressed in both - the new and old methodologies - the values of respective variables were calculated for the years 1988 and 1989 in a new arrangement (in case of having the information in the old arrangement). It concerned such variables as:

- employment,
- average wages,
- exports, imports (including sales of foreign companies, small manufacturing units, foundations and individuals).

Time series concerning imports underwent significant changes. The range of information collected in this field was extended; there were distinguished three groups of imported goods: consumer's, investment and raw materials. The total imports in current prices for 1990 were obtained as source data. They were used to compute imports in fixed prices according to:

$$MM_{i,90} = MPM_{i,90} / PMM_{i,90} \tag{6.1.17}$$

For the years 1988, 1989, 1991 imports values in fixed prices were determined using the available information on their dynamics. On the other hand , imports in current prices were determined as a product:

$$MPM_{i,j} = MM_{i,j} * PMM_{i,j} \qquad i = 1,...12 \quad j = 1988, 1989, 1991 \tag{6.1.18}$$

Data concerning imports and distinguishing the three groups of commodities: consumer's, investment and raw materials were determined as follows:

-value of transactions for 1990 was determined using data in current prices according to the SITC classification (sum of relevant SITC groups);

-then, the data were converted into fixed prices, using a deflator uniform for all groups (only till 1990);

-using the dynamics of fixed prices for the three groups, there were determined the data for 1991, 1988 and 1989 in such a way that the sum of imports by groups would add up to total value of imports, thus consumer's imports were determined as the difference between total imports and the other two groups.

Information concerning the balance of population's revenues and expenditures was ordered by introducing full, available at present classification. Data for 1989, unavailable in the assumed layout, needed completion. Having information for the whole year, it was assumed that the composition of revenues and incomes stayed constant throughout 1989 and values of particular categories were determined using total value of revenues and expenditures and the assumed shares.

Operational monthly bank was then transferred into the quarterly setup. The aggregation technique depends on the type of particular variables. The following four types can be distinguished: flows, stocks (resources), average values, and deflators. For each type of variables there was applied respective formula (symbol K at the end denotes that a variable is observed in a quarter, M denotes monthly observation):

-for variables being flows:

$$XK_{j,t} = \sum_{k=3j-2}^{3j} XM_{k,t} \qquad j=1,...,4; \qquad (6.1.19)$$

-for variables being stocks (resources):

$$XK_{j,t} = XM_{3j,t} \qquad j=1,...,4; \qquad (6.1.20)$$

-for average levels:

$$XK_{j,t} = \frac{1}{3} * \sum_{k=3j-2}^{3j} XM_{k,t} \qquad (6.1.21)$$

-for deflators:

$$PXK_{j,t} = \frac{\sum_{k=3j-2}^{3j} XPM_{k,t}}{\sum_{k=3j-2}^{3j} (XPM_{k,t} / PXM_{k,t})} \qquad (6.1.22)$$

or alternatively:

$$PXK_{j,t} = \frac{\sum_{k=3j-2}^{3j} (XM_{k,t} * PXM_{k,t})}{\sum_{k=3j-2}^{3j} XM_{k,t}} \qquad (6.1.23)$$

The choice of one of the alternative formulas concerning deflators ($PXK_{j,t}$) depends on the type of available information on absolute values of the variable X. If the information expressed in the current prices ($XPM_{k,t}$) is available, then formula (22) is applied; if only the information in constant prices ($XM_{k,t}$) is available , formula (23) will be suitable. Some of the variables demanded the use of specific transformations.

When constructing the short term data base two important conditions should be met. First, there must be the internal coherence, and second the ability to compare the monthly and quarterly information with the yearly data. The process of deep re- organisation of the statistical reporting system is, at present, the source of many incoherences in the presently published statistical information, both for short terms and when comparing data for various time intervals.

For example, for the categories: employment, wages, and output sales of the industry and construction, the monthly data cover enterprises employing over 5 workers only. In all categories referring to finances of enterprises, the monthly data concern enterprises employing over 50 workers in the industry and construction, and over 20 workers in other sectors. On the other hand, the range of particular variables shown at annual intervals in published Yearbooks is different. The socialised sector is still distinguished (e.g. in case of enterprises's finances) or data for whole economy are published (e.g. for employment). Perfect situation would be to have full information for whole economy, or for the same group of enterprises, assuming that the part of economy not covered by reports is relatively constant and only a tiny percentage of economic activities is left out. In this situation we have decided to keep definitions concerning the quarterly data for the so-called source series and to create macro aggregates for the whole economy.

The data base needed for the quarterly model of the Polish national economy WK-91 contains 87, time series (without the dummy variables) covering the period from the first quarter of 1989 to the second quarter of 1991 (see Appendix 3).

6.2. The problem of generating unobservable macro aggregates

Economic macro aggregates modelling in the period of transition from the centrally planned economy to the market economy nearly completely depends on the availability of suitable statistical data. In the last 20 years the countries with developed market economies have developed the statistics covering the data of high frequency - weeks, months, quarters the latter also in the social accounting framework. In countries with centrally planned economies, annual statistics dominated. Hence, the data on macro aggregates (GDP and its components) are available, up to now, only for annual periods. They were published for more than 40 years in the MPS framework. The time series reconstructed for the SNA system are available in Poland only for the period starting from 1980. The quarterly data cover only some of the components of macro categories and/or related variables. For example, the value added growth can be approximated by the changes in production sales, the use of the national income described by retail sales and investment outlays, the distribution of national income by money receipts of households supported by average wages in major industries, etc. In principle, it makes it possible to "generate" quarterly values of the macro categories - being unobservable - from related observable time series (indicators).

Several methods have been devised to deal with this problem. If related series (indicators) are available we can use suitable statistical techniques for interpolating and distributing a time series on the basis of movements in the related series (see, among others, C. Corrado [1988]). If only annual totals exist, the problem can be solved using purely mathematical methods (see Lisman and Sandee [1964], Glejser [1966], Boot and Feibes [1967], Boot et al. [1967]) or a simple distribution at a 25% rate.

Friedman [1962] was first to apply the regression analysis to the problem of interpolation, suggesting that the technique could be extended to the problem of distribution and extrapolation.

Following the above literature, we shall start with the quarterly variable. The generalisation to an annual variable will follow next. The application of interpolation techniques essentially involves specification of a regression relationship between the quarterly variable to be interpolated (or distributed) and a vector of monthly related series. Although, the procedures typically guarantee that the result of aggregation of the underlying monthly series into a quarterly frequency equals the original quarterly value of the variable of interest, the reliability of the estimates depends upon the validity and explanatory power of the assumed regression model.

As noted by G.C. Chow and A. Lin [1971], the three problems for which regression analysis can be used to estimate time series by related series are:

1) interpolation - determination of values at intermediate dates, given values at end points (stock data);

2) distribution - determination of values at finer intervals than available data permit, subject to temporal aggregation (flow data);

3) extrapolation - extension of a given series outside the sample period.

G. C. Chow, A. Lin obtained monthly estimates of relevant components of GNP by applying the quarterly regression of the components on some related series to monthly data. It was assumed that monthly observations of some series to be estimated satisfy a multiply regression relationship with p related series $x_1 \ldots x_p$. During the sample period of 3n months, the relation was

$$y = X\beta + u \qquad (6.2.1)$$

where y is 3n x 1, X is 3n x p, u is a random vector with mean 0 and covariance matrix V.

C is a matrix n x 3n which converts the 3n monthly observations into n quarterly. For interpolation (I) and distribution (D) matrices, it takes the form:

$$C_I = \begin{bmatrix} 1 & 0 & 0 & 0 & 0 & . & . & . & 0 & 0 & 0 \\ 0 & 0 & 0 & 1 & 0 & . & . & . & 0 & 0 & 0 \\ . & . & . & . & . & . & . & . & . & . & . \\ . & . & . & . & . & . & . & . & . & . & . \\ 0 & 0 & 0 & 0 & 0 & . & . & . & 1 & 0 & 0 \end{bmatrix}$$

$$C_D = \frac{1}{3}\begin{bmatrix} 1 & 1 & 1 & 0 & 0 & 0 & . & . & . & 0 & 0 & 0 \\ 0 & 0 & 0 & 1 & 1 & 1 & . & . & . & 0 & 0 & 0 \\ . & . & . & . & . & . & . & . & . & . & . & . \\ . & . & . & . & . & . & . & . & . & . & . & . \\ 0 & 0 & 0 & 0 & 0 & 0 & . & . & . & 1 & 1 & 1 \end{bmatrix}$$

The vector of n quarterly observations of the dependent variable to be subscripted by a dot which marks a quarterly variable will satisfy the regression model:

$$y. = Cy = CX\beta + Cu = X.\beta + u. , \qquad (6.2.2)$$

with $E(u.u.') = V. = CVC'$.

The problem is to estimate a vector z of m observations on the dependent variables, where z would be identical with y in cases of interpolation and distribution. A linear unbiased estimator $\hat{z}$ of z satisfies, for some m x n matrix A

$$\hat{z} = Ay. = A(X.\beta + u.) \qquad (6.2.3)$$

and

$$E(\hat{z} - z) = E[A(X.\beta + u.) - X_Z\beta + u_Z)] = (AX. - X_Z)\beta = 0 \qquad (6.2.4)$$

with X_Z and u_Z denoting variables in the regression model for z.

To find the best linear unbiased estimator $\hat{z}$, one needs to minimise:

$$cov(\hat{z} - z) = cov(Au. - u_Z) = AV.A' - AV_.z - V_{Z.}\ A' + V_Z \qquad (6.2.5)$$

with respect to A, subject to the m x p matrix equation:

$$AX - X_Z = 0 \qquad (6.2.6).$$

The solution for A is:

$$A = X_Z (X.'V^{-1}X.)^{-1}X.'V^{-1} + V_ZV.^{-1}\ [I - X.(X.'V.^{-1}X.)^{-1}X.'V.^{-1} \qquad (6.2.7).$$

Estimator $\hat{z}$ is:

$$\hat{z} = Ay. = X_Z\hat{\beta} + (V_{Z.}V.^{-1})\hat{u}. \qquad (6.2.8)$$

where $\hat{\beta} = (X.'V.^{-1}X.)^{-1}X.'V.^{-1}y.$ is the least squares estimate of the regression coefficient and $\hat{u}. = y. - X.\hat{\beta}$ is the n x 1 vector of residuals in the regression using quarterly data. The estimator $\hat{z}$ is applicable to interpolation of a series of stocks and to distribution of series of flows. The treatments of stocks and flows are distinguished only by matrix C.

In practice, V is unknown and has to be estimated by assuming some structure of the residuals in the monthly regression. Three alternative assumptions can be distinguished:

1) monthly regression residuals are serially uncorrelated with variance of δ;
2) monthly residuals follow a first order autoregression
$$u = au_{t-1} + \varepsilon_t\ ;$$
3) monthly residuals are serially uncorrelated, but have variances proportional to a known function of an explanatory variable.

This method constitutes a useful solution to the problem of distributing quarterly aggregates to a monthly frequency. It is not obvious how to use it in general. In case of generating a quarterly series from annual observations it might introduce an artificial step or discontinuity in the series between the last period of one year and the first period of the next (Fernandez [1981]).

To avoid this problem, Denton [1971] proposed to minimise the squared differences between the first differences of the series to be estimated and the first differences of the high frequency series. The problem is formulated by specifying a quadratic loss function in the difference between series to be created Y and linear combination of high frequency series:

$$(Y - X\beta)'A(Y - X\beta) \tag{6.2.9}$$

where

$$A = D'D \tag{6.2.10}$$

and D is

$$\underset{n\times x}{D} = \begin{bmatrix} 1 & 0 & 0 & 0 & 0 & . & . & . & 0 & 0 \\ -1 & 1 & 0 & 0 & 0 & . & . & . & 0 & 0 \\ 0 & -1 & 1 & 0 & 0 & . & . & . & 0 & 0 \\ . & . & . & . & . & . & . & . & . & . \\ . & . & . & . & . & . & . & . & . & . \\ 0 & 0 & 0 & 0 & 0 & . & . & . & -1 & 1 \end{bmatrix} \tag{6.2.11}$$

This matrix serves to convert the values of Y and X to first differences.

Fernandez [1981] considers the case with A = D'D, where D is the first difference transformation given by (11) and the regression model is expressed by $Y = X\beta + u$, but assumes that u follows the random walk model $u = u_{t-1} + \varepsilon_t$, ε_t being random variable serially independent with mean zero and constant variance. Assume also that u = 0, so for the initial period Var $u_1 = \delta^2$ Under these assumptions the residuals of the model:

$$DY = DX\beta + Du \tag{6.2.12}$$

have classical properties, E(Duu'D') is finite and equal $\delta^2 I$.

Let $\Delta Y.$ be a known annual change in dependent variable. The problem would be:

$$\Delta Y. = QDY = QDX\beta + QDu \tag{6.2.13}$$

where Q is a m x n matrix:

$$Q=\begin{bmatrix} h & 0 & 0 & 0 & 0 & . & . & . & 0 & 0 \\ 0 & g & h & 0 & 0 & . & . & . & 0 & 0 \\ 0 & 0 & g & h & 0 & . & . & . & 0 & 0 \\ . & . & . & . & . & . & . & . & . & . \\ . & . & . & . & . & . & . & . & . & . \\ 0 & 0 & 0 & 0 & 0 & . & . & . & g & h \end{bmatrix}, \quad g=\begin{bmatrix}0 & 1 & 2 & 3\end{bmatrix}, \quad h=\begin{bmatrix}4 & 3 & 2 & 1\end{bmatrix}$$

The best linear estimator is obtained by minimising covariance matrix $D\hat{Y}$ - DY under the restriction:

$$E(D\hat{Y} - DY) = E[R(QDX\beta + QDu) - (DX\beta + Du)] = 0 \qquad (6.2.14)$$

which in turn implies RQDX-DX = 0 and R is some n x m matrix which satisfies:

$$D\hat{Y} = R\Delta Y. = R(QDX\beta + QDu). \qquad (6.2.15)$$

After minimisation (using Lagrange multipliers), we receive:

$$\hat{X} = Z\beta' + (D'D)^{-1}B(B'(D'D)^{-1}B)^{-1}[Y - B'Z\hat{\beta}] \qquad (6.2.16)$$

$$\hat{\beta} = [Z'B(B'(D'D)^{-1}B)^{-1}B'Z]^{-1}Z'B(B'(D'D)^{-1}B)^{-1}Y \qquad (6.2.17)$$

where QD = B' .

This method eliminates the problem of the spurious step or discontinuity between different years and can be pursued for other frequency levels with different matrix Q.

The close idea to the Chow and Lin's one has been presented by V.A. Ginsburgh [1973]. He proposes a two step method, which is a combination of related series and mathematical interpolation.

6.2.1. Derivation of quarterly time series for macro aggregates for Poland

When constructing quarterly time series of macro aggregates for Poland, we faced many statistical obstacles. First, the annual data are published about a year later than the quarterly one. So, when we calculated the unobservable for the first time (in May 1991), annual data were not available for the sample period 1990-1991 (as the data for 1990 were published in September 1991). Moreover, short-term data for Poland are published only since 1988. Second, the annual data are inconsistent with the quarterly ones because of price base (the annual data are in constant prices of 1984, the quarterly ones in 1990 prices). Third, annual data (published in Yearbook of the GUS) and quarterly one (published in Monthly Bulletins of the GUS and Bulletin of the NBP) vary in the subjects range, the annual ones cover whole economy, whereas the quarterly data are available for many "key" categories, i.e. sales in industry and construction do not cover economic units employing up to 5 workers. So, it was impossible to use the procedures outlined above directly. We tried to follow them, assuming their simplifications. In general, we used the approach making use of related series (indicators) and were looking for simple relationships between them and the respective macro aggregates.

The values of unobservable macro aggregates for quarterly periods were calculated, making use of the relationships, which, on the basis of annual data, can be established between the above macro aggregates and the related series. The latter were either components of the macro aggregates or other variables, the values of which were observable also in quarterly periods.

Let Y_T, Y_{Ti} be values (the levels) of a macro aggregate, respectively, in year T and a quarter of T-th year, X_T, X_{Ti} values (the levels) of a related variable (indicator), observable quarterly and yearly. For the annual data we have a linear regression relationship:

$$Y_T = a_0 + a_1 X_T , \qquad (6.2.18)$$

where a_0, a_1 are the parameters. It will be called a translation (bridge) equation.

Hence, the estimated value of Y is calculated for each quarter, according to the formula of the bridge equation:

$$\bar{Y}_{Ti} = \bar{a}_0/4 + \bar{a}_1 X_{Ti} , \qquad (6.2.19)$$

where $\bar{a}_0$, $\bar{a}_1$ are the parameters estimated from equation (18).In most cases, bridge equations (18) describe relations based on symptomatic data, i.e. between a particular macro variable and a proxy for this variable. We tried to avoid the use of casual relations as it would predetermine the specification of structural equations explaining macro aggregates. It was determined by the character of indicator. The final choice of related series (indicators) was dictated by actual availability of data.

The above procedure of generating quarterly data by using the relationships established on the basis of the annual data was applied to derive:

a) gross domestic product (SNA) and national income produced (MPS) as a whole and its components, value added and respective net output originating in :
- industry,
- building industry,
- agriculture,
- in the other sectors;

b) gross domestic product (SNA) and total national income distributed (MPS) and its components:
- personal consumption,
- public consumption,
- net investment outlays,
- increase in inventories and reserves.

The following general strategy was applied. The value of the components of the SNA system were estimated first, being the base of comparisons between the Polish data and the national accounts used in Europe. Next, values of the MPS components were related to their SNA counterparts. To calculate the elements of GDP we used the following indicators as a proxy of value added (in current prices for industry and building industry and in real terms for agriculture):

- in industry - nominal sales of products in mining and manufacturing industry;
- in building industry - nominal basic output of building enterprises;
- in agriculture - purchase of cattle for slaughter and procurement of cereals.

The values of macro aggregates in constant 1990 prices were calculated from respective identities - dividing nominal values by the appropriate deflators or for MPS system components from the bridge equations.

Because of the previously mentioned discrepancy in the ranges of annual and quarterly data on the sales in industry and basic output of building industry, quarterly series used as indicators were adjusted to make them comparable with annual data - using the following formula:

$$X'_{Ti} = X_{Ti} * (X_T / \Sigma X_{Ti}), \qquad (6.2.20)$$

where: X_{Ti} is the value of sales (production) in i-th quarter of year T, including economic units employing over 5 workers, X_T - value of sales (production) in year T, covering whole economy.

A similar pattern was used to generate the components of GDP to be distributed. However, in the case of private consumption, there were no more available proxy variables as the retail sales, covering socialised trade only, which ceased to be representative. Hence, we had to use an indicator involved in casual relationship: thus the nominal value of private consumption was related to the total money incomes of households and private sector.

It was assumed, that public consumption (in nominal terms) follows the budget expenditures. On the other hand, net investment outlays were calculated as a part of gross investment outlays.

The values of the above variables in constant prices 1990 were calculated from the respective identities dividing nominal values by appropriate deflators or for MPS components from bridge equations relating them to SNA components.

The data used as the indicators were not seasonally adjusted. It means that the seasonal effects characteristic for particular indicators are transferred through the bridge equations to the generated unobservable variables. This approach may lead to biased estimates of seasonal patterns, but the short sample of quarterly data considerably restricted the chances to apply techniques suitable for the deseasonalizing the time series of indicators.

Table 6.1 presents the list of the bridge equations, which were estimated over the period 1980 - 1990, using OLS method. Short sample of quarterly data (1988.1-1991.2) made necessary the estimation of the bridge equations to a large extent outside this sample. On calculating the expected quarterly values of macro aggregates the assumption of stability of estimated parameters was used, which will be the subject of systematic testing.

Graphs 6.1 - 6.4 show the empirical results. Let us briefly comment on them. The years 1989-1991 were essential for the period of transition. In this period the Polish economy was affected by a deepening recession, particularly in the industry, the primary reason of which were the failures in the realisation of the anti-inflationary stabilisation program introduced in 1990. After abolishing nearly completely the price control the severe constrains in the domestic demand were introduced (tight fiscal control over wages, high interest rates, stabilisation of exchange rates, etc.). In 1991 the collapse of trade within the former CMEA countries reduced also the foreign demand.

The tough monetary policy (of expensive credits) restricted also the dynamics of agricultural output - based on short-term loans, (where one can easily notice seasonal fluctuations an increase in the III quarter - time of the harvest), and the output of building industry. Production in other sectors, including transportation, trade and services shows systematic decline and distinct seasonality in the IV quarter, being the result, above all, of the increased turnover in trade in this period.

The deep decline in the domestic output was accompanied initially by a decline in (complementary) imports. However, in 1991 we observed considerable growth in (competitive) imports, due to high appreciation of zloty (vis a vis US $ and other free convertible currencies), which fully absorbed the increase of personal consumption and deepened the recession. Among the components of domestic final demand, the (declining) investment outlays are characterised by regular seasonal fluctuations - a fall in the first quarter, a growth in fourth quarter.

Table 6.1 The list of estimated bridge equations

GDP component	Related series used in bridge equation
Real personal consumption (SNA) CNA	Real personal consumption (MPS) C, Real public consumption (MPS) G 1.10085 * C +0.63386 * G
Real personal consumption (MPS) C	Personal incomes VYPK, price index PC . 74482 * VYP/PC
Real public consumption (SNA) GNA	Real personal consumption (SNA) CNA 0.13642 * CNA

Real public consumption (MPS) G	Real public consumption (SNA) GNA 1.17496 * GNA
Real gross investment outlays (SNA) JNA	Real gross investment outlays (MPS) J 1.043398 * J
Real net investment outlays (MPS) JA	Real gross investment outlays (SNA) JNA 0.46028 * JNA
Nominal net investment outlays (MPS) JAP	Nominal gross investment outlays JP -1083.603471 + 0.88972 * JP
Increase in inventories and reserves (SNA) DRNA	XGNA-CNA-GNA-J
Increase in inventories and reserves (MPS) DR	XG-C-G-JA
Value added in industry (SNA) XXQNA	Sales of products in mining and manuf. industries SQQT 0.36803 * SQQT
Net output in industry (MPS) XQ	Value added in industry (SNA) XXQNA 0.91853 * XXQNA
Value added in construction sector (SNA) XXBNA	Basic output of building enterprises QPBT 0.78260 * QPBT
Net output in construction sector (MPS) XB	Value added in construction sector (SNA) XXBNA 0.98119 * XXBNA
Total output of agriculture QR	Purchase of cattle for slaughter SKZ, procurement of cereals SKZB 0.000145 + 36.50885 * SKZ + 5.41765* SKZB
Value added in agriculture (SNA) XXRNA	Total output of agriculture QR 0.412590 * QR
Net output in agriculture (MPS) XR	Value added in agriculture (SNA) XXRNA 0.824063 * XXRNA
Value added in the other sectors (SNA) XPONA	XNA-XXQNA-XXBNA-XXRNA
Net output in the other sectors (MPS) XPO	X-XQ-XB-XR
Gross domestic product (SNA) XNA	Value added in industry (SNA) XXQNA 2.36146 * XXQNA
Net domestic product (MPS) X	Net output in industry (MPS) XQ 2.05412 * XQ

Gross domestic product to be distributed (SNA)		
XGNA		XNA + M - E
National income distributed		
(MPs)	XG	X + M - E

FIG. 6.1: NET MATERIAL PRODUCT AND ITS ELEMENTS (MPS)

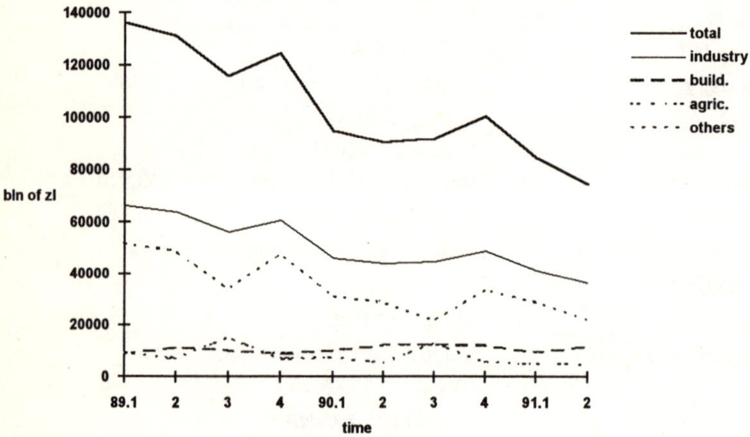

FIG. 6.2: GROSS DOMESTIC PRODUCT AND ITS ELEMENTS (SNA)

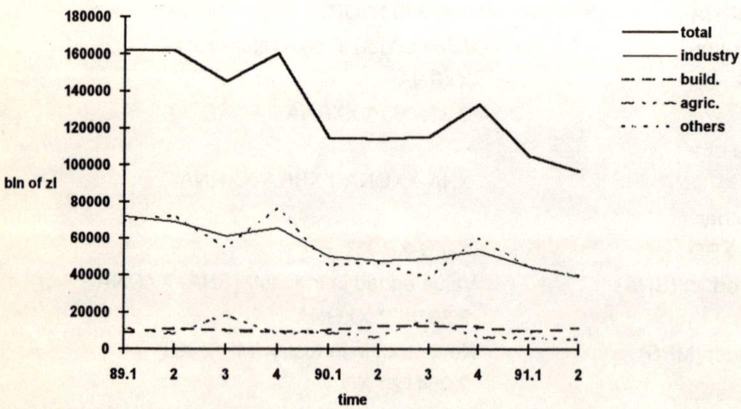

FIG. 6.3: NET MATERIAL PRODUCT TO BE DISTRIBUTED AND ITS ELEMENTS (MPS)

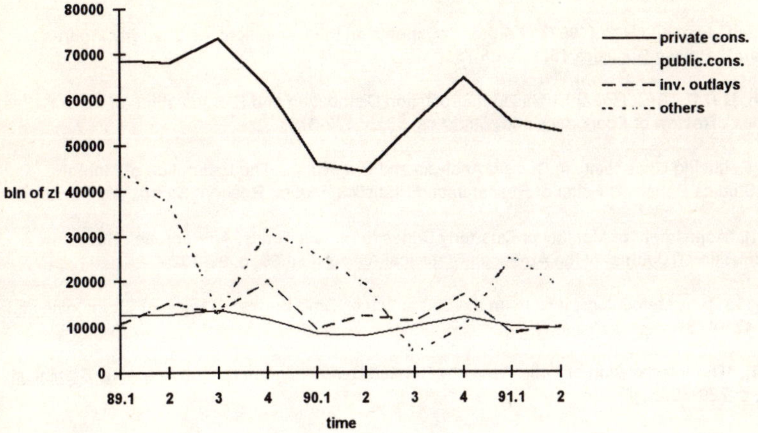

FIG. 6.4: GROSS DOMESTIC PRODUCT TO BE DISTRIBUTED AND ITS ELEMENTS (SNA)

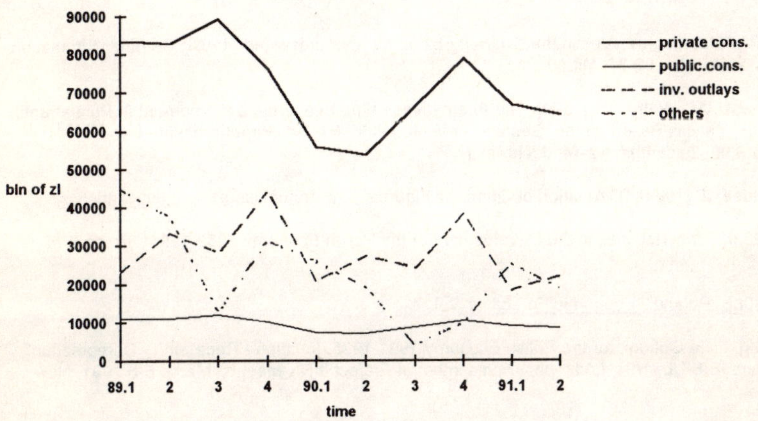

REFERENCES

Boot C.G. and Feibes W. [1967], "On Glejser's Derivation of Monthly Figures from Yearly Data", Cahiers Economiques de Bruxelles 36, p 539-546.

Boot C.G., Feibes, W. and Lisman, J.H.C. [1967], "Further Comments on the Derivations of Quarterly Figures from Annual Data", Applied Statistics 16(1), p 65-75.

Chow G. and An- oh Lin, [1971], "Best Linear Unbiased Interpolation Distribution and Extrapolation of Time Series by Related Series", Review of Economics and Statistics 53, p. 372-375

Corrado, Carol, [1988], Reducing Uncertainty in Current Analysis and Projections: The Estimation of Monthly GNP", Special Studies Paper - Division of Research and Statistics Federal Reserve Board, Washington

Denton, Frank T., [1971], "Adjustment of Monthly or Quarterly Series to Annual Totals: An Approach Based on Quadratic Minimization.", Journal of the American Statistical Association 66, p. 99-102.

Fernandez, Roque B., [1981], "A Metodological Note on the Estimation of Time Series", Review of Economics and Statistics 63, p 471-476.

Friedman, Milton, [1962], "The Interpolation of Time Series by Related Series", Journal of the American Statistical Association 57, p. 729-757.

Glejser, H. [1966], "Une methode d'evaluation de donnees meansuelles a partiar d'indices trimestriels ou annuels", Cahiers Economiques de Bruxelles 29, p 45-54.

Juszczak G., Kaźmierska M.M., Łapińska- Sobczak N., Welfe W., [1991], "Short, Term Models of Financial Flows for `the Polish Economy in Transition", Discussion Papers IEiS, 2/91, Łódź.

Juszczak G., Kaźmierska M. M., Orłowski W., Narel S., Welfe A., Welfe W. [1991], "Alternatives to the Development of Economic Situation in Poland (econometric model simulation analyses), Prace IEiS, 94, seria F, Łódź

Kazmierska M. M. [1991], "Macroaggregates in the Quarterly Model", paper presented at ACE Seminar Simulation and Financial Models, May 22-24, Mittelberg.

Kaźmierska M. M., Orłowski W., Welfe W., [1990], The Alternatives of the Economic Development in Poland until 1995. Simulation Analysis Based on the Demand - oriented W5 - Model", Paper presented at MACROMODELS'90, December 12-14, Jachranka.

Lisman, J.H.C. and Sandee, J. [1964], "Derivation of Quarterly Figures from Annual Data", Applied Statistics 13(2), p 87-90.

Welfe, Wladyslaw, [1990a], "Uncertainities in the Development of the Polish Economy 1989-1994", Prace IEiS UL, 77, Lodz

Welfe, Wladyslaw, [1990b], "Poland", Economic Forecasts, vol. 7.

Welfe, Wladyslaw, [1991], "The Outlook for the Polish Economy 1991-1995. Inflation - Recession - Deregulation", Discussion Papers IEiS UŁ, 1/91, Łódź, paper presented at Project LINK Meeting March 6-8 1991, New York.

APPENDIX 1

LIST OF VARIABLES FOR THE QUARTERLY MODEL WK-91 OF THE POLISH ECONOMY

AFDYP	- dividends paid by enterprises, (10^9 Zl)
AFDZP	- subsidies and other increases of incomes obtained by enterprises, (10^9 Zl)
AFPDP	- income tax paid by enterprises, (10^9 Zl)
AFPOZP	- turnover tax and other encumbrances of incomes paid by enterprises, (10^9 Zl)
AFPZP*	- tax on increase of wage and salary paid by enterprises, (10^9 Zl)
AFZP	- gross profits of enterprises, (10^9 Zl)
AFZNP	- net profits of enterprises, (10^9 Zl)
BCP	- total expenditures of state budget, (10^9 Zl)
BDP	- surplus or deficit of state budget, (10^9 Zl)
BYP	- total receipts of state budget , (10^9 Zl)
BZPP	- credit liability of economic units, (10^9 Zl)
C	- personal consumption - MPS (10^9, 1990 Zl)
CNA	- personal consumption - SNA (10^9, 1990 ZL)
DR	- inventory increase - MPS (10^9, 1990 Zl)
DRNA	- inventory increase - SNA (10^9, 1990 Zl)
E*	- total exports (10^9, 1990 Zl)
G	- other (social) consumption (10^9, 1990 Zl)
GNA	- other gross (social) consumption (10^9, 1990 Zl)
J	- gross investment outlays (10^9, 1990 Zl)
JA	- net investment outlays - MPS (10^9, 1990 Zl)
JAP	- net investment outlays - MPS, (10^9 Zl)
JJ	- investment outlays: constructions (10^9, 1990 Zl)
JNA	- gross investment outlays - SNA (10^9, 1990 Zl)
JNAP	- gross investment outlays - SNA, (10^9 Zl)
JP	- gross investment outlays - MPS, (10^9 Zl)
JV	- investment outlays: machinery and equipment (10^9, 1990 Zl)
KWSP	- fabrication costs of enterprises, (10^9 Zl)
LA	- total cargo transportation (10^6 t)
M	- total imports (10^9, 1990 Zl)
MH	- total imports of consumer goods (10^9, 1990 Zl)
MI	- total imports of investment goods (10^9, 1990 Zl)
MZ	- total imports of raw materials and intermediate goods (10^9, 1990 Zl)
N6	- employment in 6 major industry groups in socialized sector, (10^3)
NB	- employment in building industry, (10^3)
NH	- employment in trade, (10^3)
NO	- employment in service sector, (10^3)
NQ	- employment in manufacturing and mining industry, (10^3)
NT	- employment in transport, (10^3)
NZ	- employment in communal services, (10^3)
OLP	- total deposits of households, (10^9 Zl)
OOP	- total money stocs, (10^9 Zl)
OPP	- total deposits of enterprises, (10^9 Zl)
PC	- retail prices of consumer goods and services
PCOC	- retail prices of services supplied to households
PCX	- retail prices of commodities
PJ	- deflators of total investment outlays in socialized sector

PJJ	- deflators of investment outlays - construction in socialized sector
PJV	- deflators of investment outlays - machinery equipment installed in socialized sector
PQB	- deflators of building industry output
PSKZ	- prices of purchase of cattle for slaughter
PSKZB	- prices of procurement of cereals
PSQ	- deflators of output sold in manufacturing and mining industry
PTM*	- deflators of total imports (transaction Zl)
QPB	- basic output of building enterprises (10^9, 1990 Zl)
QR	- total output of agriculture (10^9, 1990 Zl)
RPOD	- interest rate of long term deposits and savings in banks, %
SKZ	- purchase of cattle for slaughter (10^3 t)
SKZB	- procurement of cereals (10^3 t)
SQOUP	- sales of production and services in socialized sector, (10^9 Zl)
SQQ	- sales of products of mining and manufacturing industry (10^9, 1990 Zl)
U8912	- dummy variable (1 in 1 and 2 quarter of 1989)
U894	- dummy variable (1 in 4 quarter of 1989)
U894902	- dummy variable (1 in 4 quarter of 1989 to 2 quarter of 1990)
U90	- dummy variable (1 in 1990)
U901	- dummy variable (1 in 1 quarter of 1990)
U903	- dummy variable (1 in 3 quarter of 1990)
U904	- dummy variable (1 in 4 quarter of 1990)
U91	- dummy variable (1 in 1991)
U911	- dummy variable (1 in 1 quarter of 1991)
U912	- dummy variable (1 in 1 and 2 quarters of 1991)
UJJ*	- share of investment outlays on buildings and constructions in total investment outlays
VCFP	- households expenditures on credits repaid, (10^9 Zl)
VCHP	- households expenditures on commodities, (10^9 Zl)
VCOP	- households expenditures on payments for services, (10^9 Zl)
VCP	- money expenditures of households and private sector , (10^9 Zl)
VCVP	- household expenditures on taxes and charges, (10^9 Zl)
VYAP	- households incomes from sales of agricultural products, (10^9 Zl)
VYBGP	- households incomes from social money benefits, (10^9 Zl)
VYFP	- households incomes from credits granted, (10^9 Zl)
VYNUP	- households incomes from non-agricultural private sector, (10^9 Zl)
VYP	- money incomes of households and private sector , (10^9 Zl)
VYTP	- households incomes from compensation, interest on deposits and other transfers, (10^9 Zl)
VYZP	- total labour income, (10^9 Zl)
VYZZP	- other households incomes, (10^9 Zl)
X	- net material product - MPS (10^9, 1990 Zl)
XB	- net material product in building industry - MPS (10^9, 1990 Zl)
XG	- net material product distributed - MPS (10^9, 1990 Zl)
XGNA	- gross domestic product distributed - SNA (10^9, 1990 Zl)
XNA	- gross domestic product - SNA (10^9, 1990 Zl)
XPO	- net material product in other sectors - MPS (10^9, 1990 Zl)
XPONA	- gross domestic product in other sectors - SNA (10^9, 1990 Zl)
XQ	- net material product in manufacturing and mining industry-MPS (10^9, 1990 Zl)
XR	- net material product in agriculture - MPS (10^9, 1990 Zl)
XXBNA	- gross domestic product in building industry - SNA (10^9, 1990 Zl)
XXQNA	- gross domestic product in manufacturing and mining industry SNA (10^9, 1990 Zl)

XXRNA	- gross domestic product in agriculture - SNA (10^9, 1990 Zl)
Z1	- dummy variable (1 in 1 quarter of every year)
Z2	- dummy variable (1 in 2 quarter of every year)
Z3	- dummy variable (1 in 3 quarter of every year)
Z4	- dummy variable (1 in 4 quarter of every year)
Z6P	- average monthly wage in 6 major groups of industry (including payments from profit), 10^3 Zl
ZBP	- average monthly wage in building industry, 10^3 Zl
ZHP	- average monthly wage in trade, 10^3 Zl
ZOP	- average monthly wage in services sector, 10^3 Zl
ZQP	- average monthly wage in manufacturing and mining industry, 10^3 Zl
ZTP	- average monthly wage in transport, 10^3 Zl
ZZP	- average monthly wage in communal services, 10^3 Zl

Note:

letter P at the end of a symbol means that the variable is expressed in current prices. Price indices (deflators) are defined assuming, as their base, the average 1990 price.

* indicates strictly exogenous variable

APPENDIX 2

THE STRUCTURE OF THE QUARTERLY MODEL WK-91 OF THE POLISH ECONOMY

1. Gross personal consumption (1990 Zl):

$$\mathbf{CNA} = \underset{(41.78)}{1.1009}*\mathbf{C} + \underset{(4.89)}{0.6339}*\mathbf{G}$$

$R^2 = 1.000$ DW = 0.90

2. Personal consumption (1990 Zl):

$$\mathbf{C} = \underset{(1.0)}{-329.27} + \underset{(178.0)}{0.77310}*(\mathbf{VYP/PC})$$

$R^2 = 0.999$ DW = 2.51

3. Gross other (social) consumption (1990 Zl):

$$\mathbf{GNA} = \underset{(2.4)}{4632.9} + \underset{(2.54)}{0.1229}*\{0.4*(\mathbf{BCP/PC})+0.6*[\mathbf{BCP(1)/PC(1)}]\}$$

$R^2 = 0.479$ DW = 1.73

4. Other (social) consumption (1990 Zl):

$$\mathbf{G} = \underset{(7*10^5)}{1.1338}*\mathbf{GNA}$$

$R^2 = 1.000$ DW = 2.62

5. Gross investment outlays:

$$\mathbf{JP} = \underset{(0.88)}{2172.70} + \underset{(1.5)}{0.1833}*\mathbf{AFZNP} + \underset{(11.8)}{0.5390}*\mathbf{BCP} \underset{(1.6)}{-28.765}*\mathbf{RPOD}$$

$R^2 = 0.967$ DW=2.90

6. Net investment outlays:

$$\mathbf{JAP} = \underset{(5*10^5)}{-1083.6} + \underset{(10*10^6)}{0.8897}*\mathbf{JP}$$

R2=1.000 DW=2.48

7. Gross investment outlays (1990 Zl):

J =JP/PJ

8. Net investment outlays SNA (1990 Zl):

$$\mathbf{JNA} = \underset{(2*10^6)}{1.0434}*\mathbf{J}$$

$R^2 = 1.000$ DW = 2.00

9. Net investment outlays MPS (1990 Zl):

$$\mathbf{JA} = \underset{(4*10^4)}{0.4603}*\mathbf{JNA}$$

$R^2 = 1.000$ DW = 2.00

10. Investment outlays:machinery and equipment (1990 Zl):

JV = (1-UJJ)*J

11. Investment outlays: constructions (1990 Zl):

JJ = UJJ*J

12. Inventory increase SNA (1990 Zl):

DRNA = XGNA-CNA-GNA-JNA

13. Inventory increase MPS (1990 Zl):

DR = XG-C-G-JA

14. Total imports of intermediate commodities (1990 Zl):

$$\mathbf{MZ} = \underset{(1.1)}{2548.7} + \underset{(1.9)}{0.0171}*(\mathbf{SQOUP/PSQ}) - \underset{(0.2)}{516.66}*(\mathbf{PTM/PSQ}) + \underset{(5.9)}{6372.1}*\mathbf{Z4}$$

$R^2 = 0.907$ DW = 1.73

15. Total imports of consumer goods (1990 Zl):

$$\mathbf{MH} = \underset{(2.6)}{17787.4} + \underset{(0.4)}{0.0366}*(\mathbf{VCHP/PC}) - \underset{(1.8)}{11376.7}*(\mathbf{PTM/PC}) - \underset{(1.2)}{3530.9}*\mathbf{Z3}$$

$R^2 = 0.603$ DW = 1.84

16. Total imports of investment goods (1990 Zl):

$$\mathbf{MI} = \underset{(1.4)}{3867.1} + \underset{(3.9)}{0.4717}*\mathbf{JV} - \underset{(0.8)}{1878.9}*(\mathbf{PTM/PJ}) + \underset{(4.8)}{7239.3}*\mathbf{U912}$$

$R^2 = 0.888$ DW = 2.39

17. Total imports (1990 Zl):

M = **MZ** + **MH** + **MI**

18. Sales of products in mining and manufacturing industry (1990 Zl):

SQQ + (**MH**+**MI**) = 28035.3 + 1.7101*[0.582*(**VCHP/PCX**)+0.172*$\mathbf{J}$+0.826*$\mathbf{E}$] +
(2.4) (9.7)
0.1726*$\mathbf{SQQ(1)}$ + 0.8868*$\mathbf{DR}$
(2.0) (4.0)

$R^2 = 0.974$ DW = 0.72

19. Value added in industry (SNA):

XXQNA = 0.3860*$\mathbf{SQQ}$

20. Net output in industry (MPS):

XQ = 0.9185*$\mathbf{XXQNA}$

21. Basic output of socialized building enterprises (1990 Zl):

QPB = 0.6192*$\mathbf{JJ}$ + 3719.9*(**Z1**+**Z2**) + 2149.2*$\mathbf{Z3}$ - 3573.0*$\mathbf{U894}$ -
(47.5) (16.2) (6.1) (8.7)
1978.8*$\mathbf{U8912}$ + 2963.2*$\mathbf{U903}$
(7.8) (7.2)

$R^2 = 0.983$ DW = 2.45

22. Value added in construction sector (SNA):

XXBNA = 0.9142*$\mathbf{QPB}$

23. Net output in construction sector (MPS):

XB = 0.9812*$\mathbf{XXBNA}$

24. Total cargo transportation:

LA = -109.29 + 0.0536*(0.037*$\mathbf{SQQ}$+0.011*$\mathbf{QPB}$)
(4.2) (11.4)

$R^2 = 0.942$ DW = 1.93

25. Purchase of cattle for sloughter:

SKZ = -81.950 + 200.37*(**PSKZ/PSKZ(1)**) + 0.0045*$\mathbf{C}$
(0.92) (5.6) (3.7)

$R^2 = 0.857$ DW = 2.65

26. Procurement of cereals:

$$\mathbf{SKZB} = -752.95 + 325.07*[\mathbf{PSKZB/PSKZB(1)}] + 0.0137*\mathbf{C} + 4541.4*\mathbf{Z3}$$

(1.2) (2.2) (1.4) (18.3)

$R^2 = 0.985$ DW = 1.89

27. Total otput of agriculture (1990 Zl):

$$\mathbf{QR} = 0.00014 + 36.509*\mathbf{SKZ} + 5.4177*\mathbf{SKZB}$$

(0.05) (59.1) $(2*10^7)$

$R^2 = 1.000$ DW = 0.72

28. Value added in agriculture (SNA):

$$\mathbf{XXRNA} = 0.4126*\mathbf{QR}$$

(8*10)

$R^2 = 1.000$ DW = 1.57

29. Net output in agriculture (MPS):

$$\mathbf{XR} = 0.8241*\mathbf{XXRNA}$$

$(12*10^7)$

$R^2 = 1.000$ DW = 2.00

30. Value added in other sectors (SNA):

$$\mathbf{XPONA} - \mathbf{GK} = 11457.6 + 179.19*\mathbf{LA} - 11571.1*\mathbf{Z3} + 11124.9*\mathbf{Z4}$$

(4.1) (11.9) (5.4) (5.2)

$R^2 = 0.973$ DW = 3.36

31. Net output in other sectors (MPS):

$$\mathbf{XPO} = 0.7922*(\mathbf{XPONA} - \mathbf{G})$$

(34.7)

$R^2 = 0.91$ DW = 1.73

32. Net material product (MPS):

$$\mathbf{X} = \mathbf{XQ} + \mathbf{XB} + \mathbf{XR} + \mathbf{XPO}$$

33. Gross domestic product (SNA):

$$\mathbf{XNA} = \mathbf{XXQNA} + \mathbf{XXBNA} + \mathbf{XXRNA} + \mathbf{XPONA}$$

34. National income used (MPS):

$$XG = X - E + M$$

35. GDP used (SNA):

$$XGNA = XNA - E + M$$

36. Average monthly wage in industry:

$$ZQP = \underset{(2.2)}{-798.70} + \underset{(14.2)}{947.57}*PC + \underset{(2.4)}{23.908}*(SQQ/NQ)$$

$R^2 = 0.989$ DW = 1.62

37. Average monthly wage in construction sector:

$$ZBP = \underset{(1.1)}{-224.28} + \underset{(15.4)}{780.48}*PC + \underset{(1.3)}{30.404}*(QPB/NB)$$

$R^2 = 0.981$ DW = 1.32

38. Average monthly wage in trade:

$$ZHP = \underset{(5.5)}{-509.69} + \underset{(35.2)}{792.24}*PC + \underset{(5.6)}{13.502}*((VCHP/PCX)/NH)$$

$R^2 = 0.995$ DW = 1.67

39. Average monthly wage in transportation:

$$ZTP = \underset{(3.3)}{-1074.7} + \underset{(12.0)}{1042.4}*PC + \underset{(3.3)}{4169.6}*(LA/NT)$$

$R^2 = 0.991$ DW = 2.51

40. Average monthly wage in 6 main sectors:

$$Z6P = \underset{(0.09)}{0.1773} + \underset{(507.2)}{0.9996}*((ZQP*NQ+ZBP*NB+ZHP*NH+ZTP*NT)/(NQ+NB+NT+NH))$$

$R^2 = 1.000$ DW = 2.00

41. Average monthly wage in services sector:

$$ZOP = \underset{(1.3)}{-53.529} + \underset{(26.4)}{1.0690}*Z6P$$

$R^2 = 0.989$ DW = 2.04

42. Total labour incomes (NBP source):

$$\textbf{VYZP} = 32.781 + 0.9115*[0.001*3*(\textbf{Z6P*N6+ZOP*NO})]$$
(0.07) (68.9)

$R^2 = 0.998$ DW = 1.59

43. Incomes from credits granted:

$$\textbf{VYFP} = 660.71 + 0.0908*\textbf{OLP} - 26.446*\textbf{RPOD}$$
(0.65) (12.5) (4.4)

$R^2 = 0.965$ DW = 2.65

44. Incomes from sale of agricultural products:

$$\textbf{VYAP} = -1121.O + 0.0029*(\textbf{SKZ*PSKZ}) + 0.0087*(\textbf{SKZB*PSKZB})$$
(0.92) (5.06) (1.7)

$R^2 = 0.813$ DW = 2.44

45. Incomes from social benefits:

$$\textbf{VYBGP} = 913.84 + 0.6169*\textbf{VYZP(1)}$$
(0.64) (13.0)

$R^2 = 0.966$ DW = 1.69

46. Incomes from transfers:

$$\textbf{VYTP} = -446.21 + 0.0294*\textbf{OLP} + 2.6409*\textbf{RPOD}$$
(1.2) (10.8) (1.2)

$R^2 = 0.943$ DW = 2.47

47. Incomes from private sector:

$$\textbf{VYNUP} = -1031.2 + 0.4360*\textbf{VYZP}$$
(0.93) (12.3)

$R^2 = 0.949$ DW = 2.63

48. Money incomes (receipts) of households and private sector (NBP source):

$$\textbf{VYP} = -718.23 + 1.1403*(\textbf{VYZP+VYFP+VYAP+VYBGP+VYTP+VYNUP})$$
(0.85) (105.6)

$R^2 = 0.999$ DW = 2.03

49. Households expenditures (NBP sources):

$$\mathbf{VCHP} = \underset{(1.4)}{2801.8} + \underset{(22.3)}{0.5034}*\mathbf{VYP}$$

$R^2 = 0.984$ DW = 1.10

50. Households expenditures on credit repaiment:

$$\mathbf{VCFP} = \underset{(9.3)}{-133.74} + \underset{(9.3)}{0.6753}*\mathbf{VYFP}$$

$R^2 = 0.916$ DW = 1.55

51. Households expenditures on paiment for services:

$$\mathbf{VCOP} = \underset{(1.2)}{-575.28} + \underset{(23.1)}{0.1338}*[0.3*\mathbf{VYP}+0.7*\mathbf{VYP(1)}]$$

$R^2 = 0.987$ DW = 2.02

52. Households expenditures on taxes and charges:

$$\mathbf{VCVP} = \underset{(1.3)}{-648.88} + \underset{(13.3)}{0.0804}*(0.5*\mathbf{VYP}+0.5*\mathbf{VYP(1)})$$

$R^2 = 0.962$ DW = 2.00

53. Total expenditures of households (NBP source):

$$\mathbf{VCP} = \underset{(1.3)}{-763.13} + \underset{(123.6)}{1.1009}*(\mathbf{VCHP}+\mathbf{VCFP}+\mathbf{VCVP}+\mathbf{VCOP})$$

$R^2 = 0.999$ DW = 1.78

54. Total expenditures of state budget:

$$\mathbf{BCP} = \underset{(0.13)}{369.67} + \underset{(15.0)}{1.0567}*[0.8*\mathbf{BYP}+0.2*\mathbf{BYP(1)}]$$

R2=0.970 DW=2.13

55. Total revenues of state budget:

$$\mathbf{BYP} = \underset{(0.48)}{-1702.9} + \underset{(11.9)}{1.2651}*[0.8*(\mathbf{AFPDP}+\mathbf{AFPOZP}+\mathbf{AFDYP}+\mathbf{AFPZP}+0.13*\mathbf{VYZP})+$$
$$0.2*(\mathbf{AFPDP(1)}+\mathbf{AFPOZP(1)}+\mathbf{AFDYP(1)}+\mathbf{AFPZP(1)}+0.13*\mathbf{VYZP(1)})]$$

$R^2 = 0.952$ DW = 2.34

56. Deficit of state budget:

BDP = **BYP** - **BCP**

57. Sales of products and services in material sectors:

$$\mathbf{SQOUP} = 3559.4 + 1.2551*(\mathbf{SQQ}*\mathbf{PSQ}+\mathbf{QPB}*\mathbf{PQB}+\mathbf{LA}*\mathbf{PSQ}*19.85)$$
(1.1) (49.9)

$R^2 = 0.997$ DW = 1.45

58. Fabrication costs of enterprises:

$$\mathbf{KWSP} = -684.40 + 3.4213*\mathbf{VYZP} + 2.3282*(\mathbf{MZ}*\mathbf{PTM}) + 0.2296*(\mathbf{BZPP}*\mathbf{RPOD}/100)$$
(0.13) (10.1) (1.8) (2.2)

$R^2 = 0.992$ DW = 1.31

59. Turnover tax paid by enterprises:

$$\mathbf{AFPOZP} = 1228.7 + 0.0546*\mathbf{SQOUP}$$
(2.8) (20.5)

$R^2 = 0.981$ DW = 0.80

60. Subsidies obtained by enterprises:

$$\mathbf{AFDZP} = 1662.4 + 0.0483*(\mathbf{SQQ}*\mathbf{PSQ})$$
(1.9) (6.3)

$R^2 = 0.832$ DW = 1.36

61. Gross profits of enterprises:

$$\mathbf{AFZP} = 507.59 + 1.1159*(\mathbf{SQOUP}-\mathbf{KWSP}-\mathbf{AFPOZP}+\mathbf{AFDZP})$$
(0.14) (8.8)

$R^2 = 0.906$ DW = 1.15

62. Net profits:

$$\mathbf{AFZNP} = \mathbf{AFZP}-\mathbf{AFPDP}-\mathbf{AFDYP}-\mathbf{AFPZP}$$

63. Income tax paid by enterprises:

$$\mathbf{AFPDP} = 785.22 + 0.3677*[0.7*\mathbf{AFZP}+0.3*\mathbf{AFZP(1)}]$$
(0.91) (16.9)

$R^2 = 0.976$ DW = 1.53

64. Dividends:

$$\mathbf{AFDYP} = 91.145 + 0.0717*\mathbf{AFZP} - 1882.9*\mathbf{U894} + 2643.8*\mathbf{U91}$$

(0.98) (25.8) (12.2) (22.8)

$R^2 = 0.995$ DW = 2.42

65. Deposits of enterprises:

$$\mathbf{OPP} = 3590.9 + 0.2319*\mathbf{SQOUP}$$

(0.96) (10.1)

$R^2 = 0.927$ DW = 2.47

66. Total indebtedness of enterprises:

$$\mathbf{BZPP} = 4056.9 + 2.0293*\mathbf{OPP} - 103.30*\mathbf{RPOD}$$

(0.32) (8.9) (1.4)

$R^2 = 0.927$ DW = 1.46

67. Deposits of households:

$$\mathbf{OLP\text{-}OLP(1)} = 3767.9 + 0.1103*\mathbf{VYP} + 25.355*\mathbf{RPOD} + 27826.0*\mathbf{U894}$$

(0.76) (2.9) (0.9) (4.6)

$R^2 = 0.850$ DW = 2.30

68. Total deposits of enterprises and households:

$$\mathbf{OOP} = \mathbf{OPP} + \mathbf{OLP}$$

69. Interest rate on long term deposits:

$$\mathbf{RPOD1} = -0.0130 + 0.4207*[\mathbf{PC/PC(2)}]$$

(0.08) (8.1)

$R^2 = 0.917$ DW = 1.64

$$\mathbf{RPOD} = \mathbf{RPOD1}*100$$

70. Deflators of sales products of manufacturing and mining industry:

$$\mathbf{PSQ} = -0.0192 + 0.2412*\mathbf{PTM} + 4.9143*(3*\mathbf{ZQP}*\mathbf{NQ}/100)/\mathbf{SQQ}) +$$

(0.67) (3.2) (13.6)

$$0.53*[\mathbf{AFZP(1)}+\mathbf{AFPOZP(1)}]/\mathbf{SQQ(1)}$$

(47.5)

$R^2 = 0.996$ DW = 3.01

71. Deflator of construction industry output:

$$\mathbf{PQB} = \underset{(0.44)}{0.0256} + \underset{(1.8)}{0.2643}*\mathbf{PTM} + \underset{(4.9)}{0.1266}*[(3*\mathbf{ZBP}*\mathbf{NB}/100)/\mathbf{QPB}] + \underset{(1.2)}{0.0479}*[\mathbf{AFZP(1)}+\mathbf{AFPOZP(1)}]/\mathbf{QPB(1)}]$$

$R^2 = 0.976$ DW = 3.19

72. Retail prices of consumer goods:

$$\mathbf{PCX} = \underset{(0.72)}{0.0301} + \underset{(8.6)}{1.0718}*\mathbf{PSQ} + \underset{(1.9)}{0.2386}*\mathbf{PSQ(1)}$$

$R^2 = 0.994$ DW = 1.54

73. Retail prices of services supplied to households:

$$\mathbf{PCOC} = \underset{(1.3)}{-0.2399} + \underset{(13.5)}{2.0728}*\mathbf{PCX} - \underset{(4.2)}{0.9349}*\mathbf{U90}$$

$R^2 = 0.963$ DW = 2.41

74. Retail prices of consumer goods and services:

$$\mathbf{PC} = \underset{(0.95)}{-0.00015} + \underset{(2923.6)}{0.9519}*\mathbf{PCX} + \underset{(221.4)}{0.0363}*\mathbf{PCOC}$$

$R^2 = 1.000$ DW = 2.36

75. Deflator of total investment outlays:

$$\mathbf{PJ} = \underset{(1.9)}{0.0566} + \underset{(30.2)}{0.9552}*\mathbf{PSQ}$$

$R^2 = 0.991$ DW = 2.10

76. Procurement prices of pigs for sloughter:

$$\mathbf{PSKZ} = \underset{(4.0)}{1461.0} + \underset{(11.1)}{4333.4}*\mathbf{PSQ}$$

$R^2 = 0.939$ DW = 1.67

77. Procurement prices of cereals:

$$\mathbf{PSKZB} = \underset{(6.2)}{28.995} + \underset{(7.5)}{37.325}*\mathbf{PSQ}$$

$R^2 = 0.876$ DW = 1.53

78. Employment in industry:

$$\mathbf{NQ} = \underset{(11.0)}{3231.1} + \underset{(4.7)}{0.0096}*[0.1*\mathbf{SQQ}+0.3*\mathbf{SQQ(1)}+0.3*\mathbf{SQQ(2)}+0.3*\mathbf{SQQ(3)}]$$

$R^2 = 0.818$ DW = 2.00

79. Employment in trade:

$$\mathbf{NH} = \underset{(3.4)}{556.91} + \underset{(4.7)}{0.0164}*\{0.05*(\mathbf{VCHP/PCX})+0.15*[\mathbf{VCHP(1)/PCX(1)}]+0.35*[\mathbf{VCHP(2)/PCX(2)}]+0.45*[\mathbf{VCHP(3)/PCX(3)}]\}$$

$R^2 = 0.813$ DW = 1.23

80. Employment in transportation:

$$\mathbf{NT} = \underset{(30.7)}{727.04} + \underset{(7.7)}{0.9203}*[0.05*\mathbf{LA}+0.15*\mathbf{LA(1)}+0.24*\mathbf{LA(2)}+0.55*\mathbf{LA(3)}]$$

$R^2 = 0.924$ DW = 2.03

81. Employment in construction industry:

$$\mathbf{NB} = \underset{(79.1)}{1263.04} + \underset{(0.64)}{0.0055}*[\mathbf{QPB}-\mathbf{QPB(1)}] \underset{(4.0)}{-133.97}*(\mathbf{U904}-\mathbf{U901})$$

$R^2 = 0.745$ DW = 1.50

82. Employment in 6 main sectors:

$$\mathbf{N6} = \underset{(2.2)}{206.79} + \underset{(90.2)}{1.0259}*(\mathbf{NQ}+\mathbf{NB}+\mathbf{NH}+\mathbf{NT})$$

$R^2 = 0.999$ DW = 1.71

83. Employment in service sector:

$$\mathbf{NO} = \underset{(1.7)}{1189.9} + \underset{(2.3)}{0.5487}*\mathbf{NO(1)} + \underset{(1.4)}{0.0119}*\mathbf{G} - \underset{(3.2)}{151.84}*\mathbf{U911}$$

$R^2 = 0.770$ DW = 1.14

APPENDIX 3

EXCERPT FROM THE QUARTERLY DATA BANK FOR THE PERIOD 1989.1 - 1991.2

PERIOD	AFDZP	AFDYP	AFPDP	AFPOZP	AFZP	AFZNP
1989.1	1903.700	357.100	014.200	1608.500	3274.600	1903.300
1989.2	1888.900	447.000	1522.600	1828.700	4838.700	2869.100
1989.3	2840.700	512.100	2863.200	2765.900	6947.200	3571.900
1989.4	2983.100	706.100	1154.000	6587.100	34858.000	22606.000
1990.1	9635.000	3565.200	17423.000	11109.000	45346.000	24149.000
1990.2	9766.000	2939.000	15728.000	11380.000	41204.000	21922.000
1990.3	7964.000	3108.500	15385.000	11125.000	41471.000	20009.000
1990.4	10335.000	3339.100	17121.000	14289.000	47128.000	13954.000
1991.1	8402.000	4452.000	11846.000	13987.000	25828.000	2368.000
1991.2	7173.000	4027.000	9202.000	12579.000	16166.000	-1621.000

	BCP	BDP	BYP	BZPP	C	CNA
1989.1	4554.800	-1617.300	2937.500	8859.900	68654.000	83583.000
1989.2	6174.500	-1658.100	4516.400	15853.000	68039.000	82835.000
1989.3	6082.200	19.500	6101.700	22846.000	73340.000	89288.000
1989.4	16875.000	-340.300	16534.000	29839.000	62674.000	76304.000
1990.1	35876.000	1772.800	37649.000	44063.000	45927.000	55914.000
1990.2	44761.000	4895.500	49657.000	68648.000	44219.000	53835.000
1990.3	43689.000	2067.100	45756.000	90282.000	54690.000	66583.000
1990.4	69452.000	-6317.800	63134.000	107545.000	64692.000	78760.000
1991.1	52653.000	-5006.500	47647.000	128199.000	54945.000	66893.000
1991.2	57295.000	-6942.000	50353.000	140147.000	52661.000	64113.000

	DR	DRNA	E	G	GNA	J
1989.1	44803.000	44803.000	21131.000	12739.000	11236.000	22137.000
1989.2	37431.000	37431.000	25114.000	12625.000	11136.000	31988.000
1989.3	12952.000	12952.000	21629.000	13609.000	12003.000	27110.000
1989.4	31344.000	31344.000	30961.000	11630.000	10258.000	42055.000
1990.1	25898.000	25898.000	20058.000	8522.200	7516.600	19888.000
1990.2	19047.000	19047.000	24241.000	8205.300	7237.100	26206.000
1990.3	4142.300	4142.200	25729.000	10148.000	8950.800	23200.000
1990.4	9977.700	9977.700	29952.000	12004.000	10588.000	35487.000
1991.1	25335.000	25335.000	12426.000	10196.000	8992.500	17587.000
1991.2	18483.000	18483.000	14571.000	9771.800	8618.700	21237.000

	JAK	JAPK	JJK	JNAK	JPK	JVK
1989.1	10631.000	884.100	12584.000	23098.000	2211.700	8420.800
1989.2	15362.000	2771.100	17939.000	33376.000	4332.500	12414.000
1989.3	13019.000	3600.000	14866.000	28286.000	5264.200	10857.000
1989.4	20197.000	9316.500	21942.000	43881.000	11689.000	17962.000
1990.1	9551.500	14712.000	12201.000	20752.000	17753.000	6669.900
1990.2	12586.000	21852.000	16288.000	27344.000	25779.000	8578.300
1990.3	11142.000	23522.000	13648.000	24207.000	27655.000	8365.200
1990.4	17043.000	38618.000	21732.000	37027.000	44623.000	11940.000
1991.1	8446.000	20013.000	11321.000	18350.000	23712.000	5366.300
1991.2	10199.000	27749.000	14430.000	22159.000	32406.000	5720.600

	KWSPK	LAK	MK	MHK	MIK	MZK
1989.1	13714.000	258.000	21529.000	12880.000	3882.200	4766.900
1989.2	16738.000	261.800	27644.000	10707.000	9208.200	7728.900
1989.3	23227.000	244.900	18859.000	5921.900	5582.900	7354.200
1989.4	56980.000	225.900	32348.000	8725.400	10252.000	13371.000
1990.1	125842.000	155.200	15065.000	6403.900	4895.400	3765.800
1990.2	134845.000	143.200	17946.000	6563.200	6401.500	4981.200
1990.3	144915.000	144.900	14246.000	3998.700	5079.500	5167.800
1990.4	189679.000	156.900	33152.000	12154.000	9366.700	11632.000
1991.1	205410.000	117.000	26924.000	17477.000	4841.600	4605.600
1991.2	202415.000	113.300	31249.000	13062.000	12454.000	5733.400

	N6K	NBK	NHK	NOK	NQK	NTK
1989.1	9338.500	1385.700	1505.900	2968.000	4993.500	1021.200
1989.2	9097.700	1326.900	1464.400	2968.000	4885.300	988.900
1989.3	9021.200	1306.100	1446.700	2932.000	4861.100	957.800
1989.4	8871.100	1253.500	1416.100	2992.000	4838.100	948.400
1990.1	9251.000	1390.300	1539.600	2955.000	4913.400	967.300
1990.2	8772.400	1285.800	1422.700	2891.000	4705.100	935.600
1990.3	8260.700	1176.500	1284.700	2864.000	4483.200	897.400
1990.4	7894.800	1114.900	1139.700	2952.000	4335.800	877.100
1991.1	8253.700	1266.400	1165.400	2780.000	4556.900	870.100
1991.2	8085.900	1264.200	1140.500	2814.000	4463.200	838.500

	OLPK	OOPK	OPPK	PCK	PCOCK	PCXK
1989.1	11223.000	15331.000	4107.800	0.081	0.085	0.082
1989.2	14234.000	21300.000	7066.300	0.103	0.107	0.104
1989.3	24520.000	35852.000	11333.000	0.169	0.158	0.172
1989.4	64291.000	95796.000	31505.000	0.427	0.307	0.437
1990.1	82006.000	112879.000	30873.000	1.025	1.049	1.037
1990.2	96871.000	136218.000	39346.000	1.284	1.327	1.298
1990.3	115513.000	169623.000	54110.000	1.320	1.717	1.321
1990.4	133193.000	189069.000	55876.000	1.551	2.005	1.553
1991.1	146350.000	205333.000	58983.000	1.934	3.226	1.909
1991.2	174275.000	235204.000	60929.000	2.147	4.594	2.080

	PJK	PQBK	PSKZK	PSKZBK	PSQK	PTMK
1989.1	0.100	0.102	1473.200	33.600	0.062	0.065
1989.2	0.135	0.116	2013.500	30.500	0.074	0.086
1989.3	0.194	0.160	2093.500	28.700	0.114	0.148
1989.4	0.278	0.345	2441.700	30.900	0.285	0.266
1990.1	0.893	0.789	4500.300	79.400	0.894	1.135
1990.2	0.984	0.883	6177.300	73.400	0.982	0.940
1990.3	1.192	0.948	6436.500	70.400	1.081	1.427
1990.4	1.257	1.037	7509.500	76.000	1.216	1.093
1991.1	1.348	1.150	8387.800	78.900	1.446	1.124
1991.2	1.526	1.252	6881.200	75.000	1.532	1.097

	QPBK	QRK	RPODK	SKZK	SKZBK	SQOUPK
1989.1	9839.900	27581.000	66.000	625.300	877.200	16608.000
1989.2	12543.000	20976.000	72.000	532.800	281.400	20546.000
1989.3	11355.000	45225.000	96.000	419.000	5524.200	28818.000
1989.4	10014.000	20314.000	171.000	472.300	566.900	80348.000
1990.1	11320.000	22060.000	269.000	469.900	905.300	164787.000
1990.2	13647.000	16046.000	79.500	394.700	301.900	173788.000
1990.3	13564.000	38727.000	34.800	404.600	4421.800	185138.000
1990.4	13524.000	17013.000	55.000	401.600	434.000	234499.000
1991.1	10547.000	14807.000	77.800	359.000	313.800	237831.000
1991.2	12953.000	13976.000	75.100	343.400	265.600	229781.000

	SQQK	UJJK	UJVK	VCFPK	VCHPK	VCOPK
1989.1	187316.000	0.568	0.380	135.200	4661.800	524.400
1989.2	179764.000	0.561	0.388	205.500	5930.600	796.700
1989.3	158842.000	0.548	0.400	303.500	10027.000	1169.900
1989.4	170882.000	0.522	0.427	1081.400	22298.000	2209.000
1990.1	130286.000	0.613	0.335	1820.600	32111.000	5556.500
1990.2	124053.000	0.622	0.327	1900.000	42657.000	7273.700
1990.3	125774.000	0.588	0.361	4200.000	54068.000	9881.600
1990.4	138010.000	0.612	0.336	9495.300	73590.000	13100.000
1991.1	115914.000	0.644	0.305	8400.000	70314.000	16100.000
1991.2	102200.000	0.679	0.269	10700.000	70700.000	19900.000

	VCPK	VCVPK	VYAPK	VYBGPK	VYFPK	VYNUPK
1989.1	5937.600	352.100	946.000	1033.100	249.400	878.700
1989.2	7869.100	535.000	1288.800	1407.400	339.700	1197.100
1989.3	12876.000	788.600	2265.200	2474.600	598.200	2103.400
1989.4	29269.000	1462.000	5066.100	6112.800	954.900	4506.000
1990.1	44845.000	2739.700	4883.000	12100.000	1809.900	7369.800
1990.2	60993.000	4139.100	5471.700	13168.000	5000.000	10795.000
1990.3	78828.000	5432.200	9351.300	16489.000	10600.000	13800.000
1990.4	14292.000	8678.200	9538.700	21031.000	13050.000	21500.000
1991.1	112500.000	9033.200	6306.800	29968.000	11608.000	17800.000
1991.2	126800.000	12400.000	5600.000	32900.000	14400.000	22500.000

	VYPK	VYTPK	VYZPK	XBK	XGK	XGNAK
1989.1	7242.400	217.700	3284.200	8826.300	136827.000	162719.000
1989.2	9118.900	296.600	3726.500	11251.000	133458.000	164778.000
1989.3	16105.000	522.900	6621.200	10185.000	112920.000	142529.000
1989.4	34824.000	1170.700	13612.000	8982.700	125846.000	161786.000
1990.1	61432.000	2900.000	23938.000	10154.000	89899.000	110081.000
1990.2	73835.000	3000.000	30026.000	12242.000	84057.000	107463.000
1990.3	94012.000	2500.000	32605.000	12167.000	80123.000	103884.000
1990.4	129637.000	3500.000	44434.000	12131.000	103717.000	136353.000
1991.1	138600.000	4700.000	50800.000	9460.900	98922.000	119571.000
1991.2	147100.000	4700.000	49600.000	11619.000	91115.000	113373.000

	XK	XNAK	XPOK	XPONAK	XQK	XRK
1989.1	136429.000	162321.000	51808.000	69638.000	66417.000	9377.700
1989.2	130928.000	162248.000	48806.000	72735.000	63739.000	7132.000
1989.3	115690.000	145299.000	33808.000	54943.000	56321.000	15377.000
1989.4	124459.000	160400.000	47980.000	76899.000	60590.000	6906.900
1990.1	94892.000	115074.000	31042.000	45331.000	46196.000	7500.400
1990.2	90352.000	113758.000	28669.000	46774.000	43986.000	5455.500
1990.3	91606.000	115367.000	21676.000	38437.000	44596.000	13167.000
1990.4	100517.000	133153.000	33667.000	60495.000	48934.000	5784.500
1991.1	84424.000	105073.000	28829.000	44577.000	41100.000	5034.300
1991.2	74436.000	96694.000	21828.000	39635.000	36237.000	4751.900

	XXBNAK	XXQNAK	XXRNAK	Z6PK	ZBPK	ZHPK
1989.1	8995.500	72308.000	11380.000	88.700	90.800	70.600
1989.2	11467.000	69392.000	8654.700	113.000	119.200	96.400
1989.3	10380.000	61316.000	18660.000	215.000	217.900	168.600
1989.4	9154.900	65964.000	8381.500	449.600	410.900	358.200
1990.1	10348.000	50293.000	9101.800	767.700	699.300	593.900
1990.2	12476.000	47887.000	6620.300	907.600	925.800	746.900
1990.3	12400.000	48551.000	15978.000	1071.700	1145.700	936.700
1990.4	12364.000	53275.000	7019.500	1416.200	1472.600	1225.900
1991.1	9642.300	44745.000	6109.100	1640.300	1593.600	1504.500
1991.2	11842.000	39451.000	5766.400	1711.900	1783.100	1626.500

	ZOPK	ZQPK	ZTPK
1989.1	81.500	95.400	75.900
1989.2	87.200	120.300	91.800
1989.3	189.200	236.000	170.200
1989.4	406.800	497.600	405.200
1990.1	642.600	851.200	689.800
1990.2	931.200	968.800	805.800
1990.3	1047.300	1112.100	993.200
1990.4	1602.400	1490.400	1294.800
1991.1	1723.600	1689.400	1601.900
1991.2	1712.700	1720.200	1658.000

Printing: Weihert-Druck GmbH, Darmstadt
Binding: Buchbinderei Schäffer, Grünstadt